Veritas Press

A◌
PHONICS
MUSEUM

MARLIN & LAURIE DETWEILER
DIANE COLEMAN
NED BUSTARD
EMILY FISCHER
ERIC VANDERHOOF

Third Edition

Copyright ©2006 Veritas Press
Lancaster, Pennsylvania

www.VeritasPress.com
(800) 922-5082

ISBN-10: 1-932168-59-1
ISBN-13: 978-1-932168-59-4

Printed in the United States of America.

PHONICS MUSEUM

Dear Friends,

We are very excited to be a part of your efforts to teach your students to read. Learning to read is a great thrill for young people. And what greater joy than to know that your children can read God's Word themselves. Upon completion of this program your child should be able to read the Scriptures. A portion of a canticle from an 1855 book based on an ancient verse expresses this well:

Christ His Cross shall be my speed!
Teach me, dear Mamma, to read
That I may in Scripture see
What His love hath done for me.
. . . Teach me letters—A B C.

After reviewing various phonics curricula, and after years of experience working with many of them and then doing extensive research of historical standards and methods, we became convinced that children would be much better off if the content they were reading had some meat to it. Consequently, we set out to create a program that had Biblical and historical content and also made use of the soundest phonetic principles and methods.

Teaching children to read is not a complex or complicated process. We know that alphabet tablets date back to the time of ancient Egypt and were baked tiles that had been scratched or etched. Looking back to the founding of Plymouth Colony, we see that children were taught to read from a hornbook. The hornbook was an alphabet board which was covered in front with a thin sheet of horn to prevent it from being soiled. The horn, harvested from cattle, was heated to make it malleable and then pressed until thin and translucent. Hornbooks were used because actual books were so precious children were not permitted to use them.

We want students to love reading by *quickly* learning to read early in the program. That is why the first book they read has so few consonants and only one vowel. We have found that this quick success helps them to love reading and effectively captures their interest in books. We have seen incredible results with this program. Not only do students read their first book in a matter of a few weeks, but the complexity builds to where they can actually read most anything by the end of the program.

As we surveyed the market we found that most phonetics readers were Dick and Jane*ish*—offering no real story. We thought this an unfortunate waste and sought to create readers (which we call *primers*) that had connections to meaningful events and stories. Some of these stories may not be familiar to you. In every case there is an explanation on the back cover to familiarize you with the event or topic of the primer. **You should read the back cover before the student reads the book.**

The difficulty of some words in the primers is intentional. You will be teaching phonetic word attack. Students will benefit from sounding out some unfamiliar words for which they do not know the meaning. Another great side-benefit is that they will develop their vocabulary by learning the meaning of these "new" words. There is great historic precedent for this approach from several hundred years ago, when many children learned to read with only the Bible. **After the first reading you should review the vocabulary words listed in the Teacher's Manual for that lesson and teach the meanings of the words to the students. Vocabulary cards for the most useful of these words are provided in Appendix 15.** Note that the meanings given for these words and phrases are *only* in the context of the story. The definitions are for comprehension of the story and are not all the definitions a word might have.

Have the students read each primer more than once. Don't expect immediate fluency. And realize that there are some books that are bigger jumps in difficulty from the prior book than others. For example, Book 9, *In a Camel's Eye*, is the first book with multi-syllable words.

Teaching reading should be fun and interesting—captivating the students' interest and love, hopefully for life. We have provided you with the tools to do this. The music is a supplement to help your children learn the rules. Memorization is most easily done with music. The various styles of music should not be ignored, as they provide an ancillary learning opportunity. The games are also intended to draw the student in to learn what he must to be a great reader. This Teacher's Manual provides you with a multitude of teaching ideas. Please do not rely solely on the student worksheets—much of the teaching is found in the Manual. The flashcards, like the music, will teach letters and sounds and will also introduce the student to outstanding works of art. Finally, the museum itself is intended to put the entire program into a category of something that a student will seek out in his free time, as well as when he is "schooling."

Consult the Overview that follows the Table of Contents for more specific guidance for using the Phonics Museum.

Laurie Detweiler

TABLE OF CONTENTS

PHONICS MUSEUM OVERVIEW

This brief overview is intended to provide you with a quick orientation to this thorough program.

1. Using the enclosed packing list, identify everything to acquaint yourself with the name and description of each item.

2. Open the teacher's manual (start with Kindergarten, if you have both) and familiarize yourself with it. Pay particular attention to the page that explains the icons (this page appears after the Table of Contents) as the icons will be used extensively throughout the manual.

3. Open the student workbook (again, Kindergarten if you have both). The lesson numbers in the teacher's manual will correspond to the student workbook worksheet numbers. For example, Lesson 54 in the teacher's manual corresponds to worksheets 54A, 54B, and 54C.

4. Vocabulary cards and definitions for many of the words used in each primer are found in Appendix 15 in the back of the Teacher's Manual. These cards should be photocopied (or hand-copied by the student, if possible) to be reviewed occasionally for comprehension and for phonetic word attack. Remember that some of these are intentionally difficult words and are there for the purpose of promoting decoding skills pronunciation. It is important for the student to build confidence in pronouncing unfamiliar words. After making the cards you may want to go over the unfamiliar words, allowing the student to sound out each word and explaining the meaning as found on the back of the cards.

5. Set up the pop-up museum by folding at the creases and gathering the inward folds together in the center. Use paper clips to fasten these "inside corners" together. When properly assembled, the museum will have four "rooms" and, when viewed from above, will look like four spokes of a wheel. The museum is intended for the children to play in a museum just like they would play with a doll house. The paper dolls are intended for this activity. Encourage them to hang up the fine art cards as they study each of their letters. For example when studying the letter P, they might hang up the pig card. Sticky tack works well for attaching

the cards. Note the game board portion. Refer to the packing list, if necessary, to determine which side is the game board. When you are ready to play a game, remove the paper clips and flatten the museum on a table with the game board up.

6. Make the museum bag. Take the iron-on sheet and iron this onto an old pillow case or even a fabric bag. Heat your iron to medium heat, lay the transfer squarely on the surface of the bag with the rough side down and iron over the sheet. The heat will cause the transfer to stick to the bag. This will be used as your student makes his own museum, hunting for objects that begin with the sound of the letter he is studying. If you are using this in a classroom, you will find a sheet in **Appendix 13** that explains the activity to parents. You will want to provide them each a copy.

7. Become familiar with each of the games. Look in the appendix of this teacher's manual for explanations.

8. Find the letter formation strips in Appendix 10 of either teacher's manual. Write the student's full name on it, so he can see how to form his name correctly. You may want to laminate this and tape it to his desk or have it available where he can see it.

9. Punch out the puzzle boards. We have found that a plastic box with different compartments is a good way to organize these. Place a different letter in each one. For Kindergarten if you write the uppercase letter in permanent marker on the bottom of each slot it allows the child to play an upper and lowercase matching game.

10. Vocabulary cards are in the back of the manual. These should be cut out and used to drill words before primers are read.

You are now ready to begin with the first lesson! We have tried to answer the most frequently asked questions, but please feel free to call us if you have others. May your new adventure be a blessing to you and your students.

ICON LEGEND

 Whether it is the Alphabet Quest or one of the primers, this icon will alert you to the fact that it is time to read a book.

 Singing is an important element in learning with this reading program. You will be alerted that it is time for a song with this icon.

 This icon indicates when it is time to remind the students of concepts like paper position when writing.

 Fine art flashcards are pivotal in the Phonics Museum. The flashcard icon will show you when it is time to incorporate these cards in the teaching process.

 Fun and insightful instructions for better teaching are indicated by this "bright idea" icon.

 This icon tells you that it is time to hang a painting in the museum and allow the students time to collect items to make their own museum. The paintings to hang are the 2.25" square cards with the fine art reproductions printed on them. These cards should be hung with sticky tac.

 The grapheme card icon refers to the reproducible cards found in Appendix 14 in the back of this manual. These should be photocopied onto cardstock and cut apart for use. These cards will be used throughout the program for letter recognition apart from the fine art flashcards.

 The fine art coloring pages found in the back of the student workbooks are able to be used at any time but this icon shows where the coloring activity fits best in the overall program.

ICON LEGEND *continued*

 This icon shows the teacher where tests can be introduced to help evaluate the student's progress.

 The puzzle piece icon refers to the letter puzzles. These puzzle pieces are used to teach the concepts of how different sounds link together to create words.

 All work and no play makes learning dull. There are many games to play in the Phonics Museum and this icon reminds you to play games on a regular basis, though the games can be used at any time.

 Get out your scissors and glue! This icon means that it is time for an art activity. Read through the directions before class.

PHONICS MUSEUM

LESSON 1
INTRODUCTION

ACTIVITY 1: HEARING

Discuss with the children how wonderful it is that God has given language to us so we can talk to one another and to Him. Spend a few minutes in prayer, thanking God for His great gift of language.

Describe to the children that in the past many people could only know the Word of God by hearing it read to them because most of them could not read. In order to help the people remember the great stories of the Bible, artists would paint wonderful pictures, cut huge sculptures, or create beautiful stained glass windows to put in the churches. The people would gaze at these things and be reminded of the truths of Scripture.

Today, we can all learn to read the Bible for ourselves! God speaks to us through His Word every day!

Tell the children that they will be learning to read this year and their lessons will start by careful listening to a new book: *The Alphabet Quest*. In this book, a little boy learns about letters and sounds during his visit to a very special museum full of beautiful pictures. The pictures will help him to remember the letters and sounds as he starts to read.

Read *The Alphabet Quest* aloud. It is a good idea to read this book once a week to reinforce the letter sounds and keep the museum theme fresh in the student's minds. After reading the story, call the children's attention to the flashcards (or posters posted around the room in a school setting). Read the "stimulus words" out loud for each card. Tell the children that these pictures will always be on display to remind them of the letters and sounds as they start to read.

Describe to the children that we can also sing our words with beautiful music, which also helps us to remember important things. This year they will learn songs which will name the letters and the sounds they make. Play the Alphabet Song for the children twice. Some may want to try to sing along right away, but discourage this at first. Quiet listening to the song for the first few days is preferable.

Worksheet 1A: Present the worksheet to the children and read the instructions aloud. Monitor their progress as they work independently. You may want to play the song once or twice more during this time.

ACTIVITY 2: WRITING

Tell the children that holy men who were taught by the Holy Spirit wrote down the words of God in the collection of books which became our Bible ("The Old Testament in Hebrew...and the New Testament in Greek, being immediately inspired by God, and, by His singular care and providence, kept pure in all ages, are therefore authentical..." *Westminster Confession of Faith, Chapter 1, Article 8, abridged)*. Writing letters, words, and even sentences is another skill which they will be learning this year.

Worksheet 1B: Using the mazes on Worksheet 1B as your examples, draw some large mazes on the board. Allow children to come up one at a time and follow the mazes. Describe that these mazes are like roads for the chalk (whiteboard marker, etc.) to follow and that they should try to stay "on the road."

 Tell them that they will be doing these types of mazes on their own at their desks.

THE THREE P'S

First, teach the children that there are three things they must remember when they are writing. These are called the "THREE P's." They are: Pencil grip, Paper position, and Posture. Later on we will add a fourth P—Pressure.

Pencil grip should be demonstrated at this time. It is a three-point grip, with the pencil resting on the third finger, the thumb and index fingers grasping the pencil on either side just above the "paint line." Fingers should not be on the bare wood—this is too close to the point for good control, nor should fingers be too far up the shaft of the pencil, for the same reason.

Their hands should rest comfortably on the desk with the pencil at an approximate 45 degree angle from the plane of the desk (not straight up).

Children should be instructed to use good posture. The free hand should be used to hold the paper in position. Remember that children's fine motor skills all develop at different times. Initially this may be a difficult task, but success can be gained with practice. Be patient and encourage them to do their best. If you find they are having difficulty, consider using a washable marker as they flow over the page easier.

Present Worksheet 1B and instruct right-handers that the paper should be flat on the desk with the lower left corner pointed toward them. Instruct left-handers that the lower right corner should be pointed toward them at the same angle, but in the opposite direction. Teach the children in each case to direct the point at their belly-buttons. Their writing arm—left and right hand—should then rest comfortably, parallel to the angle of the paper.

After you have checked the "THREE P's" for each student, permit them to follow the mazes in the same way they did on the board. Monitor their progress as they work independently.

LESSON 2
TARGET SOUND: SHORT A (AS IN "ADAM")

ACTIVITY 1: HEARING

Remind the children about yesterday's activities. Discuss briefly how wonderful it is that God has given language to us so we can share our thoughts and praise Him with our words and in song. Play the Museum Song for the children encouraging them to sing along while pointing to the corresponding letters on the flashcards.

Describe that spoken words are made up of many little sounds and that what they will be doing today is listening very carefully for one special little sound—the short A sound. Make this sound clearly and have the children echo it back to you. Instruct them to indicate by raising their hand (see ideas below) when they hear this sound as you say the following sounds, distinctly and slowly, one-by-one:

f , r , a , n , g , a , t , a , m , s , b , a , p , a , d , r , f , a , b , n , p , a , n , p , a , p , m , t , g , a , s , a

Show the children the flashcard with the letter A on it. Have them hear the sound of short A as in "apple." You may want to laminate the flashcards and hole punch the upper left hand corner to place them on a ring in the order of the Museum Song (A, M, B, P, T, D, N, G, S, F, R, E, I, O, U, L, H, C, K, J, Z, Y, W, Q, V, X)

A fun way to do this would be to have them raise both hands beside their faces, fingers spread out and palms facing forward, in a gesture of surprise ("aaaaaaaaa!"). Make sure that you pronounce the consonant sounds WITHOUT the "uh" after them. Produce each as precisely as possible.

This list is composed of all the sounds to be studied during the first quarter of this program. There are ten instances of the short A sound in the above list. Subsequent lists will also contain ten instances of the targeted sound for each lesson.

You may want to have the children close their eyes as you do this to discourage answers based on the responses of others. Note carefully any consistent slowness or absence of correct response by any student.

Another variation would be to instruct children to echo the targeted sound back to you when they hear it. This will reinforce their own accurate production of the sound.

Give your students the *Apple Harvest* painting and allow them to hang it in the museum. Talk to them about the story *The Alphabet Quest* and give them their museum bag. An iron-on was included in the Phonics Museum box that should be applied to an old pillow case, canvas bag, or anything that can store small household items that a student might collect to demonstrate his understanding. Allow them time to go through the house and collect items that begin with the sound of A to make their own museum. If you are teaching in a school setting, instruct the children to take the bag home and bring in objects the following day.

The child's museum should be designated as a place where they can display their "art" objects each week. A dresser top for those at home works well or set up a table in the school setting for the students to establish their own museum.

ACTIVITY 2: SEEING

Aa — Tell the children that the letter which makes the short A sound is the letter A and that God has given us the gift of being able to write down our spoken words for others to read. Show them the grapheme cards (those cards that have the printed upper and lower case "A,a." A grapheme is the written letter, the sound it makes is called a phoneme). Point out the features of each letter (the capital A is like a tent, pointed on top; the lower case A has a curl at the top and a "pocket," etc.)

Mix these cards with the other printed upper case letter cards for the first quarter. Present these to the children in random order, instructing them to indicate when they see the target letter A. Repeat this activity with the lower case letters, then with both upper and lower case letters combined.

On the board, write the written upper and lower case letters for A (see worksheet 2b for a sample of the written letters), describing and numbering your strokes as you do so. You may want to use different colors for different strokes to emphasize them, and always stick to the same sequence of colors as you teach letter formation during the year: green for stroke 1, blue for stroke 2, red for stroke 3, and so on. If you are doing this at home, use a small white dry-erase board.

Compare and contrast the printed letters and the written letters, emphasizing their similarities: both capitals look very much alike, the written lower case A is just the "pocket without the curl," etc. Leave both the printed and written examples on the board for reference as you present Worksheet 2A.

Worksheet 2A: Read the instructions aloud to the students and monitor their progress as they work independently. (This worksheet may be presented again later in the week as an assessment tool, without the examples for reference.)

ACTIVITY 3: WRITING

Worksheet 2B: Read the instructions aloud to the students and monitor their progress as they work independently. Remind them that the mazes are not to be "filled in," but are like "roads" for their pencils to follow. Tell them to do all the mazes first, then return to the top row to make the letters on their own.

 Remind them about the "THREE P's" of writing and monitor their progress carefully as they work.

Minor deviations of line within, or even slightly beyond, the letter mazes can be expected at first. However, wild or distorted letter formation should be monitored to determine if the student may have perceptual or eye-hand coordination difficulties.

You may want to give the students the coloring page (found in the back of the student workbook) along with the flashcard. Read the information about the artist to your students before they color the picture. Explain that we want to take our time and color in the lines. This is a good way to continue to work on their fine motor skills.

LESSON 3
TARGET SOUND: SHORT A

ACTIVITY 1: HEARING

Play the Museum Song for the children encouraging them to sing along when they are able.

Write the written letter "A,a" on the board and ask the children if they remember what sound this letter makes. Reinforce correct responses and have the children echo the short A sound several times, in different "voices" and pitches to maintain interest.

 Take the children back to the flashcard with the letter A on it. Have them hear the sound of short A as in "apple."

Now tell them that the short A sound can play "hide and seek" with other sounds which are very much alike. Challenge the children to "find" the short A sound among the following list of sounds which you will read aloud:

For the first time through this list, the vowels *other than* A should be read as *long* vowel sounds as follows: E as in "eat," I as in "ice," O as in "open," and U as in "flute." When you repeat the exercise, say all the vowels as *short* sounds (increasing the difficulty) as follows: E as in "end," I as in "in," O as in "hop," and U as in "up."

e, i, a, o, u, a, i, a, u, a, i, o, a, a, e, u, i, a, o, a, i, u, a, a

Again, there are ten of the target short A sounds in the above list.
You may, of course, use any of the previously suggested variations for presentation or response. (See Lesson 2, Activity 1 on page 3.)

ACTIVITY 2: SEEING

Aa   Call attention to the written "A,a" on the board and then present the printed "A,a" cards. Remind the children that printed letters may look slightly different ("wear different disguises") from written letters but that they mean the same letter and the same sound. Draw a parallel with the fact that there are many different types and kinds of cats, but we all identify them as members of the group of animals called "cats."

Mix all the printed first quarter letter cards, adding to them your own written "A,a" cards. Instruct them to indicate when they see the target letter A in either written or printed form as you present the cards in random order one-by-one. Remove the examples from their view as you present Worksheet 3A.

Worksheet 3A: Read the instructions aloud to the students and monitor their progress as they work independently.

ACTIVITY 3: WRITING

Place guidelines and perimeter lines on the board. Call on students to come to the board and make the upper and lower case letter A. Encourage proper stroke formation and sequence, prompting as necessary.

Worksheet 3B: Read the instructions aloud to the students and monitor their progress as they work independently. Explain the use of the "perimeter" lines on the paper, which are like "fences" to help them size and space their letters properly.

Continue to monitor the "THREE P's" of writing!

LESSON 4
TARGET SOUND: SHORT A

ACTIVITY 1: HEARING

 Play the Alphabet Song for the children, encouraging them to sing along when they are able.

Praise the children for being such good listeners and ask who remembers the special sound for the week. After repeating the short A sound several times as you did in Lesson 3, tell the children that this sound likes to be the leader (with other sounds) in "Follow the Leader" and form words. Instruct them to indicate by raising their hand, or some other manner when they hear the short A as the "leader" at the beginning of the following list of words:

Adam	mug	fox	ax	apple	butter	gift
alligator	donut	sun	river	puppy	animal	note
fudge	soap	attic	Alice	big	at	nurse
actor	Molly	peach	aspirin	Robert	dime	teacher

You could make a game of this by reading the list a second or third time at a faster pace, changing the order of the words, to see how quickly the children can respond correctly.

Worksheet 4A (top): Read the instructions aloud to the children. Tell them that you will name the pictures for them while they respond independently on their own papers.

Row 1: alligator, bird, apples
Row 2: sink, anchor, ax

ACTIVITY 2: SEEING AND WRITING

Demonstrate the proper letter formation on the board and have students trace both upper and lower case "A,a" in the air with their pencils before they proceed to finish the bottom half of Worksheet 4A.

Worksheet 4A (bottom): Continue to monitor letter formation and the "THREE P's."

Worksheet 4B: Display both the printed and written letters "A,a" in both cases. On the board, put a "splotch" of color (like on an artist's palette) beside the corresponding letter type as indicated in the coloring guide at the bottom of the worksheet. Leave this display on the board for reference while the children work independently.

 Have the students work over their color guide with the corresponding color.

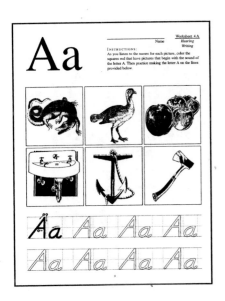

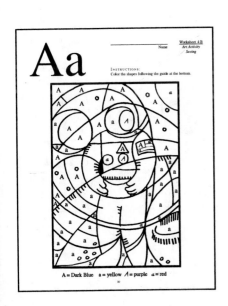

LESSON 5
TARGET SOUND: SHORT A

ACTIVITY 1: ART ACTIVITY—APPLE PRINTS

Worksheet 5A: Prepare a work table with small apples cut in half lengthwise, (Red Delicious apples work best due to their distinct apple shape), assorted washable paints on paper plates, damp paper towels, etc. Demonstrate for the children how to make an apple print by dipping the cut surface of the apple into the paint and then pressing it against the paper. Have them practice several times before putting a print on Worksheet 5A. Place the prints in a safe location to dry.

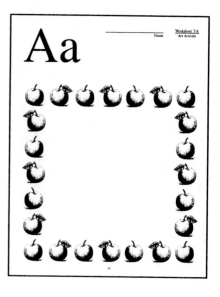

ACTIVITY 2: HEARING AND WRITING

Worksheet 5B: Tell the students that you will be working on this together as a group today. Have them trace the first letter maze, then listen carefully as you read the names of the pictures in the row that follows: monkey, apple, bell, pig. Monitor their work as they circle the pictures which begin with the short A sound.

Continue with the worksheet in the same manner (make sure students listen for the beginning, or "leader," sound and only circle those pictures!). The pictured items are:
    Row 1: monkey, apple, bell, pig
    Row 2: bull, alligator, nut, bed
    Row 3: pen, rose, anchor, baby
    Row 4: ax, duck, elephant (this one can be tricky!), fish

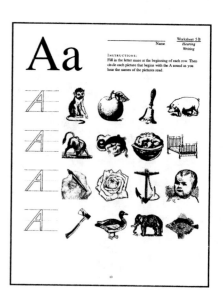

Worksheet 5C: Read the instructions aloud to the students and then call on specific students to identify the pictures. Monitor as they complete the worksheet according to the directions.

    Row 1: hat, apples, man
    Row 2: anchor, alligator, elephant
    Row 3: nose, spider, ax

ACTIVITY 3: HEARING AND SPEAKING

Play a word-generating game such as "My father owns a shop and he bought some apples" then the next child would continue the game by saying "My father owns a shop and he bought an ax" and so on, to stimulate children to come up with their own examples of words which begin with the short A sound. Write them on the board, highlighting the "A's" at the beginning and have them "echo" them after you.

Another idea would be to see how many proper names of girls, boys, last names, places, pets, etc. they can think of which begin with the short A sound.

Students can also be called to the board to write the beginning A letters for the words. This would be a good time to introduce the rule for using upper case for proper names.

LESSON 6
TARGET SOUND: M

ACTIVITY 1: HEARING

 Sing the Museum Song. Encourage them to enjoy singing the song and to sing robustly.

 Show the children the flashcard with the letter M on it. Have them hear the sound of short M as in "mummy."

Tell the children that they are such good listeners that they are now ready to listen for a new sound. This is the sound we make when something tastes very good—the sound M. Draw this out: "mmmmm." Have the children echo it back to you.

Name several foods that children like and have them respond by saying the target sound. Have them "rub their bellies" also as they make the "mmmmm."

 This may be their way of indicating when they hear this sound in the following exercise.

Say the following sounds slowly and distinctly, one-by-one as they indicate when they hear the M sound:

f, r, m, g, a, m, t, b, m, s, a, d, p, f, m, m, r, a, b, d, m, t, m, r, f, s, m, a, p, g, m, d, m

Again, make sure you pronounce the consonants quickly, without the "uh" after them.

You may repeat the list using any of the previous variations.

Give your students the reproduction of the Golden Effigy of King Tutankhamen and allow them to hang it in the museum. Talk to them about the story *The Alphabet Quest* and give them their museum bag. Allow them time to go through the house and collect items that begin with the sound of M to make their own museum. If you are teaching in a school setting, instruct the children to take the bag home and bring in objects the following day.

ACTIVITY 2: SEEING

Tell the children that the letter which makes the M sound is the letter M. Show them the cards with the printed upper and lower case "M,m." Point out the features of each letter (two mountains, or humps; the upper case is pointed, the lower case is rounded, etc.)

Mix these cards with the other printed upper case letters for the first quarter. Present them to the children in random order, instructing them to indicate when they see the target letter M.

Repeat this activity with the lower case letters, then with both upper and lower case letters combined.

On the board, write the written upper and lower case letters for M, describing and numbering your strokes as you do so. Compare and contrast the printed letters and the written letters—they look very much alike for this letter. Leave both the printed and written examples on the board as you present Worksheet 6A.

Worksheet 6A: Read the instructions aloud to the children and monitor their progress as they work independently.

ACTIVITY 3: WRITING

Place guidelines and perimeter lines on the board. Call on students to come to the board and make the upper and lower case letter M. Remind them how the strokes are made and in what order.

Worksheet 6B: Read the instructions aloud to the students. Tell them that they will draw in the letter mazes FIRST, then go back up to the top of the page to make the letters on their own. Watch that children do not attempt to do the letters independently on the first line before they have practiced in the mazes on the rest of the page.

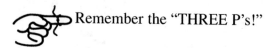 Remember the "THREE P's!"

You may want to give the students the coloring page along with the flashcard. Read the information about the artist to your students before they color the picture. Explain that we want to take our time and color in the lines.

Lesson 7
Target Sound: M

Activity 1: Hearing

Play the Museum Song for the children encouraging them to sing along while pointing to the corresponding letters on the flashcards.

Write the written letters "M,m" on the board and ask the children if they remember what sound this letter makes. Reinforce correct responses and have the children echo the sound several times, in different "voices" and pitches to maintain interest.

You may want to call attention to the different ways this can be said to mean different things, for instance, when someone is listening to another without comment. It could be fun to say this in different ways and have the children try to guess what you are indicating.

However, teach them that sounds alone are never enough to tell another person what you really mean and that it is best to use words when responding to another person. A side lesson could include instruction on polite words such as "Please," "Thank you," "Yes" (instead of "Yeah" or "okay"), etc.

Tell them that the M sound also likes to play "hide and seek" with its best buddy, the N sound. They are very much alike, so it is sometimes hard to find M when they are playing. Have them watch you carefully as you produce both sounds and identify what you do differently to make each one. Challenge them to find the M sounds in a list of randomly produced M and N. This is tricky—encourage them to watch your mouth for extra clues!

n, n, m, m, n, m, m, n, n, m, n, n, n, m, m, m, n, m, n, m

Praise them for being such good listeners. Now tell them that the M also likes to be the leader in "Follow the Leader," but he plays with lots of other sounds when he does this. Instruct them to indicate by rubbing their tummies when they hear the M sound as the "leader" at the beginning of the following list of words:

mask	apple	Mary	mittens	field	sock	top
dog	monkey	ax	moon	goose	match	note
salt	girl	math	Monday	Andy	monster	go
book	fussy	rope	pastor	garage	magnifying glass	

Worksheet 7A: Read the instructions aloud to the children. Tell them that you will name the pictures for them while they respond independently on their own papers.

Row 1: monkey, bat, moon
Row 2: car, mittens, elephant
Row 3: mask, chair, magnifying glass

ACTIVITY 2: SEEING AND WRITING

On the board, write the written upper and lower case letters for M, describing and numbering your strokes as you do so.

Place guidelines and perimeter lines on the board. Call on students to come to the board and make the upper and lower case letter M. Remind them how the strokes are made and in what order.

Worksheet 7B: Read the instructions aloud to the students. Remind them about the use of the "perimeter" lines to help them with size and spacing.

 Remember the "THREE P's!"

LESSON 8
TARGET SOUND: M

ACTIVITY 1: HEARING

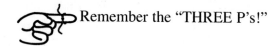 Play the Museum Song for the children encouraging them to sing along while pointing to the corresponding letters on the flashcards.

Tell the children that the M sound is going to be the "leader" in a list of new words today and that they must continue to listen carefully for it at the beginning in the following list of words:

doll	mustache	boy	mustard	arrow	gas
man	mermaid	sack	penny	table	moose
bird	saddle	flag	attic	horse	tip
animal	movie	soda	banana	rabbit	fun

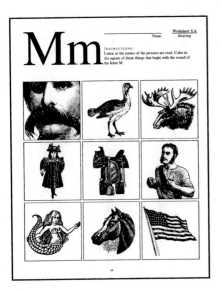

Worksheet 8A: Read the instructions aloud to the children. Tell them that you will name the pictures for them while they respond independently on their own papers.

> Row 1: mustache, bird, moose
> Row 2: doll, saddle, man
> Row 3: mermaid, horse, flag

ACTIVITY 2: SEEING

On the board, write several of the M words from the above list, using a different color for the M to highlight it within the word. Have children come to the board and circle the M in each of the words. Point out to them that the M in these words is the leader and the leader is always on the left.

Replace the written M with the printed M card and tell them that the word is the same each time because the written and printed M make the same sound, they just look slightly different.

Write the following words on the board, highlighting the M by writing it in a different color:

Mrs. Kemper   animal   Adam   summer

Discuss with them that the M is not always the leader and can be in line with the other letters.

Replace the written M with the printed M and ask them to tell you why it is acceptable to do this.
Erase the board and write the same words again, without highlighting the M. Ask who can find the M now when it is the same color as all the other letters.

Worksheet 8B: Read the instructions aloud. Remind the children that the M may not always be the leader and that there may be more than one of them in each word. Monitor as they complete the worksheet independently. Tell them to count the number of "M's" they have circled—there should be ten in all! Help them to self-edit and correct themselves if they have any oversights or errors. Watch out particularly for the "N's" on this page!

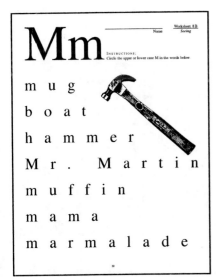

LESSON 9
TARGET SOUND: M

ACTIVITY 1: HEARING

 Play the Museum Song for the children encouraging them to sing along while pointing to the corresponding letters on the flashcards.

Tell the children that the M sound is going to be the "leader" again today and that they must continue to listen carefully for it at the beginning in the following list of words:

moon	sun	stars	fiddle	girl	ark	mask
salad	boat	push	mittens	pig	scale	mermaid
Debbie	rain	tin	basket	den	pony	minister

Worksheet 9A (top): Read the instructions aloud to the children. Tell them that you will name the pictures for them while they respond independently on their own papers.

Row 1: ark, mermaid, mask
Row 2: mittens, scale, moon

ACTIVITY 2: WRITING

On the board, write the written upper and lower case letters for M, describing and numbering your strokes. Have several children come to the board and reproduce both upper and lower case "M,m," numbering their strokes aloud as they do so.

Worksheet 9A (bottom): Monitor the children as they work independently. Make sure they are forming the letters with the strokes in the correct order.

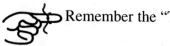 Remember the "THREE P's!"

ACTIVITY 3: ART ACTIVITY—MONSTER MASKS

Worksheet 9B: Have the children color the masks. It may be easier to glue the mask to the card stock first and then cut them out. They will need help to cut out the eye holes and make the small holes for the string.

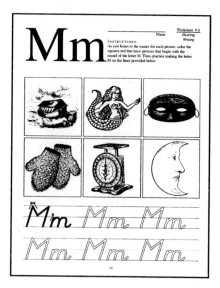

LESSON 10
TARGET SOUND M AND REVIEW

ACTIVITY 1: HEARING

 Play the Alphabet Song for the children encouraging them to sing along while pointing to the corresponding letters on the flashcards.

Remind the children that they have been listening all week for the M sound at the beginning of words. Ask them to name as many M words as they can, either by remembering those they have studied over the last few days, or thinking of new ones. List these on the board, circling the M in each word.

Worksheet 10A: Tell the children that you will be working on this together today. Read the instructions aloud, then call on different children to identify each of the pictures in order, left to right, across the rows, indicating their responses as they go. You may want them to put their finger on each picture as it is named to encourage them to keep their places. The pictures are:

Row 1: mules, apples, bed
Row 2: house, mouth, dog
Row 3: mittens, cat, mask

 Another variation would be to name all the pictures, then have children go back and indicate their responses. This may be slightly more difficult.

ACTIVITY 2: REVIEW

Put all the printed upper case letters for the first quarter on display. Ask the children to pick out the two letters which have been studied so far (A,M). Remove the rest of the upper case letters. Put all the lower case letters for the first quarter on display. Ask the children to pick out the lower case "a,m." Remove the rest of the upper case letters. Keep the target letters "A,a" and "M,m" on display.

Ask the children to echo the sounds back to you several times. Then, make a game out of it by having them make the correct sound as you point to each letter randomly. Use both the upper and lower cases as stimuli.

 You can speed this up to maintain interest, or call on various children to be the "teacher" and point to the letters for the class.

This game can be reversed also by having one student make the sounds randomly and another student point to the correct letter, in either case.

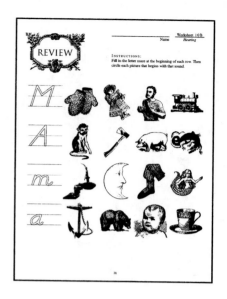

Worksheet 10B: Do this worksheet together. Have students first follow the letter maze for the upper case M. Then name the pictures following from left to right, circling the ones which have the M sound at the beginning.

Continue in the same manner for the next three rows. Remind them that the sound they are listening for will be different for each row! The correct responses are underlined below:

Row 1: mittens, doll, man, train
Row 2: monkey, ax, pig, alligator
Row 3: candle, moon, socks, mermaid
Row 4: anchor, bear, baby, teacup

An interesting note: The letters down the left side of the page, form the word "Mama." Even though the A in this word is not a true short A sound, you may want to call this to their attention.

LESSON 11
TARGET SOUND: B

ACTIVITY 1: HEARING

 Begin with both the Alphabet and Museum songs. The children should all be singing along at this point.

Inform the children that today's lesson will focus on a sound which really doesn't like to be alone. It loves to have a buddy sound with it all the time. This is the B sound. You can't really say it without adding an "uh" after it (short U). Say it several times, minimizing the "uh" as much as you can, but acknowledge that it is impossible to eliminate it entirely.

 Show the children the flashcard with the letter B on it. Have them hear the sound of short B as in "bull."

Ask the children to listen carefully for the B sound as you say the following list of sounds, one-by-one:

f, s, b, a, t, b, d, r, m, n, g, b, a, b, b, d, s, f, b, r, m, a, n, b, g, t, b, a, d, f, b, b

Describe that B is a "bursting" sound. It is very much like P, which is a "popping" sound. Both are made by forcing a little puff of air out between your lips in a small "burst" or "pop." Point out to them that the B sound is louder because it likes to use its voice, but the P sound whispers all the time. Make each sound alternately several times so they can clearly hear the difference. Now challenge them to listen for the B sound in the following list as you say the sounds aloud (again, minimizing the "uh" as much as possible):

b, b, b, p, b, b, p, b, p, p, p, b, p, p, b, p, b, p, b

Praise them for their careful listening.

A way to have them indicate hearing this sound would be to place all the fingertips of one hand on their lips and then open them rapidly like a little "burst" coming from their mouths.

Give your students the reproduction of the *Bull Leapers* and allow them to hang it in the museum. Talk to them about the story *The Alphabet Quest* and give them their museum bag. Allow them time to go through the house and collect items that begin with the sound of B to make their own museum. If you are teaching in a school setting, instruct the children to take the bag home and bring in objects the following day.

ACTIVITY 2: SEEING

Tell the children that the letter which makes the B sound is the letter B. Show them the cards with the printed upper and lower case "B,b." Point out the features of each letter (the upper case has two big bumps on the right side, the lower case only has one, etc.)

Mix these cards with the other printed upper case letters for the first quarter. Present them to the children in random order, instructing them to indicate when they see the target letter B.

Repeat this activity with the lower case letters, then with both upper and lower case letters combined.

You may notice some confusion when lower case D and P are presented. If this causes difficulty, take them out of the presentation pile for now. The similarities between the lower case B, P, and D will be addressed in more detail when these other sounds are introduced.

On the board, write the written upper and lower case letters for B, describing and numbering your strokes as you do so. Compare and contrast the printed letters and the written letters—they look very much alike for this letter. Leave both the printed and written examples on the board as you present Worksheet 11A

Worksheet 11A: Read the instructions aloud to the children and monitor their progress as they work independently.

ACTIVITY 3: WRITING

Place guidelines and perimeter lines on the board. Call on students to come to the board and make the upper and lower case letter B.Remind them how the strokes are made and in what order.

Worksheet 11B: Read the instructions aloud to the students. Remind them that they will draw in the letter mazes FIRST, then go back up to the top of the page to make the letters on their own. Monitor this carefully.

 Remember the "three Ps!"

 You may want to give the students the coloring page along with the flashcard. Read the information about the artist to your students before they color the picture. Explain that we want to take our time and color in the lines.

LESSON 12
TARGET SOUND: B

ACTIVITY 1: HEARING

 Play the Museum Song for the children encouraging them to sing along while pointing to the corresponding letters on the flashcards.

Tell the children that since the B sound loves to have a buddy with it all the time, it is the leader in a lot of words. Challenge them to listen carefully for it at the beginning of the following list of words:

banana	mother	fox	basket	feather	gate	bell
David	mustard	army	button	race	bucket	dog
bat	Richard	song	bench	potato	bed	cat
paper	fan	box	teacher	butter	six	gum

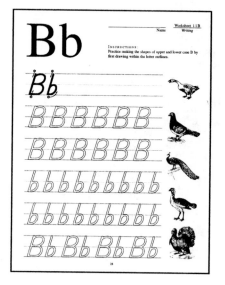

Worksheet 12A: Read the instructions aloud to the children. Tell them that you will name the pictures for them while they respond independently on their own papers.

Row 1: basket, bat, fox
Row 2: bed, cat, dog
Row 3: bucket, bench, bell

ACTIVITY 2: SEEING

Display the printed upper and lower case "B,b" for the children. Write the written letters in both cases for "A,a," "M,m," and "B,b" on the board and ask the children which set of written letters go with the printed letters on display. Erase the "A,a" and the "M,m." Leave the printed and written "B,b" on display as you present Worksheet 12B.

Worksheet 12B: Read the instructions aloud to the students and monitor their progress as they work independently.

ACTIVITY 3: REVIEW

Rewrite the "A,a" and the "M,m" on the board. Emphasize letter stroke formation and order. Ask the children if they remember the sounds which are made by those letters. Praise them for their good memories!

You may wish to create lettering lines for the students to follow. If using a whiteboard, these lines can be drawn with wet erase marker. That way children can use dry erase to make their letters and only the letters will be erased between trials. If using a chalkboard, special tape is available for putting lines on the board which will not be erased between trials.

Have students write on the board, or white board specific letters. Watch carefully how they order and produce the strokes.

Worksheet 12C: Tell the children that they will be working on this paper together today. Read the instructions at the top of the page. Name or have the students name the first picture: alligator. Ask what sound is at the beginning (or is the leader) in this word. When they respond correctly, ask which of the letters on the board makes this sound ("A,a") and point to their choice. Direct them to write this letter, in both upper and lower cases, under the picture of the alligator. Proceed with "bear" and "man" in the first row in the same manner.

Increase the difficulty of the task for the second and third rows as follows:

For the second row, only name the pictures and ask what the beginning sound is. Do not point out this choice among the examples on display. The pictures are: *monkey, apples, bucket*
For the third row, only name the pictures. Do not give any further clues

regarding sound or letter. The pictures are: *bird, ax, mask*. This will give you a good idea how well the children are matching beginning sounds with letters on their own. Monitor their work carefully. You may repeat the labels several times for students, reminding them to listen carefully to the beginning sound only, but give no further information.

LESSON 13
TARGET SOUND: B

ACTIVITY 1: HEARING

 Play the Alphabet Song for the children encouraging them to sing along while pointing to the corresponding letters on the flashcards.

Divide the board in half with a long vertical line. On the left side label the top of the board with printed and written "B,b." Leave the right side of the board blank.

Tell the children that they will be listening to the B sound at the beginning of words again today. You will read a list of words aloud and each word which begins with B will be written on the left side of the board under the "B,b" letters. Words which do not begin with the B sound will be written on the right side of the board.

Read the following list aloud, writing the word on the correct side of the board as the class (or individual students, as called upon) directs you. Circle the beginning letter of each word as you write it. Correction of inaccurate responses can be done immediately by comparing these initial letters with the "B,b" at the top of the board.

daisy	bear	mud	pie	baby	family
fish	basket	sock	ball	zebra*	name
animal	penny	bug	tickle	rug	goose

 *Watch this word. It does have a B in it, although it is not the beginning sound. Alert children may call attention to this. Reinforce that you are only listening for beginning sounds right now.

Check over the lists on the board to reinforce the study skill of reviewing finished work carefully. Present Worksheet 13A.

Worksheet 13A: Before the children cut out the pictures, name them aloud. They are: fish, baby, socks, basket, zebra, ball

Direct the students to cut them out carefully and then paste them on the correct side of the paper. The left side is for B words, just like the board display. The right side is for words which do not begin with B. Monitor their progress as they work independently.

ACTIVITY 2: ENRICHMENT ACTIVITY

Follow the directions on Worksheet 13B for making butter.

Worksheet 13B: Have the children color the label and write their name in the space provided. Affix them to their jars of butter. Call their attention to the word "butter" and its beginning sound!

ACTIVITY 3: SEEING AND HEARING

Write some of the words from Lesson 12, Activity 1 on the board, some of which start with B and some which do not. Read the words aloud. Call on individual students to come to the board and circle the beginning B in the appropriate words. Read the word to them as they do so and ask the class to echo it back to you, affirming the correct response.

Worksheet 13C: Tell the students that they will be working on this together. Read the instructions aloud. Have them put their finger on the first word in the upper left hand side of the paper ("bed"). Read this word to them, then ask if they hear the B sound and see the letter B at the beginning of this word. When they respond correctly, direct them to circle only the letter B in this word. Monitor this activity carefully.

Have them point to the next word, moving from left to right across the page ("hat"). Read it aloud and ask if they hear the B sound and see the letter B at the beginning of the word. The response should be negative. Direct them that they should not circle anything in this word.

Continue through the worksheet in this same manner, reinforcing left-to-right reading, correct responses, and accurate circling.

Note: When you come to the written words, remind them that the written letters make the same sounds as the printed ones.

LESSON 14
TARGET SOUND: B AND A IN THE MIDDLE OF WORDS

ACTIVITY 1: HEARING

 Play the Museum Song for the children encouraging them to sing along while pointing to the corresponding letters on the flashcards.

Tell the children that the B sound is going to be the leader again today and that they must continue to listen carefully for it at the beginning of words:

Worksheet 14A (top): Read the instructions aloud to the children. Tell them that you will name the pictures for them while they respond independently on their own papers.

Row 1: xylophone, wink, bench
Row 2: butterfly, shoe, boat

ACTIVITY 2: WRITING

Worksheet 14A (bottom): Remind the children to follow the letter mazes on the lower line first, then return to the upper line to make the letters on their own.

ACTIVITY 3: SEEING AND HEARING

Display both the printed and written lower case A and ask the children what sound is made by this letter. Praise them for their correct responses and their good memories.

Remind them that sometimes a letter will be the leader of other letters at the beginning of a word, and sometimes it will get in line with other letters. Ask them if they remember this when we studied the letter "M,m."

Write the following words on the board, highlighting the A by writing it in a different color:

Sam   tap   fan   stand   ram

Replace the written A with the printed A and ask them why it is acceptable to do this.

Erase the board and write the same words again, without highlighting the A. Ask who can find the A now when it is the same color as all the other letters. Permit students to come to the board and circle the A in the words. Remove all the letters from display.

Worksheet 14B: Read the instructions aloud. Have them put their finger on the first word in the upper left hand corner ("stamp"). Read the word aloud, then ask if they hear the A sound and see the A letter in this word. Direct them to circle the entire word this time if it contains the A.

Continue in the same way with the other words, reading left to right, down the page. Monitor responses for accuracy. Help them to self-edit and correct if you notice oversights or errors.

LESSON 15
TARGET SOUND: A IN THE MIDDLE OF WORDS AND B

ACTIVITY 1: HEARING

Remind the children about the last activity you did together when they listened for the A sound and looked for the A letter in the middle of words. Challenge them to be good listeners again and tell you when they hear the A in the middle of the following words as you read them aloud:
(Caution them to be careful! Some of these words sound a lot alike!)

pat	mad	put	mud	fat	fit
had	bad	sad	send	ram	rim
hum	ham	cat	man	men	bet
bat	tap	tip	bug	big	fast

Ask the children if they noticed that the meaning of a word can depend on only one sound or letter. Give the words "hum" and "ham" as examples. Other examples may be: "cat" and "cut," "bug," "bag," and "big," etc.

Worksheet 15A: Read the instructions aloud. Ask which picture should be named first to see if they have developed left-to-right prereading behavior. Name all the pictures in order for them, having them repeat the labels as you go along. Then permit them to complete the worksheet independently as you monitor their work. You may repeat the label for any picture if requested, but do not give any other clues.

Row 1: dog, bat, pig
Row 2: sun, wolf, ram
Row 3: cat, tie, man

ACTIVITY 2: WRITING, SEEING AND HEARING

Call to the children's attention that we are back to listening for B again. It will be the leader at the beginning of the words which name the pictures on this page.

Worksheet 15B: Read the instructions aloud. Have the children follow the letter maze at the beginning of the first row. Then name the pictures for the children as they circle the pictures as instructed. Continue with the remainder of the worksheet in the same manner, one row at a time.

Row 1: barrel, apple, hat, bench
Row 2: horse, bear, bed, ax
Row 3: bat, bicycle, fan, rabbit (not bunny)
Row 4: bird, bell, anchor, ball

Worksheet 15C: Read the instructions aloud, then allow the children to complete the worksheet entirely on their own.

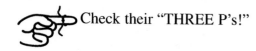 Check their "THREE P's!"

Worksheet 15D: Read the instructions aloud, then allow the children to complete the worksheet on their own. Monitor carefully and encourage neatness and accuracy.

Teaching tip: This may be a good time to encourage a "light" hand when writing and the importance of erasing completely when a mistake is made. Some children tend to press very hard when writing, which makes erasure more difficult and messy. Help children to have a firm, but not tense, grip on their pencils and gentle pressure. If they are writing correctly, their hands won't get tired so easily!

Worksheet 15E: Test. This test is optional and is added to evaluate your students if you feel it is necessary at this time. The answers are worth 2 points each.

LESSON 16
REVIEW AND TARGET SOUND: P

ACTIVITY 1: REVIEW

Present the three upper case printed letters A, M, and B to the children. On the board, write the written upper case counterparts. Call on students to come to the board and draw a line from the printed letter to its correct written form.

Repeat this exercise with the lower case printed and written letters.

Draw an artist's palette on the board with six "paint splotch" areas on it. Write one of the above letters on each area in either upper or lower case, in the colors indicated on the key at the bottom of Worksheet 16A.

Worksheet 16A: Read the instructions aloud and call their attention to the palette on the board. Remind the children that the letters on the board are the written letters and the ones on the page are the printed letters. They should be able to translate the written letter color key on the board to the printed letters used in the picture.

Allow them to work independently.

ACTIVITY 2: HEARING

 Play the Museum Song for the children encouraging them to sing along while pointing to the corresponding letters on the flashcards.

Ask the children if they remember which of the sounds they have studied so far is the "bursting" sound. This is the B sound. Make this sound several times for them. Challenge them to listen carefully as you "whisper" this sound, making the P sound. Are they able to hear the difference?

Use the indication gesture for B when you produce this sound (fingertips of one hand against your lips, opening fingers wide as the sound is produced). Now make the P sound several times using the same gesture, only using your index finger and thumb and minimizing the movement to make it "smaller." Describe that this is a "popping" sound, very quiet and small.

 Show the children the flashcard with the letter P on it. Have them hear the sound of P as in "pig."

Challenge them to indicate, using the above gesture, when they hear the P in the following list of sounds:

> f, s, p, a, t, p, d, r, m, n, g, p, a, p, p, d, s, f, p, r, m, a, n, p, g, t, p,
> a, d, f, p, p

Praise them for good listening. Now tell them that B and P are going to play hide-and-seek in the next list of sounds and that they must listen very carefully to find the P sound this time:

> p, p, p, b, b, b, p, p, b, b, p, b, p, b, b, b, p, p, p, b, b, p, b, p, b, p, p

Remember to make each sound distinctly, eliminating the "uh" after it as much as possible.

ACTIVITY 3:SEEING

Aa Tell the children that the letter which makes the P sound is the letter P. Show them the cards with the printed upper and lower case "P,p." Point out the features of each letter (the upper case has one big bump at the top on the right, the lower case is just like the upper except that it is placed lower on the line and is slightly smaller, etc.)

Display the upper and lower case "B,b." Point out the similarities and differences between these two letters in each case. Remind the students that just as B is louder, it also has more "bumps" in its letter.

Mix these cards with all the other printed upper case letters for the first quarter. Present them to the children in random order, instructing them to indicate when they see the target letter P.

Repeat this activity with the lower case letters, then with both upper and lower case letters combined.

Once again, you may notice some confusion when lower case B and D are presented. If this causes difficulty, take D out of the presentation pile for now. You may want to narrow the focus of this activity to ONLY the lower and upper case "B,b" and "P,p" to give more practice in discriminating between these two very similar letters.

On the board, write the written upper and lower case letters for P, describing and numbering your strokes as you do so. Compare and contrast the printed letters and the written letters—they look very much alike for this letter. Leave both the printed and written examples on the board as you present Worksheet 16B .

Worksheet 16B: Read the instructions aloud to the children and monitor their progress as they work independently.

MUSEUM Give your students the reproduction of *Portrait of Pig* and allow them to hang it in the museum. Talk to them about the story *The Alphabet Quest* and give them their museum bag. Allow them time to go through the house and collect items that begin with the sound of P to make their own museum. If you are teaching in a school setting, instruct the children to take the bag home and bring in objects the following day.

ACTIVITY 4: WRITING

Place guidelines and perimeter lines on the board. Call on students to come to the board and make the upper and lower case letter P. Remind them how the strokes are made and in what order.

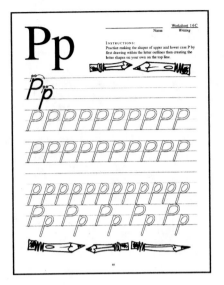

Worksheet 16C: Read the instructions aloud to the students.

Remind them that they will draw in the letter mazes FIRST, then go back up to the top of the page to make the letters on their own. Remember the "THREE P's!"

You may want to give the students the coloring page along with the flashcard. Read the information about the artist to your studentss as they color the picture. Explain that we want to take our time and color in the lines.

LESSON 17
TARGET SOUND: P

ACTIVITY 1: HEARING

Play the Museum Song for the children encouraging them to sing along while pointing to the corresponding letters on the flashcards.

Tell the children that the P sound is going to be the "leader" in the word list today and that they must continue to listen carefully for it at the beginning of these words:

penny	lock	target	David	fan	girl
cards	piano	peacock	match	pear	add
popsicle	top	ditch	paddle	rock	nut
sit	paste	music	faucet	gum	puddle

Worksheet 17A (top): Read the instructions aloud to the children. Tell them that you will name the pictures for them while they respond independently on their own papers.

Row 1: peacock, cards, piano
Row 2: top, pear, lock

ACTIVITY 2: WRITING

On the board, write the written upper and lower case letters for P, describing and numbering your strokes as you do so. Call students to the board to make the letters.

Worksheet 17A (bottom): Monitor their progress as they work independently.

ACTIVITY 3: SEEING

Worksheet 17B: Read the instructions aloud. Caution them that there is another letter on this page which looks almost like printed upper case P (the letter B), but do not tell them what it is. Monitor their work.

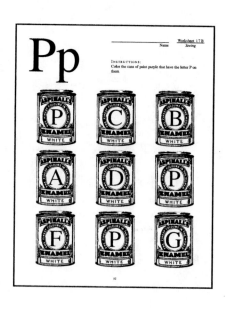

Lesson 18
Target Sound: P

ACTIVITY 1: HEARING

 Play the Museum Song for the children encouraging them to sing along while pointing to the corresponding letters on the flashcards.

Praise them for being such good listeners, especially with the quiet, little sound of P. Today, ask the children to think of as many words as they can which start with this sound. You may suggest categories such as toys, games, names, foods, etc. Write the words on the board, circling the written letter P in each word. Reinforce the use of upper case with proper names (make sure you have a few in the list!)

Worksheet 18A: Tell them that you will be doing this lesson together today. Read the instructions aloud. Ask them which picture name should be "read" first (upper left hand corner—"potatoes"). Beginning there, call on various students to identify the pictures in "reading order":

    Row 1: potatoes, dog, paint
    Row 2: wagon, pipes, pot
    Row 3: penguin, tent, frog

Allow them to complete the worksheet according to the directions.

ACTIVITY 2: WRITING

Place guidelines and perimeter lines on the board. Call on students to come to the board and make the upper and lower case letter P. Remind them how the strokes are made and in what order.

Worksheet 18B: Read the instructions aloud to the students.

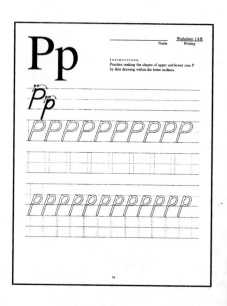

Remind them that they will draw in the letter mazes FIRST, make their own letters in the "fences" next, then go to the top of the page to make the letters on their own. Watch that children do not attempt to do the letters independently on the first line before they have practiced in the mazes and within the perimeter lines on the rest of the page.

LESSON 19
TARGET SOUND: P AND B

ACTIVITY 1: HEARING AND WRITING

 Play the Alphabet Song for the children encouraging them to sing along while pointing to the corresponding letters on the flashcards.

Tell the children that today's hearing list will have words which only begin with the B or P sound and that they must listen very carefully to only indicate those words which begin with P. Read the following list aloud, giving adequate time for proper response:

battle	picnic	porcupine	beast	pony
pizza	baby	ball	pinch	pirate
bear	pear	pin	bin	pet

Ask if anyone noticed that changing the beginning sound of some words (like "bear" and "pear," "pin" and "bin") changes their meanings. Ask if anyone can tell you how the word "bat" changes if the B sound is replaced with a P. (It becomes "pat.") Try this with some other word pairs such as "pig" and "big," "pack" and "back," etc.

Worksheet 19A: Read the instructions aloud to the students. Have them fill in the letter maze at the beginning of the top row of pictures. Name the pictures in order from left to right as the children respond on their papers, after first filling in the letter mazes at the beginning each time:

Row 1: rabbit, pizza, ring, pan
Row 2: baby, pin, cat, bear
Row 3: porcupine, apples, hammer, watch
Row 4: zebra, moose, pirates, ball

ACTIVITY 2: ART ACTIVITY

Bring the children to a common table in order to demonstrate the technique of "pointillism." Dip the eraser end of a pencil into shades of purple paint and dab gently on the pansy outline, filling in the areas with dots of color in various shades. Remind the children to practice first before working on their own papers.

Worksheet 19B: Encourage them to take their time and work neatly. Place the finished paintings in a safe place to dry.

Lesson 20
Review and Reading Aloud

ACTIVITY 1: REVIEW

Display the printed lower case P, B, and M for the children. Review the sounds which are made by each letter and give examples of common words which begin with each letter sound.

Read the following list of words to the children one at a time. After each word, point to each of the letters on display and ask which letter makes the beginning sound of that word. Do not say the letter name or sound as you point to it—simply ask "Is it this one?" and solicit their response. Repeat the word after the children have come to agreement about the correct letter and reinforce their responses.

man	bell	pig	baby	mermaid
piano	monster	pansy	butter	parade
math	park	barrel	minister	puddle

Aa Distribute a set of lower case P, B, and M letter cards to each child. Tell them to hold up the proper letter which makes the beginning sound of each of the words as you read through the above list a second time.

Note those students who are slower or frequently incorrect in their responses; further guided practice may be warranted.

Collect the letter cards and present Worksheet 20A.

Worksheet 20A: Read the instructions aloud. Call on specific students to name the pictures for the class. Repeat the label once or twice and monitor as students respond independently. Continue with the rest of the worksheet in the same manner.

Row 1: man, bell, pig
Row 2: baby, mermaid, piano

ACTIVITY 2: WRITING

Call on students to come to the board and write specific letters as in Lesson 12. Remind them of the order and direction of the strokes.

Worksheet 20B: Ask the children what they will do first on this page (the letter mazes at the beginning of the first row: "A,a"). They may go on to write their own letters on the lines provided for practicing "A,a," and then proceed to the letter "B,b," and so on.

This is a good time to remind students about pencil pressure, neatness, careful erasing, etc.

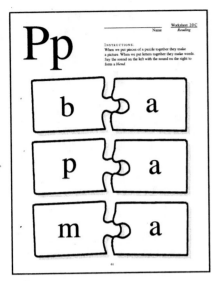

ACTIVITY 3: READING ALOUD

Distribute Worksheet 20C for them to reference as you present this lesson.

Ask the children if they remember when you told them that the B·sound did not like to be alone. For that reason, the next letter in line wants to "stick" to B when it is the leader and their sounds "run together."

 Show the children the puzzle pieces B and A. Make the letter sounds separately, then bring the pieces together and interlock them. Now say the sounds as an open syllable "ba" (remember, this is the short A sound as in "apple") without gap or "uh" between the sounds. Have the students echo this several times.

Although 'ma' and 'pa' can have the 'aw' sound, use the short A sound in this exercise.

Ask if they remember how some words changed in meaning when the beginning sound changed from B to P. Remind them of some of the example word pairs (Lesson 19). Ask if anyone can tell you what "ba" would sound like if the B were replaced with P. Praise the correct response "pa."

Show them the puzzle pieces P and A. Put them together and repeat the "pa" syllable several times, having the children echo it after you.

Now challenge the children to tell you how they should say it if the P were replaced with M. Display the two puzzle pieces M and A and bring them together. Praise their correct responses and tell them that this is a great accomplishment—THEY ARE READING!

If teaching in a school setting, tell them that they may take this worksheet home and read it to their parents tonight.

LESSON 21
TARGET SOUND: T

ACTIVITY 1: HEARING

Play the Alphabet Song for the children encouraging them to sing along while pointing to the corresponding letters on the flashcards.

Inform the children that the sound they will be listening for today is another quiet sound. Demonstrate the T sound and tell them it is made by "touching the tip of the tongue behind the top teeth." Ask them to count the number of T sounds in that phrase. Have them echo the phrase after you several times, faster and faster. Tell them this is their first "tongue twister," two more words that begin with T!

Show the children the flashcard with the letter T on it. Have them hear the sound of T as in "table."

Tell them that because they are such good listeners you will be having them listen for the T sound at the *beginning* of words right away this time. Make an upper case T with the index finger of one hand on top of the index finger of the other hand and have the children copy this gesture. This will be their way of indicating when they hear the T in the following list:

table	Tim	bag	rug	tennis	tub
scale	bike	top	banana	sun	tent
tacks	fox	gift	man	tie	bone
name	animal	Tony	tease	bat	mail

Worksheet 21A: Read the instructions aloud to the children and tell them you will be completing this together today. Say the names of the pictures one by one, asking them if they hear the T sound at the beginning of each label:

Row 1: top, tent, bike
Row 2: scale, tie, rabbit
Row 3: tacks, top, turtle

Give your students the reproduction of the *The Supper at Emmaus* and allow them to hang it in the museum. Talk to them about the story *The Alphabet Quest* and give them their museum bag. Allow them time to go through the house and collect items that begin with the sound of T to make their own museum. If you are teaching in a school setting, instruct the children to take the bag home and bring in objects the following day.

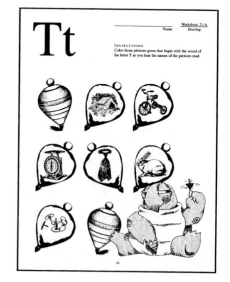

ACTIVITY 2: SEEING AND WRITING

Ask them to make the gesture for T again and tell them that this is the way to make an upper case T. Display the upper and lower case printed "T,t," drawing attention to the features of each letter (the upper case has two straight lines with the top horizontal one balanced on the bottom vertical one, the lower case is like a cross with a hook, etc.)

On the board, write the written upper and lower case letters for "T,t," describing and numbering your strokes as you do so. Compare and contrast the printed letters and the written letters—again, they look very much alike for this letter.

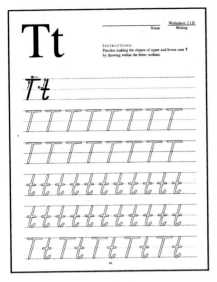

Place guidelines and perimeter lines on the board. Call on students to come to the board and make the upper and lower case letter T. Remind them how the strokes are made and in what order.

Worksheet 21B: Read the instructions aloud to the students. Remind them that they will draw in the letter mazes FIRST, then go back up to the top of the page to make the letters on their own.

 Remember the "THREE P's!"

 You may want to give the students the coloring page along with the flashcard. Read the information about the artist to your students before they color the picture. Explain that we want to take our time and color in the lines.

LESSON 22
TARGET SOUND: T

ACTIVITY 1: HEARING AND SEEING

 Play the Museum Song for the children encouraging them to sing along while pointing to the corresponding letters on the flashcards.

Ask the children if any of them remember the little "tongue twister" from the last lesson ("touch the tip of the tongue behind the top teeth"). See if anyone remembers the sound which is made when you follow those directions. Echo the T sound several times.

Remind them that it is time for careful listening again. You will be saying a new list of words and they are to indicate when they hear the T at the *beginning:*

food	teacher	fan	ruby	mask
tiger	turkey	gum	parasol	ring
light	cow	bull	wagon	hat
gown	tuba	red	towel	doll

Worksheet 22A: Read the directions aloud. Have the students complete the first letter mazes. Name the pictures in order, left to right, for them and allow them to circle the correct pictures:

Row 1: tiger, gun, parasol, tie
Row 2: hat, cow, tent, bike
Row 3: ring, table, wagon, turkey
Row 4: top, rabbit, cat, light(bulb)

Monitor their work carefully and assist them to self-correct as necessary.

ACTIVITY 2: SEEING AND ART ACTIVITY

 Remind the children that the letter which makes the T sound is the letter T. Show them the cards with the printed upper and lower case "T,t."

Mix these cards with the other printed upper case letters for the first quarter. Present them to the children in random order, instructing them to indicate when they see the target letter T.

Repeat this activity with the lower case letters, then with both upper and lower case letters combined.

Write all the upper and lower case letters they have studied so far on the board, including the "T,t." Ask the class which written letter corresponds to the printed upper case T. Do the same with the printed lower case T.

Worksheet 22B: Using the templates provided on this worksheet, cut the shapes out of wallpaper or construction paper, pasting the elements onto another piece of paper. Remind the students that "tulip" begins with the letter T.

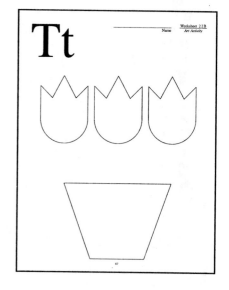

ACTIVITY 3: READING ALOUD

Bring out the puzzle pieces for B, P, T, and M. Review with the children the sounds that are made by each letter. Bring out the puzzle pieces for A. Review the sound of short A. Ask the children if they remember how to make the sounds very quickly together. Have them echo as you display and read "ta," "ba," "pa," and "ma" in that order.

Replace the beginning sound with the puzzle piece with T on it. Call on one student to tell you what it sounds like now ("ta"). Keep this on display as you present Worksheet 22C.

Worksheet 22C: Read the instructions aloud to the students. Have them read the open syllables in order from the top to the bottom of the page. Using the worksheet as a display, point to different syllables at random and call on individual students to read them. Once again, remind them that this is really READING!

Have them put Worksheet 22C aside, or turn it over on their desks.

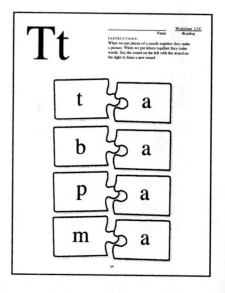

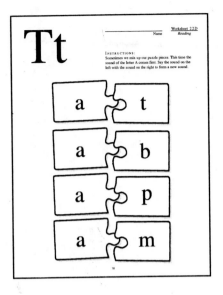

Ask them if they remember when the A sound was the leader in words. Give them some simple examples of words with the beginning A sound and ask them to supply a few more. Write these on the board, circling or highlighting the A in a different color.

Show them the puzzle piece for A. Tell them that sometimes the sounds we have studied so far will come after the A in line. Display the puzzle piece for M and make the M sound. Bring the pieces closer together as you say each sound, until they are hooked together and you are saying the syllable "am." Have the children echo it several times.

Now ask what it would be if you replaced the M with the B sound. Put the pieces for A and B together and have the children echo the syllable "ab." Repeat this process with "ap" and "at."

Worksheet 22D: Read the instructions aloud. Ask for a student volunteer to read the first syllable at the top ("at"). Continue in the same manner for the other three syllables.

Praise the children for their good reading and tell them to take both worksheets home to read to their parents tonight.

LESSON 23
REVIEW

ACTIVITY 1: HEARING

Play the Museum Song for the children encouraging them to sing along while pointing to the corresponding letters on the flashcards.

Divide the board into five equal columns. At the top of each column write one of the following letter pairs: "A,a," "M,m," "B,b," "P,p," "T,t."

Ask who can tell you what sound is made by each of those letters.

Have the children brainstorm to come up with common words which begin with any of the above five sounds. Write these words in the proper columns, circling or highlighting the beginning letters.

To encourage careful editing skills, occasionally write a word in the wrong column and see if the students can "catch" you in your error. Praise them for every mistake they can find before you can!

Erase the board. Now draw five circles in a vertical line down the board and beside each circle write one of these five letters in lower case.

Say the following word: "box." Tell them that since "box" starts with the sound B, you will fill in the circle beside the letter B on the board. Demonstrate this, filling in the circle completely. Erase this (redrawing the circle if necessary) and call on students to fill in the board circles beside the correct letters for the beginning sound as you say the following words:

basket	table	park	mother	ashes
alligator	ball	puppy	man	baby
moose	top	tiger	bed	pizza
piano	apple	toe	pocket	bake

Worksheet 23A: Read the instructions aloud and monitor their responses as you name each picture:

Row 1: bed, top, tiger
Row 2: ape, moose, pizza
Row 3: piano, ball, boot
Row 4: man, baby, alligator

ACTIVITY 2: WRITING

Write the upper and lower case "T,t" and "A,a" on the board, numbering and ordering your strokes carefully. Call on individual students to practice the letters for the class, numbering and describing their strokes in the same manner. Permit students to make the letters independently on the board as you call on them.

Write the letters T, A, and P on the board. Read the word for the children and have them echo it. Explain to the children that when we put letters together they make words. Put lines on the board and write it again on the lines with the letters spaced closer together as a word unit. Call on individual students to come to the board and copy this word on the lines.

Worksheet 23B: Read the instructions aloud. Monitor their work as they write the letters independently, especially watching their spacing on the final word "tap."

 Percival's Pairs: Using A, M, B, P, and T

LESSON 24
TARGET SOUND: T, MEDIAL (MIDDLE) A, AND REVIEW

ACTIVITY 1: HEARING

 Play the Alphabet Song for the children encouraging them to sing along while pointing to the corresponding letters on the flashcards.

Instruct the children to listen carefully to the following paragraph as you read it slowly and to indicate when they hear the T sound alone or at the beginning of any word:

Today we will talk about the T sound. T is a teeny, tiny sound made by touching the tip of the tongue behind the top teeth. Tons of words start with T. Here are ten of them: tuna, tumbleweed, tassel, taste, tinsel, terrible, temple, tin, toybox, tugboat. You can tell a friend to touch his toes, tickle his tummy, or talk on the telephone using the T sound. Don't you think the T sound is totally terrific?

Praise the children for being great listeners.

Worksheet 24A: Read the instructions aloud. Name the pictures for the children as they respond independently.

ACTIVITY 2: HEARING (MEDIAL A)

Read the following list of words aloud in succession, not pausing for any response:

cat	fan	sad	pad	bat	mad
nap	sat	tack	map	tap	fat

Ask if anyone can tell you what is the same in all those words. Whether or not you get a correct response (there is a short A sound in all of them), write several of them on the board in a vertical column, with the "a's" right below each other. Call their attention to the medial A by circling each one. Read them again. Ask if anyone can give you any more words that have A in the middle.

You may get more than a few incorrect responses. Usually these will be using other short vowel sounds instead of short A. Repeat these carefully and then make the short A sound to help students contrast the two sounds. Try replacing the incorrect vowel sound with the short A to form a possible new word. Write these words on the board, circling or highlighting the A in each one.

Worksheet 24B: Read the instructions aloud. Name the pictures one at a time for the children and have them put a dot of blue in one corner of the box if they hear the short A sound in the label. After you have named all the pictures, have them go back and color in all the boxes with blue dots.

Row 1: rat, cat, dog
Row 2: bat, bed, gun
Row 3: hat, fan, pig

ACTIVITY 3: READING ALOUD

Write the following open syllables on the board: "ma," "ba," "pa," "ta." Ask the children what letter is in all of them (A). Ask what sound it makes (short A). Now ask which one of them starts with the M sound. Have a student come up and point to the correct syllable. Ask the children how we would say, or read, this ("ma").

Lead them to read the rest of the syllables aloud, based on the pattern of "ma."

Erase all the consonants, leaving the A letters on the board. Ask what would happen if you let the A sound be the leader and put all the other sounds after it. Write M after the first A. Sound it out slowly for the children, then blend the sounds quickly to form the syllable. Have the children echo it. Write B after the second A. Ask them "If this first pair of letters says 'am', what does the second pair say?" Continue with "ap" and "at" in the same manner.

Worksheet 24C: Write the syllables on the board in the order they are presented on the worksheet. Point to them one at a time, first going down the left column, having the children echo them after you. Repeat this, asking them to read without echoing you.

Proceed to the right column, echoing first, then independently reading. Finally, point randomly to syllables, first in the right column, then in the left, and call on specific students to sound out the syllables and read them aloud.

Tell them they may take this sheet home to read to their parents and praise them for their hard work!

LESSON 25
TARGET SOUND: D

ACTIVITY 1: HEARING

 Play the Museum Song for the children encouraging them to sing along while pointing to the corresponding letters on the flashcards.

Ask the children if they remember when you studied the B and P sounds. Remind them that one was louder than the other and ask if they know which was the "bursting" sound and which was the "popping" (whispering) sound.

Tell them that the T sound has a louder buddy too. Demonstrate that if they use their voices to make the T sound louder, it becomes the sound D. Make the D sound several times, minimizing the "uh" after it as much as possible. Have them experiment with this, pointing out that their tongue is in the same position in their mouths as with the T sound, but all they are doing differently is adding their voices.

 An additional reinforcement of this concept would be to have the children put one hand on their throat (larynx) while they experiment going back and forth between the T and D sounds. They should feel the vibration when they are using their voices for D. They may also try this for B and P.

Using your right hand, show them the sign language hand signal for D: index finger straight up, other fingers curved to meet the tip of the thumb. Hold your hand so that it looks like a lower case D when viewed by the students. Assist them to make the same hand signal with their right hands. Tell them this will be their way to indicate when they hear the D sound in today's listening activities.

Because T and D are so much alike, they like to play hide and seek with each other. Challenge the children to listen for the D sound in the following list of sounds:

t, t, t, d, d, t, t, d, t, d, d, t, t, d, d, d, t, t, d, t, d

Praise them for their good listening. Now read the following list of words aloud, asking them to indicate when they hear the D sound at the *beginning* of the words:

fox	dog	mule	sun	ram	unicorn
duck	basket	man	donut	doctor	animal
nurse	dime	fudge	damp	apple	dice
desk	soap	deep	river	Dan	mug

Worksheet 25A (top): Read the instructions aloud. Name the pictures for the children, or call on individual students to name them, as you monitor their responses.

Row 1: dog, ram, mule
Row 2: sun, duck, unicorn

Give your students the reproduction of *The Dancer* and allow them to hang it in the museum. Talk to them about the story *The Alphabet Quest* and give them their museum bag. Allow them time to go through the house and collect items that begin with the sound of D to make their own museum. If you are teaching in a school setting, instruct the children to take the bag home and bring in objects the following day.

ACTIVITY 2: SEEING

Tell the children that the letter which makes the D sound is the letter D. Show them the cards with the printed upper and lower case "D, d." Point out the features of each letter (one large bump on the right side of the upper case letter, small bump on the left side of the lower case letter)

Mix these cards with the other printed upper case letters for the first quarter. Present them to the children in random order, instructing them to indicate when they see the target letter D. Repeat this activity with the lower case letters, then with both upper and lower case letters combined.
Now is the time to do careful instruction on the differences between the letters B, P, and D. Display all three printed lower case letters for the children. Above the B and P, place their upper case counterparts. Draw attention to the fact that the bump on the lower case B is on the same side as the two bumps on the upper case B. Show them that the single bump on the upper case P is on the right side also and that the lower case P looks just like its "mom," only smaller and lower on the line.

Now point out that upper case D has its bump on the right side like the other upper case letters, but that lower case D is different. Demonstrate the hand signal for D again, using your right hand and orienting it so children can view it properly as forming the lower case D.

Tell them that if they forget which is which, they can make the hand signal with their right hands and be reminded of the correct letter D.

At this time, present only the lower case B, P, and D in a random mix-up activity as above to reinforce the discrimination of these three letters.

On the board, write the written upper and lower case letters for "D,d," describing and numbering your strokes as you do so. Compare and contrast the printed letters and the written letters—they look very much alike for this letter. Leave both the printed and written examples on the board.

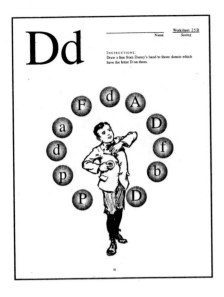

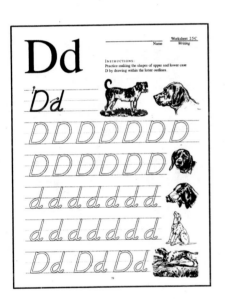

ACTIVITY 3: WRITING

Place guidelines and perimeter lines on the board. Call on students to come to the board and make the upper and lower case letter D. Remind them how the strokes are made and in what order.

Worksheet 25A (bottom): Read the instructions aloud to the students.

 Tell them that they will draw in the letter mazes FIRST, then go back up make the letters on their own. Watch that children do not attempt to do the letters independently on the first line before they have practiced in the mazes on the rest of the page.

Worksheet 25C: Allow them to work independently on this practice page.

 Remember the "THREE P's!"

 You may want to give the students the coloring page along with the flashcard. Read the information about the artist to your students before they color the picture.

LESSON 26
TARGET SOUND: N

ACTIVITY 1: HEARING

 Play the Alphabet Song for the children encouraging them to sing along while pointing to the corresponding letters on the flashcards.

Tell the children that today's sound is made the same way as the T and the D, but will sound very different. Make the N sound several times. Point out that the "tip of your tongue is behind the top teeth" but that instead of pushing the air out of your mouth, you let it come out your nose!

Show the children the flashcard with the letter N on it. Have them hear the sound of N as in "nuts."

Demonstrate again and have the children echo it several times. Ask them if they use their voices for this sound (yes).

Remind them that they have studied another sound where the air comes out their noses: M. Make both sounds alternately and have the children echo, noticing the differences in production.

A fun optional activity would be to ask if anyone has ever had a stuffy nose when they have had a bad cold. Demonstrate for the children how funny N and M sound when the air can't come out your nose by saying the following sentence, blocking the nasal airflow: "I know it's not nice when your nose is in a knot!" They may repeat it after you, holding their noses to block the airflow.

Because M and N are "nose sounds," they can often be confused. Challenge the children to find the N as you read the following list of sounds aloud. They can indicate the N sound by touching their noses.

n, n, m, m, m, n, m, n, m, m, n, n, n, m, n, n, m, m, n

Tell the children that the N sound is going to be the "leader" in a list of new words today and that they must continue to listen carefully for it at the *beginning* of these words:

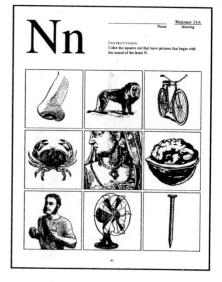

doll	nose	boy	nut	lion	next
man	new	crab	penny	nail	moose
bird	necklace	flag	attic	note	bike
animal	nothing	soda	Ned	near	fox

Worksheet 26A: Read the instructions aloud to the children. Tell them that you will name the pictures for them while they respond independently on their own papers.

Row 1: nose, lion, bike
Row 2: crab, necklace, nut
Row 3: man, fan, nail

Give your students the reproduction of *Free Sample—Try One* and allow them to hang it in the museum. Talk to them about the story *The Alphabet Quest* and give them their museum bag. Allow them time to go through the house and collect items that begin with the sound of N to make their own museum. If you are teaching in a school setting, instruct the children to take the bag home and bring in objects the following day.

ACTIVITY 2: SEEING

Aa | Tell the children that the letter which makes the N sound is the letter N. Show them the cards with the printed upper and lower case "N,n." Point out the features of each letter (one pointed mountain and valley in the upper case, the lower case has a rounded hill or hump, etc.)

Mix these cards with the other printed upper case letters for the first quarter. Present them to the children in random order, instructing them to indicate when they see the target letter N.

Repeat this activity with the lower case letters, then with both upper and lower case letters combined.

Monitor carefully their discrimination of "M,m" and "N,n." If they show signs of difficulty between the two, present only those four letters and call attention to the similarities and differences between them. Then repeat the above activity, using only those four letters.

On the board, write the written upper and lower case letters for "N,n," describing and numbering your strokes as you do so. Compare and contrast the printed letters and the written letters—they look very much alike for this letter. Leave both the printed and written examples on the board as you present Worksheet 26B.

Worksheet 26B: Read the instructions aloud. Monitor as they work independently.

ACTIVITY 3: WRITING

Place guidelines and perimeter lines on the board. Call on students to come to the board and make the upper and lower case letter N. Remind them how the strokes are made and in what order.

Worksheet 26C: Read the instructions aloud to the students.

Remind them that they will draw in the letter mazes FIRST, then go back up to the top of the page to make the letters on their own. Remember the "THREE P's!" Remind them about gentle pencil pressure and good erasing also.

You may want to give the students the coloring page along with the flashcard. Read the information about the artist to your students before they color the picture. Explain that we want to take our time and color in the lines.

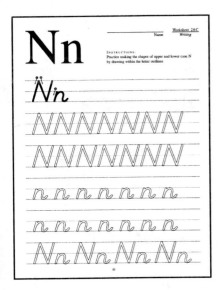

LESSON 27
REVIEW AND READING ALOUD

ACTIVITY 1: HEARING AND SEEING

Display the lower case printed letters A, M, B, P, T, D, N. Have the children echo the sounds which are made by each letter as you point to them in random order. Ask the group to make the correct sound without your demonstration when you point to various letters. Call on specific students to do this independently.

Choose two of the letters to keep on display and remove the others. Say a word which begins with one of the letters on display.

 (Be careful—do not use words with consonant blends! Stick to simple single syllable words such as "nut," "bag," etc.)

Ask individual students to come up and point to the letter which makes the beginning sound of that word.

Change the two letters on display and repeat the activity. Continue in this manner until students have had adequate practice associating the beginning sounds with the correct letters.

Worksheet 27A: Tell the children that you will be doing this page together as a group. Read the instructions aloud. Call on a student to label the first picture ("nest"). Ask if they can tell you what sound is at the beginning of the word "nest." Have them put their finger on the letter under the picture which makes this sound. Check that they are all pointing to the same letter, then instruct them to circle the N.

Continue in the same way for the rest of the page.

   Row 1: nest, bell, bear, top
   Row 2: dog, alligator, pizza, dice
   Row 3: potatoes, ax, nose, turtle

 Pay particular attention to the discrimination of the letters under the pictures of "dice" and "potatoes." This will be where visual errors will be more likely to occur. Students who are showing continued difficulty with discrimination of similar letters should be carefully monitored for possible visual problems.

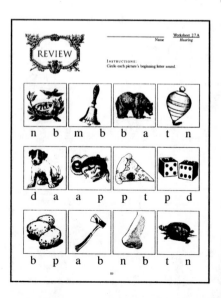

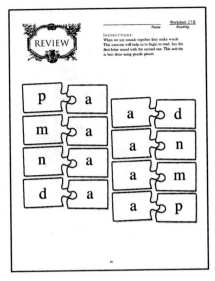

ACTIVITY 2: READING ALOUD

 Display the puzzle pieces for all of the consonants studied so far. Review the sounds of these letters with the children, both by echoing and by independent response.

Using the A piece as the second sound, place it next to each of the consonants in turn, sounding out the syllable which is formed and having the children echo each one. Repeat this exercise in random order, both by echoing and by independent response. Ask what happens when we place the letter M in line after the A. Help the children to sound this out on their own. Replace the M with one of the other consonants and sound this out. Continue with the rest of the consonants.

Worksheet 27B: Present the worksheet and call on specific students to read the syllables in order down one column and then down the other.

Praise them for their terrific reading and if teaching in a school setting, tell them that they may take this worksheet home and read it to their parents tonight.

LESSON 28
TARGET SOUND: G

ACTIVITY 1: HEARING

 Play the Museum Song for the children encouraging them to sing along while pointing to the corresponding letters on the flashcards.

Tell the children that today they will be studying a very "good" sound. This sound is so "good" that it even starts the word "God!" See if the children can tell you what sound this is. Reinforce the correct response, emphasizing the sound several times and having the children echo it.

Show the children the flashcard with the letter G on it. Have them hear the sound of G as in "goat."

Challenge the children to indicate to you when they hear the G sound as it plays hide-and-seek with these other sounds:

f, t, g, r, a, g, g, m, n, g, a, s, f, g, b, g, p, g, g, n, d, g, a, g

Tell the children that the G sound is going to be the "leader" in some of the words in the following list and that they should indicate to you when they hear it:

girl	garage	boat	paper	gum
carrot	goose	gun	fish	plane
goat	guitar	animal	doll	game
apple	fox	gate	gift	keys*

 *Be careful with this one—it begins with K which is the unvoiced equivalent of G.

Worksheet 28A: Read the instructions aloud to the children. Tell them that you will name the pictures for them while they respond independently on their own papers.

Row 1: gun, goose, keys, carrot
Row 2: plane, gate, fish

 Give your students the reproduction of the *Children at Play* and allow them to hang it in the museum. Talk to them about the story *The Alphabet Quest* and give them their museum bag. Allow them time to go through the house and collect items that begin with the sound of G to make their own museum. If you are teaching in a school setting, instruct the children to take the bag home and bring in objects the following day.

ACTIVITY 2: SEEING

Aa Tell the children that the letter which makes the G sound is the letter G. Show them the cards with the printed upper and lower case "G, g."

Point out the features of each letter (the upper case letter is a half circle with a short straight line into it, the lower case is a circle with a "paddle tail" like a beaver, etc.)

Mix these cards with the other printed upper case letters for the first quarter. Present them to the children in random order, instructing them to indicate when they see the target letter G.

Repeat this activity with the lower case letters, then with both upper and lower case letters combined.

On the board, write the written upper and lower case letters for "G,g," describing and numbering your strokes as you do so. Compare and contrast the printed letters and the written letters. The upper cases look much alike,

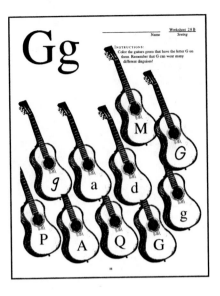

but the lower cases have several differences. The printed lower case G is fancier and would be very hard to write. So the lower case written G is simpler. It still has the circle part and the tail, but both are easier to make. Leave both the printed and written examples on the board as you present Worksheet 28B.

Worksheet 28B: Read the instructions aloud to the children and monitor their progress as they work independently.

ACTIVITY 3: WRITING

Place guidelines and perimeter lines on the board. Call on students to come to the board and make the upper and lower case letter G.

Worksheet 28C: Read the instructions aloud to the students.

 Watch that children do not attempt to do the letters independently on the first line before they have practiced in the mazes on the rest of the page. They should know the "routine" for doing these pages by now!

ACTIVITY 4: ART ACTIVITY

Worksheet 28D: Follow the directions at the top of the page. Assist the children to assemble their "goggles" when they are completed.

You may want to give the students the coloring page along with the flashcard. Read the information about the artist to your students before they color the picture. Explain that we want to take our time and color in the lines.

LESSON 29
REVIEW AND READING ALOUD

ACTIVITY 1: HEARING, SEEING AND WRITING

Put the letter mazes for upper and lower case "N,n" and "G,g" on the board in a vertical column as on Worksheet 29A. Call on a student to come to the board and follow the letter maze for upper case N, numbering and ordering the strokes.

To the right of this letter, write the following words, all in upper case letters: NOSE, PIANO, HORSE, NUT. Ask the student at the board to circle each upper case N which occurs at the beginning of any of those words.

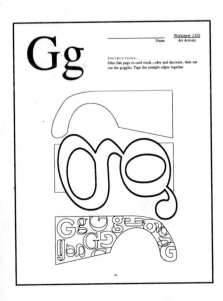

(Watch the word PIANO—point out, if necessary, that the N in this word is not at the beginning.)

Continue in the same manner for the upper case G, using these words all in upper case: UMBRELLA, GOAT, SLED, GUN.

Continue for lower case N, using words written all in lower case: necklace, lock, nest, ball.

Continue for lower case G, using these words written in lower case: keys, guitar, pig (watch out here also!), girl. Erase the board before presenting Worksheet 29A.

Worksheet 29A: Read the instructions aloud. Permit them to follow the first letter maze (N), then read the labels for the pictures. They are the same as the words you wrote on the board for the upper case N exercise. Monitor their work as they circle the correct pictures according to the designated beginning sound.

Remind the students that in each row there may be more than one picture which starts with the sound at the beginning of the row. Continue with the rest of the page in the same manner.

    Row 1: nose, piano, horse, nut
    Row 2: umbrella, goat, sledding, gun
    Row 3: necklace, lock, net, ball
    Row 4: keys, guitar, pig, girl

ACTIVITY 2: REVIEW

Write all the consonants which have been studied so far on the board in lower case: m, b, p, t, d, n, g. Point to the letters randomly, asking the children to tell you what sound each one makes. If they have any difficulty with any letter, have them echo the sound several times, then return to it at the end of the exercise for independent response.

Read the following words one at a time and ask specific students to come to the board, point to the letter which makes the beginning sound of that word, and then write it on their own on the board under its example. (The lines should be present as a writing guide.)

mask	duck	goose	teeth	box	nose
piece	girl	neck	Dave	toy	park

Leave the written lower case letters on the board as you present Worksheet 29B.

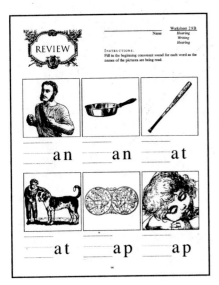

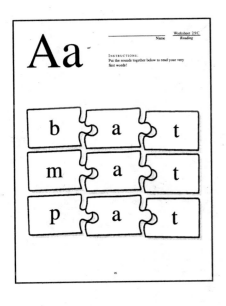

Worksheet 29B: Read the instructions aloud. Call on students to tell you what sound is at the beginning of the label for each picture. Call their attention to the letters on the board, but do NOT tell them which letter represents that sound. Prompt them to decide which of the letters should be written on the lines under the pictures and have them write their responses independently on their papers. Monitor carefully.

Row 1: man, pan, bat
Row 2: pat, map, nap

ACTIVITY 3: READING ALOUD

 Display the puzzle pieces for M, B, and P. Review the sounds. Hook them up with the letter piece for A and guide the children to blend the sounds to form the syllables. Repeat these several times, echoing, and pointing at them randomly.

Now tell the students that the line of sounds is going to get longer! Place the puzzle piece for T next to, but not adjoining, the "ma" pieces. Slowly sound out the "ma" syllable, adding the T at the end. Bring the T closer to the "ma" as you say the word more quickly, finally joining the T to the "ma" and saying the word "mat" clearly, without emphasis on or prolongation of any sound. Have the children echo this several times.

This is a word! It means something—ask if anyone knows what a "mat" is. They have just read their first real word! Praise them for this accomplishment. Continue in the same way with "bat" and "pat." Discuss briefly the meanings of each of these words, perhaps putting them into sentences to draw out their uses. Help them to notice that two of the letters in each word are the same and it is the beginning letter that makes the difference, both in sound and in meaning.

Worksheet 29C: Present the worksheet and call on students to read the words aloud to the class.

Before passing out Worksheet 29D, sign them in the space provided.

Worksheet 29D: Have the children write their first names on the appropriate space and allow them to cut it out.

LESSON 30
TARGET SOUND: G

ACTIVITY 1: HEARING

Instruct the children to take out a green crayon. Tell them that you will be reading a list of words to them and they are to hold up the green crayon each time they hear the G sound at the beginning of one of the words:

goat	funny	nest	guitar	golf	ball
rabbit	nose	gun	goose	sun	necklace
game	dime	gas	nibble	nap	neat

Praise them for their careful listening. Now instruct them to take out a red crayon. Now they are to hold up the red crayon every time they hear a word which begins with the N sound. Read the above list again.

Finally, tell them that this time they will be listening for either the G or the N at the beginning of the words and that they are to either hold up the green crayon for the G words or the red crayon for the N words. Remind them that some of the words won't begin with either G or N and that they should not hold up any crayon for those words. Read the above list again, monitoring their responses carefully. Repeat the words which may have given them more difficulty and continue until they are prompt and confident in their responses.

Worksheet 30A: Read the instructions aloud. Instruct them to put a dot of either green or red in the corner of each picture as you label them, according to the directions. After all the names have been given and dots placed, they may go back and color the pictures with the proper color.

Row 1: necklace, goat, golf
Row 2: gun, nest, guitar
Row 3: nose, goose, nut

ACTIVITY 2: WRITING

Put the letter mazes for B, A, T on the board. Draw writing lines beside this set of letters and add perimeter lines, as on Worksheet 30B. Call on students to come to the board and either write in the mazes or write the letters independently on the lines provided, numbering and describing the strokes as they do so. Assist the children to read the word aloud by sounding out as instructed.

Repeat with the letters P, A, T and M, A, T.

Worksheet 30B: Read the instructions aloud and permit the children to work independently. Remind about proper pencil pressure and careful erasing.

ACTIVITY 3: READING ALOUD

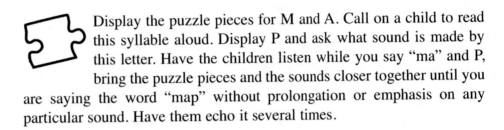 Display the puzzle pieces for M and A. Call on a child to read this syllable aloud. Display P and ask what sound is made by this letter. Have the children listen while you say "ma" and P, bring the puzzle pieces and the sounds closer together until you are saying the word "map" without prolongation or emphasis on any particular sound. Have them echo it several times.

Repeat this process with "mad" and "bat."

Worksheet 30C: Call on students to read the words on the page as you point to them randomly.

Praise them for their terrific reading and if teaching in a school setting, tell them that they may take this worksheet home and read it to their parents tonight.

 Worksheet 30D: Test. This test is optional and is added to evaluate your students if you feel it is necessary at this time. The answers are worth 2 points each.

LESSON 31
TARGET SOUND: S

ACTIVITY 1: HEARING

Play the Museum Song for the children encouraging them to sing along while pointing to the corresponding letters on the flashcards.

Today's sound is a "serpent" sound and it hisses: "ssssss." Instruct the students that the tip of the tongue is behind the top teeth, but that the air just leaks out slowly to make this sound. Have them echo the sound several times.

This is a sound whose production is later to develop in some children. You may hear some "lisping" where the air is directed to the side of the mouth, or some substitution of "th," where the tongue is placed too far forward. Most children self-correct this sound as they mature. Describing the correct placement of the tongue and direction of airflow will assist most of them in this process.

Show the children the flashcard with the letter S on it. Have them hear the sound of S as in "sun."

Tell them they are such good listeners that you think they can find the S in the beginning of words right away. Instruct them to indicate by making a "squiggle" in the air with their index fingers (in the rough form of the letter S) when they hear S as the leader in these words:

sand	girl	button	family	sun	mother
puppy	socks	saddle	rug	gate	father
sister	bone	pet	seal	bear	sunglasses
dart	tune	piano	soap	farm	buddy

Worksheet 31A: Read the instructions aloud. Call on students to label the pictures one by one as you monitor their responses.

Row 1: dog, fox, sun
Row 2: sunglasses, saddle, rooster
Row 3: seal, bear, socks

Give your students the reproduction of the *Le Semeur* and allow them to hang it in the museum. Talk to them about the story *The Alphabet Quest* and give them their museum bag. Allow them time to go through the house and collect items that begin with the sound of S to make their own museum. If you are teaching in a school setting, instruct the children to take the bag home and bring in objects the following day.

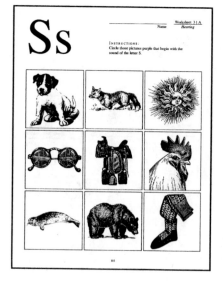

ACTIVITY 2: SEEING

Tell the children that the letter which makes the S sound is the letter S. Show them the cards with the printed upper and lower case "S,s." Point out the features of each letter (a "squiggle" like a serpent, which starts at the upper right and curves down and around to the left). The lower case is just a smaller version.

Mix these cards with the other printed upper case letters for the first quarter. Present them to the children in random order, instructing them to indicate when they see the target letter S.

Repeat this activity with the lower case letters, then with both upper and lower case letters combined.

On the board, write the written upper and lower case letters for S, describing your strokes as you do so. Compare and contrast the printed letters and the written letters—they look almost identical for this letter. Leave both the printed and written examples on the board as you present Worksheet 31B.

Worksheet 31B: Read the instructions aloud to the children and monitor their progress as they work independently.

ACTIVITY 3: WRITING

Place guidelines and perimeter lines on the board. Call on students to come to the board and make the upper and lower case letter S.

Worksheet 31C: Read the instructions aloud to the students and monitor their progress as they work independently.

 Remember the "THREE P's."

 You may want to give the students the coloring page along with the flashcard. Read the information about the artist to your students before they color the picture. Explain that we want to take our time and color in the lines.

LESSON 32
TARGET SOUND: S AND REVIEW

ACTIVITY 1: HEARING AND WRITING

Play the Alphabet Song for the children encouraging them to sing along while pointing to the corresponding letters on the flashcards.

Write the upper and lower case letters for "S, s" on the board and ask the children if they remember what sound is made by this letter. Brainstorm with the children to come up with words which begin with this letter. Write them on the board and have children come up and erase the beginning S and write one of their own in its place.

They will probably come up with a few examples which have blends in them, such as "Stephen," or "splash." These are fine to use for this exercise. However, do not use words which start with SH—although S is used as the beginning letter, SH makes a completely new sound which they will not study until later in the year.

Worksheet 32A: Read the instructions aloud to the students. Have them follow the first letter mazes at the upper left. Read the labels for the pictures and monitor their responses. Continue with the rest of the page in the same manner, following the letter mazes first, then circling the pictures with beginning S.

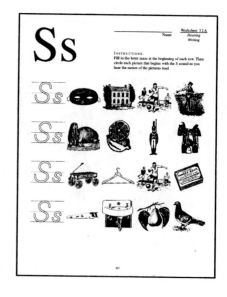

Row 1: mask, house, soccer, seeds
Row 2: walrus (not "seal!"), orange, soldier, saddle
Row 3: wagon, hanger, soccer, soap
Row 4: saw, sink, pear, bird

ACTIVITY 2: READING ALOUD

 Cut the four pictures out of Appendix 2 for your use as display items. Write these four words in a column on the board in different order than that on the worksheet: bat, Dad, map, pat.

Affix the picture of the map to the board to the right of the word column and ask if anyone can identify it. Reinforce the correct response, then call their attention to the four words on the board. Say the word "map" several times. Call on a student to draw a line from the correct word to the picture.

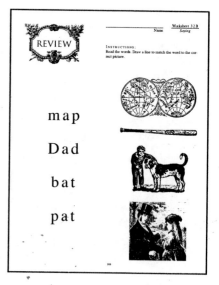

Reinforce the correct response, then erase the line. Continue in the same manner with the rest of the pictures and words, erasing the response line each time to prevent response based on the "process of elimination."

Worksheet 32B: Read the instructions aloud and permit the children to complete the worksheet independently.

LESSON 33
TARGET SOUND: F AND SPECIAL EXHIBITS

ACTIVITY 1: HEARING

 Play the Museum Song for the children encouraging them to sing along while pointing to the corresponding letters on the flashcards.

Instruct the children to watch your mouth carefully as you read the following list of words aloud, slightly exaggerating the F sound each time:

family   father   fish   fix   fudge   funny

Ask if anyone can make the sound which started those words and praise correct responses. Have all the children echo this sound several times.

Show the children the flashcard with the letter F on it. Have them hear the sound of F as in "fan."

Challenge them to find this sound as it plays hide-and-seek with the other sounds in the following list:

s, b, f, a, f, t, d, r, f, m, a, n, f, f, r, g, f, p, f, s, f, s, f, f

Now instruct them to indicate when they hear it at the beginning of words:

socks	fox	box	sun	fun	fish
dish	man	fan	tan	fix	six
foam	dome	roam	sin	fin	pin

Ask if they noticed that many of those words sounded alike except for the first sound. Repeat some of the word pairs/triplets and remind them that sometimes changing only one sound or letter can make a big difference in the meaning of the word.

Worksheet 33A: Read the instructions aloud and allow the children to work independently.

Row 1: deer, faucet, fan
Row 2: grapes, feet, strawberry
Row 3: hive, fist, fork

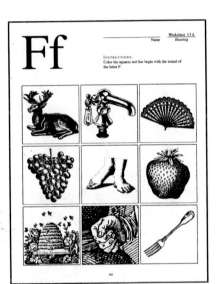

 Give your students the reproduction of the *Lady with a Fan* and allow them to hang it in the museum. Talk to them about the story *The Alphabet Quest* and give them their museum bag. Allow them time to go through the house and collect items that begin with the sound of F to make their own museum. If you are teaching in a school setting, instruct the children to take the bag home and bring in objects the following day.

ACTIVITY 2: SEEING

Tell the children that the letter which makes the F sound is the letter F. Show them the cards with the printed upper and lower case "F,f." Point out the features of each letter (upper case has two shorter lines coming out to the right side, lower case has a hook at the top and a short crossbar, etc.)

Mix these cards with the other printed upper case letters for the first quarter. Present them to the children in random order, instructing them to indicate when they see the target letter F.

Repeat this activity with the lower case letters, then with both upper and lower case letters combined.

On the board, write the written upper and lower case letters for F, describing and numbering your strokes as you do so. Compare and contrast the printed letters and the written letters—they look very much alike for this letter. Leave both the printed and written examples on the board.

Worksheet 33B: Read the instructions aloud and allow the children to work independently.

ACTIVITY 3: WRITING

Place guidelines and perimeter lines on the board. Call on students to come to the board and make the upper and lower case letter F. Remind them how the strokes are made and in what order.

Worksheet 33C: Read the instructions aloud to the students and permit them to complete the page independently. Monitor their stroke order and direction.

ACTIVITY 4: SPECIAL EXHIBITS

In the Special Exhibit wing of the *Phonics Museum* you will find odd and unique words. We call them "Special Exhibits" because we recognize that we cannot identify them by their letter sound like Percival did in the museum. These words can not be explained or sounded out. They must be memorized. Appendix 6 lists the Special Exhibit words used for each primer.

Write the eight Special Exhibits from Worksheet 33D on the board. Read them aloud to the students and have them echo them. Call attention to the fact that A as a Special Exhibits is pronounced "uh" (not like short A in "apple" or as long A in "ape") and that "the" is pronounced "thuh," not "thee."

Go through the list in order several times, asking the children to read them aloud independently as you point to them. As they develop proficiency with this, try pointing to the words randomly to insure that they are not just memorizing the list in order, but are truly recognizing each word.

Worksheet 33D: Read the instructions aloud. Repeat the above activity using the worksheet.

Praise them for their terrific reading and if teaching in a school setting, tell them that they may take this worksheet home and read it to their parents tonight.

 You may want to give the students the coloring page along with the flashcard. Read the information about the artist to your students before they color the picture. Explain that we want to take our time and color in the lines.

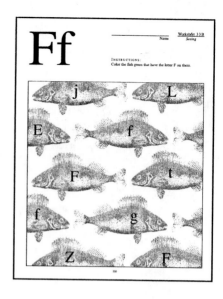

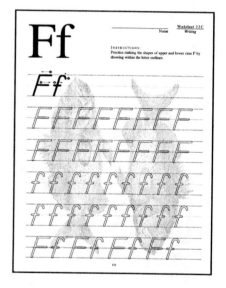

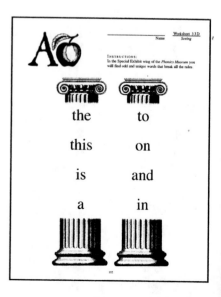

LESSON 34
REVIEW, WRITING F AND S, FINAL T

ACTIVITY 1: REVIEW

Have all the first quarter lower case letters ready to use for this activity (a, m, n, b, p, t, d, g, s, f). Instruct the children that you are going to say a word and hold up two letters. They are to indicate to you which letter makes the beginning sound of that word. Read aloud the following word list, displaying only two lower case letter choices at a time. You may have them respond as a group, or individually. Have them point to the correct letter, then encourage them to make the correct sound and name the letter also.

map	nut	pot	top	dog	goat
bat	sun	baby	family	apple	alligator
nest	Sam	dime	mom	penny	gift

Avoid using N and M or B and D together as choices until the end of the exercise. You may want to do several additional "n/m," "b/d" words with these two similar letter choices for further practice since these letters are so easily confused.

Worksheet 34A: Read the instructions aloud. Have the students put their finger on the first picture at the upper left ("bat"). Say the word several times and direct the children to respond independently on their papers. Do not prompt with the beginning sound in isolation or the name of the letter. Continue with the rest of the page in the same manner.

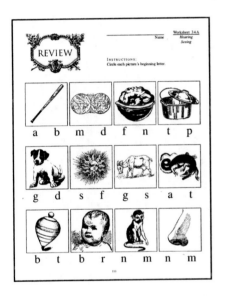

Row 1: bat, map, nut, pot
Row 2: dog, sun, goat, alligator
Row 3: top, baby, monkey, nose (watch these last two!)

ACTIVITY 2: WRITING

Call on individual students to come to the board and write both upper and lower case letters F and S.. Monitor their stroke order carefully.

Worksheet 34B: Present the worksheet, drawing attention to the fact that this one is a little different from the ones which they have had before. They may do the letter mazes on each line and then go ahead and make their letters independently, in the same manner as the board work was done.

Remind them to be neat and use gentle pencil pressure.

At this time, you may want to encourage them to do some self-judging of their work by having them circle the letter on each line which they think is their "best" one. This can be helpful in controlling perfectionism—some children may have a tendency to labor endlessly over each letter, erasing constantly, until it is "just right." Remind them that they are practicing and that every effort, although diligent, will not be perfect. This will also encourage the less skilled child to do his personal best to improve and form at least one excellent letter in each row.

ACTIVITY 3: HEARING (FINAL T)

Write the following words on the board: bat, mat, pat. Have the students read them aloud.

Ask them what is the same in all those words (A and T). Guide them to notice that it is the leader or beginning letter which changes, but that they all have A in the middle and T at the end. Say the words again, slightly emphasizing the final T.

Tell them that today they will be listening very carefully for this "teeny, tiny 't' sound" at the END of words. When they hear it, they can indicate this by making the upper case T with their index fingers (like they did in Lesson 21). Read the following list aloud:

pig	cat	sun	hat	bat	man
rat	gun	bug	fit	light	sad
fun	rut	put	mad	top	

Praise them for their great listening—pointing out that the word "great" also ends in T!

Worksheet 34C: Read the instructions aloud. Call on students to label the pictures in order and monitor their responses.

Row 1: hat, gun, cat
Row 2: sun, rat, man
Row 3: pig, top, bat

Percival's Pairs: Using A, M, B, P, T, D, N, G and S

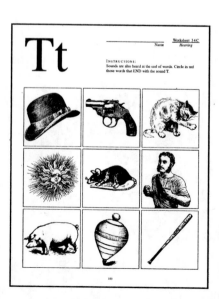

LESSON 35
REVIEW

ACTIVITY 1: HEARING

 Play the Alphabet Song for the children encouraging them to sing along while pointing to the corresponding letters on the flashcards.

Give each child two cards, one with lower case S on it and the other with lower case F. Tell them that you will be reading a list of words today and all of them will start with either S or F. It will be their job to decide which letter represents the beginning sound and hold it up for you to see.

Demonstrate this for them by saying the word "sand" and holding up the letter S. Then say "father" and hold up the letter F. You may use other examples and have them respond appropriately for more practice if needed.

Read the following list aloud, watching for correct responses from each student:

soccer	fan	soap	sink	fox
socks	fish	sun	saddle	fence
fish	faucet	fin	sat	family
silly	seed	feed	fill	sill

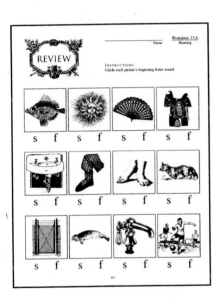

Worksheet 35A: Read the instructions aloud. Name all the pictures for the children first, then permit them to respond independently. You may repeat the picture labels for children who have forgotten them, but do not give any other clues or prompts.

Row 1: fish, sun, fan, saddle
Row 2: sink, socks, feet, fox
Row 3: fence, seal, faucet, soccer

ACTIVITY 2: ART ACTIVITY

Worksheet 35B: Read the instructions aloud and permit them to color the fans according to their preferences. Demonstrate how to fold them and assist as necessary.

ACTIVITY 3: READING ALOUD

Write the words from Worksheet 35C on the board in a different order. Guide the children to sound them out. Discuss briefly the meaning of each word and call on students to use each one in original sentences. For fun, see if you can create silly sentences using more than one word within the same sentence ("The sad bat sat on the fat fan."). Leave the written words on the board as you present Worksheet 35C.

Worksheet 35C: Read the instructions aloud. Call on students to read the words, then guide them to choose the picture which represents that concept. Monitor their responses.

REVIEW

Name _____ Worksheet 35C
Saying

INSTRUCTIONS:
Read the words. Draw a line to match the word which best describes the picture.

sat

sad

fat

fan

bat

mat

LESSON 36
TARGET SOUND: R

ACTIVITY 1: HEARING

 Play the Museum Song for the children encouraging them to sing along while pointing to the corresponding letters on the flashcards.

Ask the children if they have ever heard a rabbit "roar." You may get lots of interesting answers to this! Affirm that rabbits do not roar, but that "rabbit" and "roar" both start with the same sound—the R sound.

This is a hard sound to make and many children do not produce it clearly until third or fourth grade. Different people actually produce it in different ways and the only judge of correct production is actual clarity in speech. It will be normal to have a certain percentage of students who will not be able to approximate this sound in their speech at this time.

What you do want to emphasize to them, however, is that this is NOT a W sound. The lips are not pursed together when making R. Encourage children to experiment with tongue placement in the mouth to get closer to the R sound and avoid using their lips. Gentle prompting like this is enough to encourage the development of this difficult sound, but do not insist on clear production from every student.

It may be helpful to do an additional listening activity with children who are using W for R substitutions. Have them watch your mouth carefully as you say these two sounds alternately and at random. Have them indicate to you when they hear the true R sound. Praise their ability to hear and see the difference. Repeat this activity from time to time throughout the year to encourage continued discrimination of these two sounds.

 Show the children the flashcard with the letter R on it. Have them hear the sound of R as in "rabbit."

Tell the children that God gave rabbits very long ears so that they would be very good listeners. Challenge them to be good "rabbits" and listen for the R sound at the beginning of the following words, indicating by putting their hands on the top of their heads like rabbit ears:

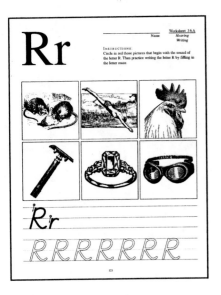

banana	top	rooster	rug	basket
popsicle	goggles	ring	salad	fudge
rats	ants	dive	recipe	beast
money	teeth	rain	rope	ax

Worksheet 36A (top): Read the instructions aloud and label the pictures as follows:

Row 1: rats, dive, rooster
Row 2: razor, ring, goggles

Give your students the reproduction of Dürer's depiction of a Rabbit and allow them to hang it in the museum. Talk to them about the story *The Alphabet Quest* and give them their museum bag. Allow them time to go through the house and collect items that begin with the sound of R to make their own museum. If you are teaching in a school setting, instruct the children to take the bag home and bring in objects the following day.

ACTIVITY 2: SEEING

Tell the children that the letter which makes the R sound is the letter R.

Show them the cards with the printed upper and lower case "R,r." Point out the features of each letter (upper case has one round bump on the right, like a P, with a diagonal line extended from this bump, the lower case is a stick with a very short hook at the top).

Mix these cards with the other printed upper case letters for the first quarter. Present them to the children in random order, instructing them to indicate when they see the target letter R.

Repeat this activity with the lower case letters, then with both upper and lower case letters combined.

On the board, write the written upper and lower case letters for R, describing and numbering your strokes as you do so. Compare and contrast the printed letters and the written letters—they look very much alike for this letter. Leave both the printed and written examples on the board.

Worksheet 36B: Read the instructions aloud and permit the students to work independently as you monitor.

ACTIVITY 3: WRITING

Call the students to come to the board to practice writng both the upper and lower case letter R.

Worksheet 36A (bottom): Read the instructions aloud and allow the children to complete the worksheet, following the letter mazes first, then writing the letters independently on the first line.

You may want to give the students the coloring page along with the flashcard. Read the information about the artist to your students before they color the picture. Explain that we want to take our time and color in the lines.

LESSON 37
TARGET SOUND: R

ACTIVITY 1: HEARING

Play the Alphabet Song for the children encouraging them to sing along while pointing to the corresponding letters on the flashcards.

Prompt the children to put on their "rabbit ears" again today and listen for the R sound at the beginning of words. They can "wiggle" their ears every time a word starts with R: (pay special attention to the W and R word pairs)

race	boy	sit	Ralph	rose
pail	reach	mask	run	won
wag	rag	sing	wing	ring

Worksheet 37A: Read the instructions aloud and monitor their work.

Row 1: kite, ring, girl
Row 2: rooster, piano, rabbit
Row 3: man, ark, ram

ACTIVITY 2: WRITING

Call students to the board to write the upper and lower case R.

Worksheet 37B: Read the instructions aloud and monitor their work.

Remind them about the "THREE P's" if you haven't done so in a while.

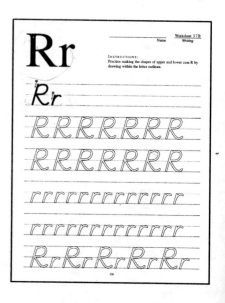

LESSON 38
TARGET SOUND: R AND SPECIAL EXHIBIT REVIEW

ACTIVITY 1: HEARING

 Play the Alphabet Song for the children encouraging them to sing along while pointing to the corresponding letters on the flashcards.

Ask the children if they remember what sound they were listening for in the last lesson. Praise their good memories! Tell them to put on their "listening rabbit ears" again and wiggle them when they hear the R at the beginning of words in the following list: (there are some tricky ones which have R in the medial or final positions—watch these!)

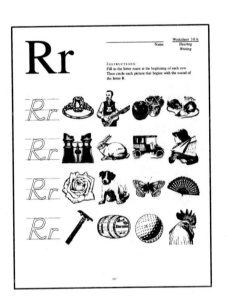

razor	ball	automobile	boat	rose
barrel	ring	rabbit	guitar	apples
rats	fan	binoculars	dog	butterfly
rooster	Ricky	relax	soup	restaurant

Worksheet 38A: Read the instructions aloud. Have them follow the first letter mazes at the top left. Read the picture labels across this row and monitor their responses. Continue with the rest of the page in the same manner.

Row 1: ring, guitar, apples, rats
Row 2: binoculars, rabbit, automobile, boat
Row 3: rose, dog, butterfly, fan
Row 4: razor, barrel, ball, rooster

ACTIVITY 2: WRITING

Call on students to come to the board and practice writing the letter R.

Worksheet 38B: Read the instructions aloud and permit the children to work independently. Remind them that they should work within the mazes before writing the letters on their own.

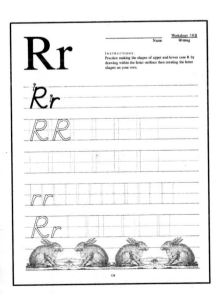 Remind them about pencil pressure, neatness, and careful erasing.

ACTIVITY 3: SPECIAL EXHIBITS REVIEW

Write the eight Special Exhibits on the board. Present each of the words in printed form and call on students to come to the board and point to the written word which corresponds to the printed word.

Read through the list several times, instructing the children to echo the words after you. Have them read the list independently several times. Then ask them to read the words as you point to them randomly. Use both the printed and written words.

Worksheet 38C: Distribute the worksheet and show the children how to number the words: 1, the; 2, this; 3, is; 4, a. Call on individual students to read the word which you ask for by number. For instance: "Meg, will you please tell us what number 3 is?" You may point to the words on the board for extra assistance if necessary.

Praise their excellent reading and their good "rabbit ears and eyes!"

LESSON 39
READING ALOUD

ACTIVITY 1: READING

 Cut out Appendix 3. Ask what letter all of the words have in common (A). Ask if they remember what sound is made by this letter.

Now ask which two words start with the same letter (rat, ran). Ask what sound is made by this letter. Guide them to the understanding that both of these words will begin with "ra."

Ask which two words end with the same letter (ran, man). Ask what sound is made by this letter. Guide them to the understanding that both of these words will end with the sounds "an."

Ask who can tell you what sound comes at the end of the first word (T). Now ask if anyone knows what sound comes at the beginning of the last word (M).

Challenge them to put all this information together and sound out the first word. Point to the word and slide your finger or the pointer across the word as the children say the letter sounds. They should be blending the sounds without pause or undue emphasis on any sound. Have them echo the word "rat" several times.

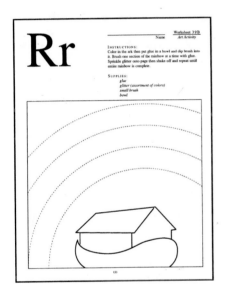

Continue in the same manner with "ran" and "man." Display the word "the" with the first letter in lower case. Ask if anyone remembers this Special Exhibit. Praise correct responses. Now write the word using an upper case T. Tell them that when this word comes at the beginning of a sentence it uses the upper case letter. Describe that a sentence is a line of words which make sense together and tell you something. It is a very important job to start a sentence and every word which is the leader in a sentence must use its upper case letter at the beginning!

Write the two sentences "The man ran." and "The rat ran." on the board. Guide the children to read the sentences and have them echo them several times. Point to them alternately in random order for independent response.

Worksheet 39A: Read the instructions aloud. At the top of the page, have students read the words and monitor their responses. Call on individual students to read the two sentences at the bottom of the page.

Praise their accomplishment and tell them to take this page home to read to their parents.

ACTIVITY 2: ART ACTIVITY

Worksheet 39B: Follow instructions on worksheet.

LESSON 40
REVIEW, WRITING AND READING

ACTIVITY 1: HEARING AND SEEING

Take the Letter Bingo card found in Appendix 4 and photocopy one for each student. Have each student write in the spaces any of the following: a, m, b, p, t, d, n, g, s, f, r, the, this, is, a. Give some markers (edible ones such as Cheerios are fun) to each student.

Instruct the students that you will be making the sounds of the letters or saying one of the Special Exhibits. If it is on their card, they are to place a marker on it. When they have 3 or 4 markers in a row (depending upon how you make your cards), either across, down, or diagonally, they should call out "Bingo!"

They must read back to you the sounds of the letters or the words on which they have placed markers to verify their choices before you declare them the winner of that round.

You may also do this using the letter names, since they have been learning both simultaneously during this quarter.

ACTIVITY 2: WRITING

Write each of the words on Worksheet 40A on the board with lines and perimeter lines to the right. Call on individual students to come to the board and write the words. Assist them to sound out the words and reinforce by echoing.

Worksheet 40A: Read the instructions aloud and monitor their progress as they work independently.

ACTIVITY 3: READING SYLLABLES

 Display the puzzle pieces for P, R, T, D, and M and affix them to the board in a vertical column. Have the children tell you both the letter names and sounds as you point randomly to them.

Present the puzzle piece for A and have the children name the letter and make the sound of short A. Place the A to the right of the top consonant on your column display and ask a volunteer to read the syllable aloud. Continue in this same manner, moving the A down the column and pairing it with each beginning sound.

Call on various students to come to the board and place the A beside any consonant and call on another student to read the syllable formed.

 If your students are doing very well with this, the activity may be enriched by asking students to come up with longer words which begin with the syllables "pa," "ra," "ta," "da," and "ma." You could keep a list of these on the board and afterwards underline or highlight the initial two letters to impress upon them the idea that big words are just strings of little syllables.

Worksheet 40B: Read the instructions aloud and call on students to read the syllables aloud.

Percival's Pairs: Using A, M, B, P, T, D, N, G, S, F, and R

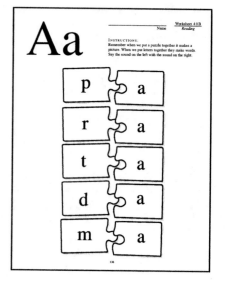

LESSON 41
REVIEW: WRITING AND READING

ACTIVITY 1: READING SYLLABLES

 Display the puzzle pieces for P, R, T, D, and M and affix them to the board in a vertical column. Have the children tell you both the letter names and sounds as you point randomly to them.

Present the puzzle piece for A and have the children name the letter and make the sound of short A. Place the A to the right of the top consonant on your column display and ask a volunteer to read the syllable aloud. Continue in this same manner, moving the A down the column and pairing it with each beginning sound.

Then ask the students to come up with longer words which begin with the syllables "pa," "ra," "ta," "da," and "ma."

 You could keep a list of these on the board and afterwards underline or highlight the initial two letters to impress upon them the idea that big words are just strings of little syllables.

Worksheet 41A: Read the instructions aloud and call on students to read the syllables aloud.

 An alternative way to use this sheet would be for you to say the syllables aloud and have the children point to the correct one on their papers.

ACTIVITY 2: READING WORDS

Take the puzzle pieces for N and M. Ask the children to tell you both the letter name and sound for each of these. Link the N piece to the "pa" syllable. Guide the children in reading the word which is formed. Continue with the rest of the syllables in the same manner.

 When you get to "dan," remind the children that this is a person's name and ask if anyone remembers what kind of letter we must use to start proper names (upper case). Ask if anyone can come to the board and write an upper case D in place of the lower case D puzzle piece. This is extra reinforcement of this rule.

Link the M piece to the syllables in turn (eliminate the "ma" from this exercise since it is meaningless) and repeat the above activity.

 Again, the word "pam" should be capitalized. Hopefully, they will all catch this on their own this time! Also, you could explain that a "tam" is a round, flattish Scottish cap with a wide headband and a tassel, also called a "tam-o-shanter."

Worksheet 41B: Read the instructions aloud. You may have them read the words in unison, call on students to read them independently, have students point to the correct word as you say them randomly, etc.

ACTIVITY 3: READING MORE WORDS

 Take away the pieces for M, T, and D and replace them with F, S, and N. Elicit the letter names and sounds from the children and go through the procedure to sound out the syllables which are formed when each is paired with A.

Present the puzzle pieces for T and P. Elicit the letter names and sounds from the students. Using each piece in turn, pair it with the syllables on display, reading each aloud as you do so (eliminating "fap" from the list for P since it is meaningless).

 Again, some vocabulary explanation may be necessary for "rap," "sap," and "pap"—focus on "rap" as a "knock on the door" rather than a popular music form and "pap" as a familiar nickname for "father" or "grandfather." Point out that "nat" can be a nickname for "Nathan" or "Nathaniel" and follow the previous procedure for replacing the lower case with the upper case.

Worksheet 41C: Read the instructions aloud and follow the previous procedure for eliciting responses. Praise their wonderful reading!

ACTIVITY 4: WRITING WORDS

Write the words which are listed on Worksheet 41D on the board. Provide perimeter and guidelines on the board for students to use and call on various students to write the words in turn.

Emphasize proper stroke order and direction.

Have students read the words on display, then erase the board.

Worksheet 41D: Read the instructions aloud and monitor their progress as they work independently.

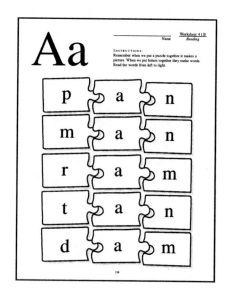

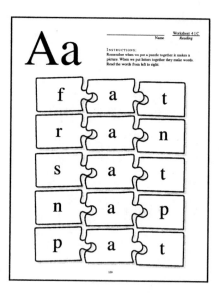

At this point, you may want to add the fourth P—pressure—to the reminder to "watch the 'P's! Therefore the four things to monitor are: pencil hold, posture, paper position, and pencil pressure (not too hard, not too soft—like Baby Bear's bed!)

 Archives: Picture/Initial Sounds
Use only cards with pictures that begin with the sound of the letters: A, S, M, F, R, G, N, B, T, P, and D

LESSON 42
TARGET SOUND: SHORT E
(AS IN "ELEPHANT")

ACTIVITY 1: HEARING

 Play the Museum Song for the children encouraging them to sing along while pointing to the corresponding letters on the flashcards.

Explain to the children that so far this year they have been learning mostly about sounds which are called "consonants" (m, b, p, t, d, n, g, s, f, r) and one sound which is called a "vowel" (short A). Tell them that today they will learn their second vowel—the short E sound. Make this new sound several times, having the children echo it after you.

 Show the children the flashcard with the letter E on it. Have them hear the sound of short E as in "egg."

Have them listen to the two vowels—short A and short E—as you repeat them alternately. They make very, very similar sounds and caution the children that they will have to be excellent listeners today in order to catch the E sound in the listening list.

 At this point in the program, you will probably be able to say this list the first time through using all short vowel sounds (see Lesson 3, Activity 1). If you notice difficulty, return to all long vowels, except for short E, until the children are firm in their ability to differentiate the short E.

 Here are two optional ways for having the children indicate when they hear this sound. Since short E starts the word "egg" and that is the stimulus picture for this letter, you may have them pretend they are holding an egg, hand upturned with fingers extended upward as if the egg is perched on their fingertips. Another way may be to have them make a "nest" for the "eggs" with their hands.

Read the following aloud, instructing the children to indicate when they hear the short E sound:

i, a, o, e, e, u, i, e, a, e, o, i, u, e, i, e, o, a, u, e, e, a, e, o, e

Praise their fine listening. Tell them that just like the other letters, short E sometimes likes to be the "line leader" in words. Give examples by reading the following words:

exit   end   elevator   Exodus

Ask them to listen carefully again as you read the following word list, indicating to you when they hear the short E at the beginning of the words:

elf   mask   ax   elephant   moon
fish   eggs   chicks parasol excellent
butter elbow attic engine Mark
extra   rabbit Eskimo   soap   every

Worksheet 42A: Read the instructions aloud. Name the pictures for the children and tell them to make a small dot of purple at the top of the picture if they hear the short E at the beginning of the picture label. After all the pictures are named and marked, they may go back and color the appropriate eggs purple.

Row 1: mask, elf, ax
Row 2: moon, parasol, elephant
Row 3: chicks, eggs, fish

Give your students the reproduction of the Fabergé Egg and allow them to hang it in the museum. Talk to them about the story *The Alphabet Quest* and give them their museum bag. Allow them time to go through the house and collect items that begin with the sound of E to make their own museum. If you are teaching in a school setting, instruct the children to take the bag home and bring in objects the following day.

ACTIVITY 2: SEEING

Tell the children that the letter which makes the short E sound is the letter "E,e." Draw attention to the stimulus picture on the wall and display the flashcard. Point out the features of the letter (the upper case has three lines extending to the right from the vertical line, the lower case is almost a circle with a small opening on the right and a line through it, etc.).

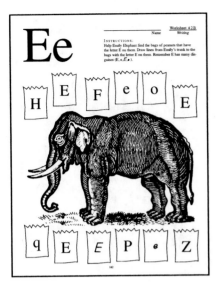

Mix the printed upper case E card with the other upper case letter cards which have been studied so far. Present these to the children in random order, instructing them to indicate when they see the target letter E.

Repeat this activity with the lower case letters, then with both upper and lower case combined.

On the board, write the written upper and lower case letters for E, describing and numbering your strokes as you do so. Compare and contrast the printed letters and the written letters. Leave both the printed and written letters on display as you present the worksheet.

Worksheet 42B: Read the instructions aloud and monitor their progress as they work independently.

ACTIVITY 3: WRITING

Place guidelines and perimeter lines on the board. Call on students to come to the board and make the upper and lower case letter E.

Worksheet 42C: Read the instructions aloud to the students and permit them to complete the page independently. Monitor their stroke order and direction.

You may want to give the students the coloring page along with the flashcard. Read the information about the artist to your students before they color the picture. Explain that we want to take our time and color in the lines.

LESSON 43
TARGET SOUNDS: SHORT E AND SHORT A (REVIEW)

ACTIVITY 1: HEARING AND SEEING

Play the Museum Song for the children encouraging them to sing along while pointing to the corresponding letters on the flashcards.

Aa Display the cards for both "E,e" and "A,a" and elicit the letter names and sounds from the children. Affix the cards to the top of the board as labels for columns.

Read the following word list aloud and ask the children to tell you on which column to place each word, based on its beginning sound. Write these words under the appropriate letters on the board, highlighting the initial E with a yellow marker or chalk and the initial A with a green one.

eggs	alligator	ax	elephant	apples
elf	enter	elbow	accident	exercise
Adam	aspirin	Emily	animal	echo

Praise them for their careful listening. Erase the board, but leave the flash-cards on display.

Worksheet 43A: Read the instructions aloud. Make certain each child has a yellow and green crayon. Call on children to label the pictures from left to right and determine if it begins with short E or A. Monitor as they color the pictures as instructed.

Row 1: eggs, whale, lightbulb
Row 2: alligator, elf, bat
Row 3: apples, ax, elephant

ACTIVITY 2: READING

Take down the card for "E,e" and call attention to the remaining one for "A,a." Remind the children that short A is often found in the middle of words. In random order, write the words found on Worksheet 43B on the board, highlighting the medial A by writing it in green marker or chalk. Assist the children to sound out the words and have them echo each several times. Leave the display on the board as you present Worksheet 43B.

Worksheet 43B: Read the instructions aloud. Call on students to read the words down the columns first, then up. Using the board display, point to words randomly and have students locate that same word on the sheet and then read it aloud.

This also serves as a good printed-to-written matching exercise.

LESSON 44
REVIEW

ACTIVITY 1: HEARING, SEEING, AND WRITING

 Play the Museum Song for the children encouraging them to sing along while pointing to the corresponding letters on the flashcards.

 Present the flashcards for the following letters: m, g, b, t, r, s, d. Elicit the letter names and sounds from the children, using the stimulus pictures to remind them of the use of the sounds at the beginning of words.

Write these same letters in lower case on the board, numbering and describing your strokes. Affirm that the written letters make the same sounds as the printed letters. Leave both the printed and written examples on display as you present Worksheet 44 A.

Worksheet 44A: Read the instructions aloud. Tell the children you will be doing this sheet together. Call on a student to label the first picture (moon). Ask the children to identify the beginning sound and the letter we use to write that sound. Monitor as they write this letter in the space provided. Continue in the same manner with the rest of the sheet.

Row 1: moon, golf
Row 2: bench, donkey
Row 3: turkey, rat
Row 4: gate, sun

ACTIVITY 2: WRITING

Call on students to write the upper and lower case letters A, E, and M on the board. Monitor stroke direction and order carefully.

Worksheet 44B: Read the instructions aloud and monitor their progress as they work independently.

Worksheet 44C: Read the instructions aloud and monitor their progress as they work independently.

Lesson 45
Target Sound: Short E and Special Exhibits

Activity 1: Hearing

Play the Alphabet Song for the children encouraging them to sing along while pointing to the corresponding letters on the flashcards.

Remind the children that they have now studied two vowel sounds: short A and short E. Just like the short A, short E often likes to be in the middle of words also. Ask them to listen carefully for the short E sound in the following words:

> met   fed   pet   bed

Tell them it is very hard sometimes to tell the difference between short A and short E in the middle of words, but you know that they are such good listeners that they will not be fooled! Instruct them to listen for only the short E sound in the middle of the following words, indicating when they hear it by using the short E gesture you have previously taught:

web	bat	leg	pig	bed	man
pen	fan	vest	hot	run	get
red	can	mud	mop	net	ten

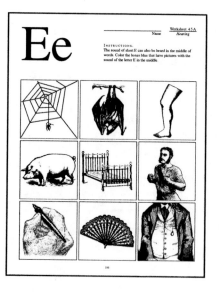

Worksheet 45A: Read the instructions aloud. Read the labels for the children, directing them to place a dot of blue on the pictures whose names have the short E in the middle. They can go back and color those boxes when all the pictures are named.

> Row 1: web, bat, leg
> Row 2: pig, bed, man
> Row 3: pen, fan, vest

Activity 2: Reading Syllables

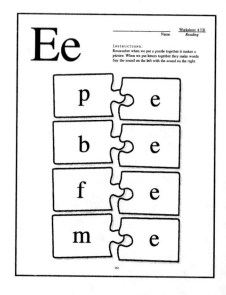

Present the puzzle pieces for P, B, F, and M. Have the children tell you the letter names and sounds. Present the E piece, making the short E sound. Link short E with each of the consonant pieces in turn, assisting the children to sound out the syllables formed.

Worksheet 45B: Read the instructions aloud. Guide the children through the reading of the syllables. Say the syllables randomly, asking them to point to the correct letter combinations.

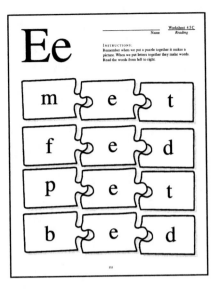

ACTIVITY 3: READING WORDS

Present the letter pieces for T and D. Name these letters and the sounds they make. Place the T at the end of the "me" syllable. Assist the children to sound out the word which is formed. Repeat this process with the T at the end of the "pe" syllable. Use the D piece for the "fe" and "be" syllables.

Worksheet 45C: Read the instructions aloud. Call on students to read the words in order from top to bottom, then randomly as you point to the display examples. You may also read words randomly and ask students to point to the correct ones on their papers.

ACTIVITY 4: READING SPECIAL EXHIBITS

Remind the children what "Special Exhibits" are (see Lesson 33), using the material in *The Alphabet Quest* book.

Write the words A, "the," and "is" on the board. Remind them how the Special Exhibits A and "the" are pronounced (using "uh," not short or long A or E). Ask if anyone can read "is" and praise this effort. Have the children echo these words several times and then read them spontaneously as you point to them.

Write the following on the board: and, this, on, a, is, the, in, to. Read them aloud to the children and have them echo back to you. Make up brief sentences using each of these words, demonstrating their use and meaning.

Worksheet 45D: Read the instructions aloud. Have students read the words first down, then up, the columns. Point to the display words on the board randomly and have students find the printed word on their sheets and read them.

Praise them for their great reading!

LESSON 46
READING AND ENDING CONSONANT REVIEW

ACTIVITY 1: READING

Present the cards for all the sounds studied so far: a, m, b, p, t, d, n, g, s, f, r, e. Play "Around the World" with the students, first with letter names as responses, then sounds. To play "Around the World," place the students in a circle with one child being "it." The one who is "it" stands behind one of the students in the circle. The teacher presents one of the cards and the one who is "it" and the one he is standing behind each try to identify the letter first. If the student who is "it" identifies the card first, he moves one place clockwise around the circle and plays again, the goal being to make it all the way around the circle. If the student who is standing behind the one who is "it" identifies the card first, he then becomes "it" and the former "it" takes his place.

Offer and elicit examples of words with each of the sounds in the beginning positions. You may use words from any of the previous lesson lists or worksheets. If the word ends with one of these sounds, draw their attention to this also. If either of the two short vowels A or E occurs in the middle of any word, point that out. Use this as a time to brainstorm and informally assess how well the students are beginning to apply the phonics knowledge they have so far acquired.

 You may decide to write any or all of the appropriate words they suggest on the board for additional reinforcement, highlighting different letters as you go along, or asking students to circle letters/sounds which you designate.

Write the words on Worksheet 46A on the board in columns just as they are presented on the worksheet.

Worksheet 46A: Read the instructions aloud. Assist the children to read the words from top to bottom of each column, following along on the worksheet as you point to the corresponding written word on the board. Repeat the activity going from bottom to top of each column. Finally, point randomly to the words on the columns and call on students to read them.

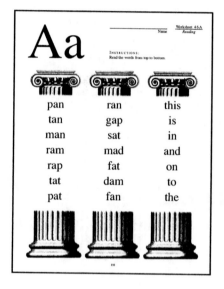

 An additional way to use this sheet for further reinforcement is to erase the words from the board and then have students point to or circle the correct word as you randomly say them. You may want to do this on an individual or small group basis to more carefully monitor their responses.

ACTIVITY 2: HEARING AND WRITING

Read the list of words below to the students and ask them to raise their hand to answer which makes the ENDING sound of each word.

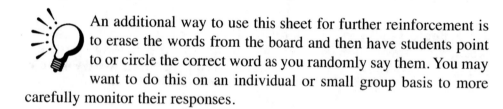

ten	bed	cat	pen	fan	rat
fun	red	sad	pat	mad	get

Praise them for their careful listening. Now tell them that you will be writing only the first two letters of each of those words on the board and that they will again show you which letter should be written at the end to finish each word.

Write the same list on the board, one word at a time, eliciting the correct ending sound and letter. You may write the letter in on the lines, or call on students to do this.

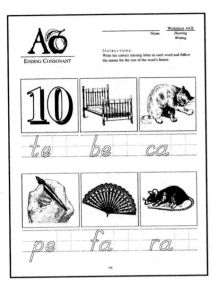

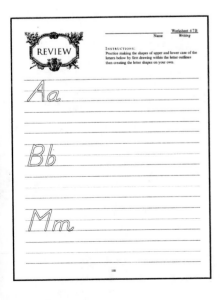

 Reinforce correct letter stroke formation and order.

Erase the board before you present the worksheet, however, you may want to keep the written lower case N, T, and D on the board for reference.

Worksheet 46B: Read the instructions aloud. Tell the students that these words all end in either N, D, or T. Call on students to label the pictures, but do not allow them to tell the class what letter or sound is at the end. Monitor their work as the students write their responses, assisting them to self-correct as necessary.

LESSON 47
READING AND WRITING REVIEW

ACTIVITY 1: READING

Write the words on Worksheet 47A on the board or if homeschool simply use the worksheet. Call on students to read the words aloud. Discuss the meanings of each word and elicit sentences from the students in which each word is properly used.

 You may want to put these words in columns or groups based on beginning, middle, or ending sounds to reinforce similarities and assist them in categorization skills.

Worksheet 47A: Read the instructions aloud. Have the students read the words in order in unison and respond as directed. Caution them that one of the words will not have a picture which matches!

ACTIVITY 2: WRITING

Place guidelines and perimeter lines on the board. Call on students to come to the board and make the upper and lower case letters A, B, and M.

 Remind about stroke direction and order.

Worksheet 47B: Read the instructions aloud and monitor their progress as they work independently.

 Remind about the "FOUR P's!"

LESSON 48
READING, WRITING, AND SPECIAL
EXHIBITS REVIEW

ACTIVITY 1: READING

 Play the Museum Song for the children encouraging them to sing along while pointing to the corresponding letters on the flashcards.

Draw three circles on the board in a vertical column. To the right of each circle write one of the following words: fan, man, fat. Tell the children that they must be careful listeners and readers today. You will be reading one of the words on the board and they must choose which word is the one you have read. Read the word "fat." Call on a student to come to the board and fill in the circle beside the correct word. After the correct response is completed, have students read the other words also to reinforce reading skills.

 You may want to point out the small differences in the words, reminding them of past lessons when they learned that just one letter can change the entire meaning of a word.

Using the words as they are presented on Worksheet 48A, continue this activity. Do NOT read the words which are used as stimulus pictures on this worksheet, but choose one of the other two in each example.

Worksheet 48A: Read the instructions aloud. Assist those students who may have difficulty labeling the pictures, perhaps by encouraging them to read the words first and then figure out which word names the picture.

ACTIVITY 2: WRITING REVIEW

Place guidelines and perimeter lines on the board. Call on students to come to the board and make the letters studied to this point.

 Remind about stroke direction and order.

Worksheet 48B: Read the instructions aloud and monitor their progress as they work independently.

 Remind them about the "FOUR P's!"

ACTIVITY 3: WRITING SPECIAL EXHIBITS

Write the lower case letter A on the board. Ask who can tell you how we say this when it is used as a Special Exhibits. Have a student come to the board and reproduce this independently. Write "is" on the board and call on a student to read this word. Erase the S and call on a student to come to the board and complete the word "is" with a written S. Write "to" on the board and call on a student to read it. Erase the T and have a student come to the board and rewrite it. Write the word "the" on the board and call on a student to read it. Erase the T and the E and have students come to the board and rewrite the missing letters. Write the word "and" on the board and call on a student to read it. Have a student volunteer come up and copy the entire word.

 Monitor stroke formation carefully.

The reason why you are only having them rewrite certain letters in this activity is because students have not yet been taught the proper stroke order and direction for writing the letters I, O, H.

Worksheet 48C: Read the instructions aloud. Point out that they are not to attempt to produce the letters which are "filled in" or are in bold type. They are only to write the missing letters for each word.

Archives: Picture/Initial Sounds
Use only cards with pictures that begin with the sound of the letters: A, E, S, M, F, R, G, N, B, T, P, and D

LESSON 49
READING AND WRITING

ACTIVITY 1: READING PAN AND THE MAD MAN

Celebrate with the children that they are now ready to read their very first book. It is called *Pan and the Mad Man* and they will be able to read all of the words in this story all by themselves!

The children will read their very first book today, but that does not mean that they will necessarily understand it. This should not alarm or worry you. Historically children learned to read using Scripture without understanding what was written. The goal at this point is to have them read correctly—sounding out words using the skills they have been developing and identify special exhibit words. Reading comprehension will be developed in the next lesson when the children reread the story.

Pan was originally an Arcadian god of hills and woodlands, the protector of herds, shepherds, and hunters. He was imagined to wander the countryside during the morning and sleep during the midday, awakening to play his pipe (Pan's pipe) in the evening hours and taking pleasure by scaring passers-by. The Greeks attributed various historic and legendary events to his influence or power. His name, meaning "the universe," led to his designation as a symbol of the universe. Explain to the children that this story is based on Greek mythology and is legend and is not true. Remind them who the one true God is.

Throughout this program's primers, you may find unusual words and phrases. This is due to the sequence of when sounds and concepts are introduced. For example, one primer is entitled *Pepin the Not-Big*. Because the students have not yet learned the SH sound, we render "short" as "not-big." This story, *Pan and the Mad Man*, contains a hyphenated created word "tan-man-ram" to replace the word "satyr." Explain to the children that a hyphen is a way to link words which need to be together to be understood. In this story, Pan is not just tan, a man, or a ram. He is a combination of all three and the hyphenated "word" is a way to show this.

Guide the children through the reading of the book by the "round robin" technique, giving every child an opportunity to read aloud. Have the students reread the book aloud in order to become more fluent in their reading. Each book should be reread two times before the next book is introduced.

This will be the time to informally assess children for the purpose of forming reading groups, based on their ability to decode, identify Special Exhibits with ease, and comprehend main ideas.

Discuss the story briefly as you read through it, drawing attention to the pictures and the words which label them. Explain any words which may be unfamiliar or uncommon, using them in sentences to further demonstrate their meanings.

For instance, the word "gap" may be unusual to them. Using the sentence "Sally has a gap where her tooth used to be." will make the meaning more concrete and relevant for young children. Apply that idea of a "gap" being an empty or open space to the columns in the story.

Worksheet 49A: Read the instructions aloud. Monitor as they work independently.

ACTIVITY 2: WRITING

Write the following words on the board: Pan, a, tan, man, ram. Call on volunteers to copy individual letters or entire words on the board beside the examples.

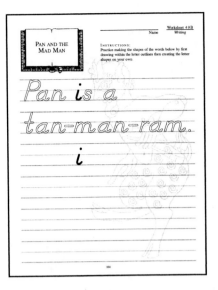

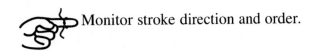Monitor stroke direction and order.

Erase the board and rearrange the words in the order of the sentence: Pan is a tan-man-ram. Leave a space for the word "is" and ask if anyone can tell you what Special Exhibits should go into the space. Add "is" to the sentence. Have the children read the sentence aloud several times.

Worksheet 49B: Read the instructions aloud. Challenge them to write the entire sentence as they see it, leaving space between words, capitalizing the first word and putting a period at the end. Instruct them not to attempt to make the I; it has been put on the sheet in bold so they will not have to write it.

Praise them for completing their first real book!

LESSON 50
READING COMPREHENSION

ACTIVITY 1: ORDER OF EVENTS

Begin with an introductory explanation of what it means for things to be done "in order." Discuss the activities of their school day—what do they do first in the morning? What do they do next? Continue in this manner, listing events as they occur from top to bottom on the board, drawing pictures if possible to depict the events, along with key words.

Describe that stories also tell about events which happen over time and in a certain order. Lead the children in a review of the story *Pan and the Mad Man*. Help them to retell it in the order in which the main events occurred, listing these events on the board using the vocabulary in the book. Number the events from top to bottom.

Erase the board and present Worksheet 50A.

Worksheet 50A: Read the instructions aloud. Look over the pictures and elicit responses regarding the events depicted in each picture. Help the children to decide which event is first, second, third, and fourth and have them number the pictures with a small numeral in the right upper corner. Allow them to work independently to cut them out and paste them in the blocks on the left side of the page in order from top to bottom.

ACTIVITY 2: ART ACTIVITY

Worksheet 50B: Read the instructions aloud and allow students to work independently.

LESSON 51
TARGET SOUNDS: SHORT A AND E REVIEW

ACTIVITY 1: HEARING AND SEEING

 Play the Alphabet Song for the children encouraging them to sing along while pointing to the corresponding letters on the flashcards.

Draw two large squares on the board. In the middle of one, write a large upper case A. In the middle of the other, write a large upper case E. Tell the children that you will be reading a list of words aloud and they are to tell you if the word has the short A or the short E in the middle, using the gestures they have been previously taught for these sounds. You will write the word in the box with the correct letter.

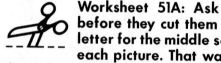

man	pet	hat	bell	cat
rat	bed	pen	Ben	Pat

If they direct you to the wrong letter box, help them to self-correct by pointing out the letter differences in the word and having them echo it several times to reinforce both sight and sound simultaneously. Leave this display on the board when you present the worksheet.

Worksheet 51A: Ask the children to name the pictures before they cut them out and write the proper lower case letter for the middle sound in the upper right hand corner of each picture. That way it is easy for them to glue them in the proper frame after they are cut out.

ACTIVITY 2: WRITING

Erase the box containing the words with medial short A. Have students come to the board and circle the middle short E in each of the remaining words in the E box. Erase all the words except "pet," "Ben," "bed," and "pen." Put lines on the board and call on students to come up and copy these words on the lines, paying careful attention to their stroke order and direction. Ask the students why the word "Ben" is capitalized.

Worksheet 51B: Read the instructions aloud. Call on students to read the words and allow them to work independently to copy them in their neatest writing.

Row 1: man, bell,pen, cat
Row 2: rat, pet, hat, bed

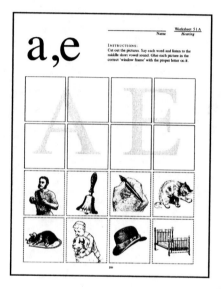

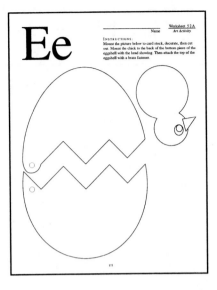

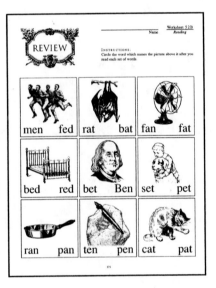

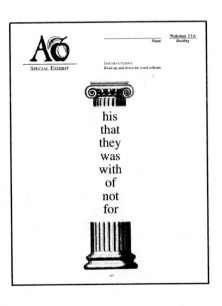

LESSON 52
TARGET SOUND E AND REVIEW

ACTIVITY 1: ART ACTIVITY

Worksheet 52A: Read the instructions aloud and have a finished example handy for the children to see. Assist them as necessary to complete the project. Encourage use of a variety of colors and designs for the eggs (like Easter eggs!)

ACTIVITY 2: READING

Worksheet 52B: Read the instructions aloud. Have them put their finger on the first picture (men). Have a volunteer read the two words at the bottom of this box: men, fed. Ask which of these words names the picture and monitor as they circle the word "men." Continue with the rest of the page in the same manner, naming the pictures from left to right across each row.

LESSON 53
SPECIAL EXHIBITS AND READING

ACTIVITY 1: SPECIAL EXHIBITS

Write the following words on the board in a vertical column: his, that, they, was, with, I. Read the words aloud to the children from top to bottom and have them echo them back to you. Discuss the meaning of each word, using it in a familiar sentence or eliciting sentences from the children. Repeat the echo reading, going from bottom to top. Do this several times in both directions.

Worksheet 53A: Present the worksheet and have the children read the words aloud as you point to them on the board display, following along on their sheets. Read words randomly from the board and ask students to point to the same word on their papers. Point to words on the board without reading them aloud and ask students to match the written board word with the corresponding printed word on the paper. Have students read the words in order from top to bottom and then again from bottom to top.

ACTIVITY 2: WRITING

Worksheet 53B: Read the instructions aloud and monitor their progress as they work independently.

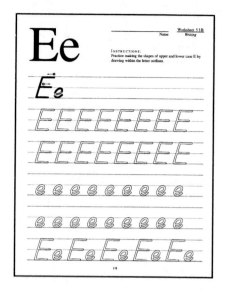

LESSON 54
READING COMPREHENSION

ACTIVITY 1: READING

Introduce the story *Bad Meg!* Guide the children in reading it aloud in "round robin" style. Discuss any vocabulary which may be necessary and assist with Special Exhibits as needed. Have the students reread the book aloud in order to become more fluent in their reading. Each book should be reread two times before the next book is introduced.

ACTIVITY 2: READING COMPREHENSION

Write the following words on the board: Pat, rat, bat, net. Lead the children to read each of the words, pointing out similarities and differences between them. Ask again why the word "Pat" is capitalized.

You may want to further this understanding by writing the word "pat" with a lower case P and pointing out that this means "to touch lightly" or "a small amount, like a pat of butter." Explain to them that just changing the case of a letter can change its meaning!

Worksheet 54A: Read the instructions aloud and monitor their progress as the children work independently.

ACTIVITY 3: READING COMPREHENSION

Worksheet 54B: Read the instructions aloud. Have the children put their finger on Question 1. Read this question to them and call on a student to label the picture. Draw their attention to the three names printed under the picture and have them put their finger on the word which is the correct name. Have them circle their responses. Repeat this with Question 2.

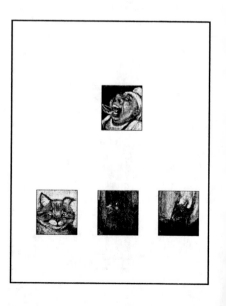

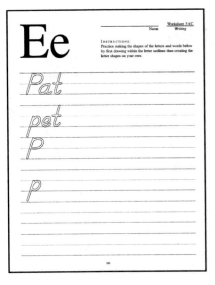

ACTIVITY 4: WRITING

Write the upper case P on the board. Invite students to come up and write this letter. Add the lower case A and T beside the upper case P. Guide the chidren to read the word and then invite students to write the word. Change the upper case P to lower case P and switch the A to E. Invite volunteers to write this new word (pet) and read it to the class.

Worksheet 54C: Read the instructions aloud and monitor their progress as they work independently.

Carefully check stroke direction and order and the "FOUR P's!"

Lesson 55
Hearing/Writing Review and Special Exhibits

ACTIVITY 1: HEARING AND WRITING

Play a quick game of "My Father Owns a Shop" (also known as "I'm Going on a Trip," etc.). Each child in turn says "My father owns a shop, and he sells _____" and insert the name of an item beginning with the initial sounds A, B, G, M, N, R, S, T. Praise their ability to think of words which begin with these sounds.

Worksheet 55A: Read the instructions and allow the students to work independently. They should be able to do this page with ease. You may assist any students with labeling if they are uncertain, but do not help them to determine beginning letters or sounds.

> Row 1: monkey, ax, alligator, saw
> Row 2: nail, man, ball, basket
> Row 3: apples, goat, frog, guitar
> Row 4: ring, mask, table, mouth

After they have completed Worksheet 55A, allow them to continue to work independently on Worksheet 55B.

Worksheet 55B: Read the instructions and allow the students to work independently.

> Row 1: nut, turtle, piano, nest
> Row 2: rabbit, seal, tiger, rooster
> Row 3: moon, socks, sun, paint
> Row 4: shoe, tie, tent, boat

ACTIVITY 2: SPECIAL EXHIBITS

Write the following Special Exhibits on the board: his, that, they, was, with. Read them in order from top to bottom, having the children echo them. Repeat this activity from bottom to top, and then randomly as you point to the words. Check to see how many students can read them independently and praise their efforts.

Worksheet 55C: Read the instructions aloud. Point to the word "his" at the top of the left column. Ask if anyone is able to find the same word in type printed on the right column. Have them draw a line to the correct word.

ACTIVITY 3: READING

Write the words found on Worksheet 55D on the board in vertical columns as shown on the worksheet. Call on children to read the words one at a time in order from top to bottom of each column. Read again from bottom to top and then randomly as you point to various words. Praise their fine reading!

Worksheet 55D: Read the instructions aloud. Point to words on the board and have students find them on their sheets. Call on students to read the words you have indicated.

 Archives: Picture/Initial Sounds
Use only cards with pictures that begin with the sound of the letters: A, E, S, M, F, R, G, N, B, T, P, and D.

LESSON 56
TARGET SOUND: SHORT I
(AS IN "IGLOO")

ACTIVITY 1: HEARING

Play the Short Vowels Song for the children encouraging them to sing along while pointing to the corresponding letters on the flashcards. The students have been formally introduced to the short vowel sounds of A, E, and I but not O and U. They have seen and heard these both in the Museum Song and *The Alphabet Quest*. Explain to the children that they will be learning about these two letters in the next few weeks.

 Show the children the flashcard with the letter I on it. Have them hear the sound of short I as in "Indian."

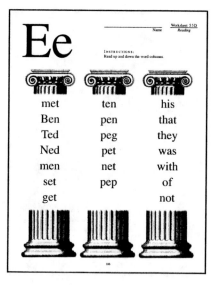

Remind them that because this is a vowel sound, it is very good at playing "hide and seek" with other vowels. Challenge them to "catch" the short I in the following list of sounds:

i, e, a, o, u, i, i, a, i, e, i, o, u, i, a, e, i, i, o, i, u, i

Give your students the reproduction of the Indian Boy and allow them to hang it in the museum. Talk to them about the story *The Alphabet Quest* and give them their museum bag. Allow them time to go through the house and collect items that begin with the sound of I to make their own museum. If you are teaching in a school setting, instruct the children to take the bag home and bring in objects the following day.

ACTIVITY 2: SEEING

Tell the children that the letter which makes the short I sound is the letter "I, i." Draw attention to the stimulus picture on the wall and the flashcard. Point out the features of the letter (the upper case has one long vertical line and two small horizontal lines at the top and bottom, the lower case has a dot over it, etc.)

Mix the printed upper case I card with the other upper case letter cards which have been studied so far. Present these to the children in random order, instructing them to indicate when they see the target letter I.

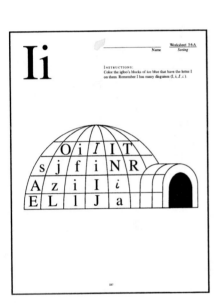

Repeat this activity with the lower case letters, then with both upper and lower case combined.

On the board, write the written upper and lower case letters for I, describing and numbering your strokes as you do so. Compare and contrast the printed letters and the written letters. Leave both the printed and written letters on display as you present the worksheet.

Worksheet 56A: Read the instructions aloud and monitor as the children work independently.

ACTIVITY 3: WRITING

Place guidelines and perimeter lines on the board. Call on students to come to the board and make the upper and lower case letter I.

Worksheet 56B: Read the instructions aloud and monitor their progress as they work independently.

You may want to give the students the coloring page along with the flashcard. Read the information about the artist to your studentss as they color the picture.

LESSON 57
TARGET SOUND: SHORT I

ACTIVITY 1: HEARING

Tell the children that just like all the other letters, the letter "I,i" loves to be the leader in line and begin lots of words. Challenge them to listen carefully to the following word list and indicate when they hear the short I sound at the beginning of any word:

Indian	candle	ax	fly	dart
butter	mother	ink	itch	igloo
animal	egg	ill	enter	inside
Alex	imagine	nose	gate	if

Worksheet 57A: Read the instructions aloud. Label the pictures for the children as they respond as directed.

Row 1: Indian, ax, candle
Row 3: dart, fly, igloo

ACTIVITY 2: WRITING

Invite children to come up and practice upper and lower case I. Monitor their stroke order and direction carefully.

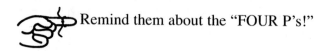

Worksheet 57B: Read the instructions carefully. Make sure they use all the letter mazes first before they write the letters independently on the first line.

Remind them about the "FOUR P's!"

Percival's Pairs: Using A, M, B, P, T, D, N, G, S, F, R, E, and I

LESSON 58
TARGET SOUND: SHORT I

ACTIVITY 1: HEARING

Tell the children that short I is another sound which is often right in the middle of words, just like short A and E. Challenge them to listen very carefully to the short I sounds in the middle of the following words:

fish   pig   pin   lips   hill

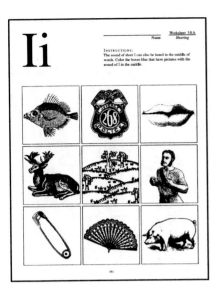

Sometimes short A, E, and I like to change places in words with the same consonants and change the whole meaning of the word. Say the following word groups to the children, discussing how the meaning changes as the middle vowel changes:

pan, pen, pin   tan, ten, tin   bag, beg, big

Challenge the children to indicate only when they hear short I in the middle of words in the following list:

peg   pig   rip   rap   Ben   bin
red   rid   sin   pet   pit   pat

Praise them for their careful listening!

Worksheet 58A: Read the instructions aloud and monitor their progress as they work independently, assisting if necessary with the labeling of the pictures.

Row 1: fish, badge, lips
Row 2: deer, hills, man
Row 3: pin, fan, pig

ACTIVITY 2: READING SYLLABLES

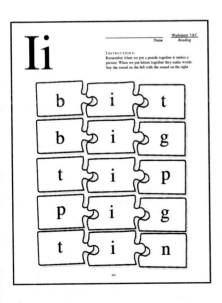

 Present the puzzle pieces for B, P, D, S. Review the letter names and sounds with the children. Place the piece for I beside each of these consonants in turn, guiding the chidren to read the syllables formed.

Worksheet 58B: Read the instructions aloud. Call on children to read the syllables in order and randomly as you display them with the puzzle pieces.

ACTIVITY 3: READING WORDS

Take out the pieces for T, G, P, and N. Review these letter names and sounds with the children. Link these consonants with the syllables on display in a manner which will form meaningful words (such as "big," "bit," "pin," "dig," "sit," etc.). Play with these puzzle pieces, forming words and having children read them until you have exhausted most of the word possibilities for this combination of sounds.

Worksheet 58C: Read the instructions aloud. Call on students to read the words on the page. Write the words on the board and ask them to match the written word which you indicate on the board with the printed word as it is shown on the sheet.

Lesson 59
Target Sound: Short I and Vowel Review

Activity 1: Middle Vowel Sound Review

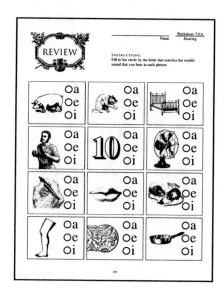

Aa Give each child a set of cards with lower case A, E, and I on them. Review with them the sounds each one makes. Read the following word list and instruct the children to hold up the card which shows the letter making the middle sound in each of the words:

pig	cat	bed	man	ten	fan
pen	lips	rats	leg	map	pan
pin	sad	fed	fin	rag	rid

Worksheet 59A: Read the instructions aloud. Remind the children how they are to respond, filling in the circle beside the letter which makes the middle sound of each picture name. Label all the pictures for the children as they respond independently.

Row 1: pig, cat, bed
Row 2: man, ten, fan
Row 3: pen, lips, rats
Row 4: leg, map, pan

Activity 2: Art Activity

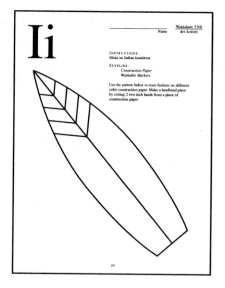

Worksheet 59B: Display a finished Indian headress containing three or four feathers of different colored paper. Assist the children to make their own using the pattern on Worksheet 59B. Encourage them to trace carefully and use different colors.

Lesson 60
Special Exhibits and Writing Review

Activity 1: Special Exhibits Review

Cut out the printed and written Special Exhibits of Worksheet 60A from Appendix 5/6 and glue to card stock to make cards.

Present the printed Special Exhibits cards: his, that, they, was, with. Lead the children in echoing, and then reading independently. Present the written word cards and repeat the activity.

Affix the printed cards to a display board (chalk, white, flannel, etc.) Present the written cards one at a time and invite children to find the corresponding printed word on the display. Repeat with the rest of the cards and then switch the activity (written on display, printed by presentation).

Now mix all the cards face down on a display board. Play the Memory game with the children. They must make pairs of matching printed and written Special Exhibits.

 You may also do this with all the Special Exhibits which have been studied so far. This will make the game more challenging, but will be a great review and reinforcement activity.

Worksheet 60A: Read the instructions aloud and monitor their progress as they work independently.

ACTIVITY 2: WRITING

Invite students to the board to write all the lower case letters studied so far in groups of two or three on the board. Repeat until all the letters have been practiced.

 Carefully watch stroke formation!

If you have students who are persisting with incorrect stroke order or direction, additional practice may be necessary. This is important because later use of cursive writing is dependent upon proper stroke formation for efficiency and legibility.

Worksheet 60B: Read the instructions aloud and monitor their progress as they work independently.

 Remind them about the "FOUR P's!"

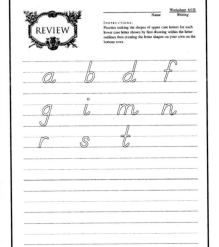 If you have students who are persisting with incorrect pencil hold, give them triangular grips for their pencils for reinforcement of the correct finger position. Students whose writing is very dark may find the use of a harder lead pencil (lighter impression) or a mechanical pencil to be helpful (the lead in a mechanical pencil will break with too much pressure).

LESSON 61
REVIEW

ACTIVITY 1: SEEING

Present the flashcards for the letters "A,a," "E,e," and "I,i." Present the written upper and lower case cards and call on children to match the written letters with the printed letters and give the names and sounds. Following the key on Worksheet 61A, draw an artist's palette on the board with the corresponding colors for each of the letter types. Leave the display on the board for the worksheet activity.

Worksheet 61A: Read the directions aloud and monitor their progress as they work independently.

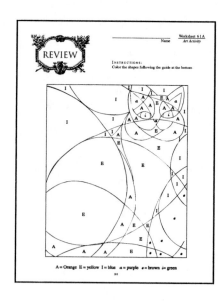

ACTIVITY 2: SEEING, READING AND WRITING

Play a game of letter/sound bingo with the children today, using the following sounds in the beginning of words: m, b, n, r, a, t, s, g.

Children may make these cards on their own by writing the lower case letters independently in the blocks of prepared sheets similar to Tic-tac-toe. Since there are only eight letters, the middle (ninth) space can be a "free" space.

Worksheet 61B: Read the instructions aloud and call on students to name the pictures. Monitor their progress as they work independently.

   Row 1: mermaid, nail, baby, ring
   Row 2: goat, sun, turtle, apples

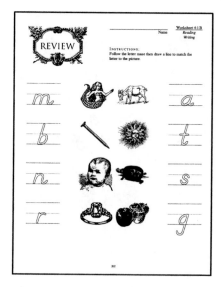

LESSON 62
READING COMPREHENSION
AND SPECIAL EXHIBITS

ACTIVITY 1: READING

Divide the board into two sections. In one section write the following: The, a, to. On the other section write the following: fat, men, fed, fig, pig. Challenge the children to read the words as you point to them randomly. Ask why they think you have divided the words into groups (one group are Special Exhibits, the other group are words that can be sounded out).

The fat men fed a fig to a pig.

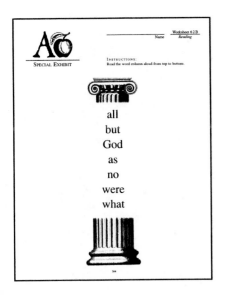

all
but
God
as
no
were
what

Introduce a little grammar lesson here! Discuss briefly that words have different jobs in sentences. Ask the children if they can find the word on the board which tells what someone does (fed). Ask if they can find the word which describes something (fat). The other three words in that group (men, fig, pig) all name things. At this point, you can just say that the Special Exhibits are extra helpers to make the sentences sound right.

Rearrange the words on the board to make the sentence: The fat men fed a fig to a pig. You may need to define a "fig" for them.

 Bring in Fig Newtons for them to try! Read the sentence several times by echoing and independently.

Worksheet 62A: Read the instructions aloud and monitor their work.

ACTIVITY 2: SPECIAL EXHIBITS

Write the words from Worksheet 62B on the board in a column. Have the children echo them down and up again; then randomly call on students to read them aloud independently. Put the words in sentences and elicit sentences from the students to reinforce meaning.

You may also want to review the previously introduced words which are in the next story, listed with List 3 in Appendix 6.

Worksheet 62B: Read the instructions aloud. Assist the children to read the words from top to bottom of the column, following along on the worksheet as you point to the corresponding written word on the board. Repeat the activity going from bottom to top of the column. Finally, point randomly to the words on the column and call on students to read them.

An additional way to use this sheet for further reinforcement is to erase the words from the board and then have students point to or circle the correct word as you randomly say them. You may want to do this on an individual or small group basis to more carefully monitor their responses.

LESSON 63
READING AND WRITING REVIEW

ACTIVITY 1: READING

Draw three circles on the board in a vertical column. To the right of each circle write one of the following words: fan, man, dam. Tell the children that they must be careful listeners and readers today. You will be reading one of the words on the board and they must choose which word is the one you have read. Read the word "fan." Call on a student to come to the board and fill in the circle beside the correct word. After the correct response is completed, have students read the other words also to reinforce reading skills.

 You may want to point out the small differences in the words, reminding them of past lessons when they learned that just one letter can change the entire meaning of a word.

Using the words as they are presented on Worksheet 63A, continue this activity. Do NOT read the words which are used as stimulus pictures on this worksheet, but choose one of the other two in each example.

Worksheet 63A: Read the instructions aloud. Assist those students who may have difficulty labeling the pictures, perhaps by encouraging them to read the words first and then figure out which word names the picture. Monitor their progress as they work independently.

ACTIVITY 2: WRITING REVIEW

Call on a student to come to the board to write the letters I and G.

Write lower case IG on the board. Place B, P, D, F, and R in front of the "ig" and ask the children if a word is made. Allow volunteers to come to the board and make the letters. Elicit sentences which use each word appropriately.

Worksheet 63B: Read the instructions aloud. Monitor stroke formation and order carefully as they work independently.

LESSON 64
READING AND ALPHABETICAL ORDER

ACTIVITY 1: READING

Write the words on Worksheet 64A on the board in columns just as they are presented on the worksheet.

Worksheet 64A: Read the instructions aloud. Assist the children to read the words from top to bottom of each column, following along on the worksheet as you point to the corresponding written word on the board. Repeat the activity going from bottom to top of each column. Finally, point randomly to the words on the columns and call on students to read them.

An additional way to use this sheet for further reinforcement is to erase the words from the board and then have students point to or circle the correct word as you randomly say them. You may want to do this on an individual or small group basis to more carefully monitor their responses.

It would also be a good idea to classify the words in various ways: by beginning, middle, or ending sounds. This should be handled as a group exercise. You could write the words on the board as they suggest them, highlighting the selected letter/sound, or having students circle them.

ACTIVITY 2: ALPHABETICAL ORDER

Sing the Alphabet Song again with GUSTO! Explain briefly that many things in our culture are ordered in this way: dictionary entries, telephone books, their names in the teacher's grade book! Knowing the order of our letters will help them to be good students.

On the board draw 10 to 12 dots in a simple pattern. Label each with a letter of the alphabet in the order in which you wish the picture to be formed. Have the students call out the letter names in order as you connect them on the board.

Worksheet 64B: Read the instructions aloud. Allow the children to sing the song quietly to themselves as they complete the sheet.

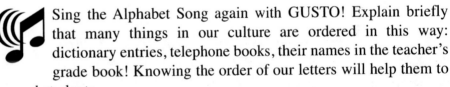 **Percival's Pairs: Using A, M, B, P, T, D, N, G, S, F, R, E, and I**

LESSON 65
READING AND COMPREHENSION

ACTIVITY 1: READING WORDS

Write the words from Worksheet 65A on the board in columns just as they are presented on the worksheet.

Worksheet 65A: Read the instructions aloud. Assist the children to read the words from top to bottom of each column, following along on the worksheet as you point to the corresponding written word on the board. Repeat the activity going from bottom to top of each column. Finally, point randomly to the words on the columns and call on students to read them.

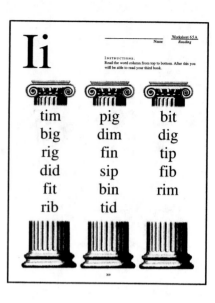

 An additional way to use this sheet for further reinforcement is to erase the words from the board and then have students point to or circle the correct word as you randomly say them. You may want to do this on an individual or small group basis to more carefully monitor their responses.

 There are a lot of new words on this list which you will want to briefly define for students. Put them into sentences to help convey meaning and elicit sentences from the students.

Congratulate them on being prepared to read another book!

ACTIVITY 2: READING

This book chronicles the voyage of the Mayflower. The following vocabulary and expressions are used:

big rig—large sailing vessel
rib to rib—close together
dim—dark
gab—talk, discuss
rap—talk
pep—energy, vigor
dip—to sink or drop down
fit—in good shape
bit of fin—some fish
sip at the bag—drink water from a wine skin
bin—manger, feed trough
ran not a bit—the ship was stalled
in a fit—confused or uncertain
tid bit—small amount
tad bit—small amount

rim—coastline
sat as a dam—rose up before them
fib—lie

The art for this story is styled after Amercian Primative. At this time there were no art schools so any painting was done by self-taught artists. Perspective and anatomy are not used in a realistic fashion and there is a great deal of repeated decorative patterns.

Present the book *To the Rim of the Map* and read aloud in "round robin" style. You may prefer to do this in your informal reading groups at this time to accommodate differences in progress.

Worksheet 65B: Read the instructions aloud and monitor their progress as they work independently.

Praise them for their fine reading!

LESSON 66
TARGET SOUND: SHORT O (AS IN "OX")

ACTIVITY 1: HEARING

 Play the Museum Song for the children encouraging them to sing along while pointing to the corresponding letters on the flashcards.

 Show the children the flashcard with the letter O on it. Have them hear the sound of short O as in "ox."

Remind them that because this is a vowel sound, it is also very good at playing "hide and seek" with other vowels. Challenge them to "catch" the short O in the following list of sounds:

 An idea for indicating O would be to open their mouths wide as if they were saying short O, but making no sound.

a, o, i, o, o, u, e, a, o, e, o, i, o, o, u, u, a, i, o, e, o, o

Praise their careful listening!

Give your students the reproduction of *The Ox Driver, an Old Time Figure of the West* and allow them to hang it in the museum. Talk to them about the story *The Alphabet Quest* and give them their museum bag. Allow them time to go through the house and collect items that begin with the sound of O to make their own museum. If you are teaching in a school setting, instruct the children to take the bag home and bring in objects the following day.

ACTIVITY 2: SEEING

Write the upper and lower case "O,o" on the board. Ask if anyone can tell you what the shape of these letters is (circle). These are so easy to make, and both cases look alike except for their size!

 Mix the printed upper case O card with the other upper case letter cards which have been studied so far. Present these to the children in random order, instructing them to indicate when they see the target letter O.

Repeat this activity with the lower case letters, then with both upper and lower case combined.

On the board, rewrite the written upper and lower case letters for O, describing the direction of the circle stroke as you do so.

Worksheet 66A: Read the instructions aloud. Ask how many legs an octopus has (eight). Tell them that each leg will be able to "grab" one letter O.

 You may also want to discuss briefly that the suction cups on the underside of an octopus' legs are round like "o's!"

ACTIVITY 2: WRITING

Invite students to come up to the board to write the upper and lower case O. Watch that they are going counterclockwise with their stroke.

Worksheet 66B: Read the instructions aloud and then monitor as they work independently.

 Remind them to work down the page first, then return to the top to make the letters on their own. Monitor the "FOUR P's"!

 You may want to give the students the coloring page along with the flashcard. Read the information about the artist to your students before they color the picture.

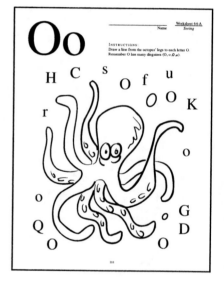

LESSON 67
TARGET SOUND: SHORT O

ACTIVITY 1: HEARING

 Play the Short Vowels Song for the children encouraging them to sing along while pointing to the corresponding letters on the flashcards.

Tell the children that the short O sound is going to be the "leader" in words today and that they must listen carefully for it at the beginning of the following list of words:

octopus	zebra	bear	fish	horse
ostrich	ax	ox	otter	kangaroo
apple	igloo	egg	if	operation
off	in	an	on	elevator

Worksheet 67A: Read the instructions aloud to the children. Tell them that you will name the pictures for them while they respond by placing a dot of orange on the ones which begin with the short O sound. They may go back then and color in the marked pictures.

> Row 1: otter, zebra, bear
> Row 2: fish, octopus, ox
> Row 3: horse, kangaroo, ostrich

ACTIVITY 2: WRITING

Worksheet 67B: Read the instructions aloud and allow children to work independently.

LESSON 68
TARGET SOUND: SHORT O

ACTIVITY 1: HEARING

Remind the children that vowel sounds also love to be in the middle of words. Review with them the vowels they have learned so far: short A, E, I, and O. Discuss briefly how much alike they are, but that they can make a big difference in a word. Read the following word pairs and ask them to indicate whether the first word or the second word has the short O sound:

hit, hot	pod, pad	fog, fig	rat, rot
Tim, Tom	Don, den	pet, pot	mop, map

Worksheet 68A: Read the instructions aloud. Have students name the pictures and monitor as they respond as instructed.

Row 1: pot, bed, pig
Row 2: map, top, queen
Row 3: lock, boxing, skate

ACTIVITY 2: READING

 Present the puzzle pieces for M, P, T, N. Review the letter names and sounds with the children. Pair the piece for O with each of the consonants and have the children blend the sounds to form syllables.

Worksheet 68B: Read the instructions aloud. Call on students to read the syllables in order, and randomly as you use the display pieces.

 Since they have begun to work on order of events in their reading comprehension exercises, you could introduce the concept of numbering these syllables from 1-4 from top to bottom. Then you could designate the syllable to be read by its number. Present the P and T pieces. Use these pieces to form the words as shown on Worksheet 68C and lead the children in reading them aloud.

Briefly discuss the meaning of the word "not." It does not mean the "knot" in their shoelaces! Make up some sentences with and without the word "not" to demonstrate how it changes the meaning: You may go to the party; you may NOT go to the party.

Worksheet 68C: Read the instructions aloud and use various ways as previously described to elicit responses from the students. Write the words on the board and pair the written with the printed. Encourage fluent sound blending and praise their efforts!

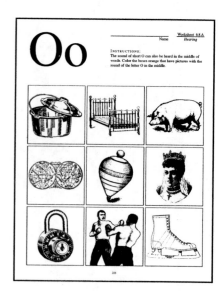

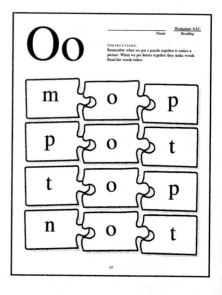

LESSON 69
TARGET SOUND: SHORT O AND SPECIAL EXHIBITS

ACTIVITY 1: ART ACTIVITY

Worksheet 69A: Have the student color in the otter parts on the worksheet then cut them out. Glue the pieces with craft glue onto a bar of soap and allow to dry.

ACTIVITY 2: READING SPECIAL EXHIBITS

Write the words on Worksheet 69B on the board in a column just as they are presented on the worksheet. Have the students echo the words and then read them independently in order, top to bottom. Repeat this exercise from bottom to top and then independently.

Worksheet 69B: Read the instructions aloud. Assist the children to read the words from top to bottom of each column, following along on the worksheet as you point to the corresponding written word on the board. Repeat the activity going from bottom to top of each column. Finally, point randomly to the words on the columns and call on students to read them.

💡 An additional way to use this sheet for further reinforcement is to erase the words from the board and then have students point to or circle the correct word as you randomly say them. You may want to do this on an individual or small group basis to more carefully monitor their responses.

LESSON 70
TARGET SOUND: SHORT O AND READING COMPREHENSION

ACTIVITY 1: READING

 Play the Museum Song for the children encouraging them to sing along while pointing to the corresponding letters on the flashcards.

Write the words from Worksheet 70A on the board in a column just as they are presented on the worksheet.

Worksheet 70A: Read the instructions aloud. Assist the children to read the words from top to bottom of each column, following along on the worksheet as you point to the corresponding written word on the

board. Repeat the activity going from bottom to top of each column. Finally, point randomly to the words on the columns and call on students to read them.

ACTIVITY 2: READING

Introduce the story *Pepin the Not-Big*. Guide the children through the reading of this book aloud in "round robin" style. Discuss the pictures and events as they occur. Have the students reread the book aloud in order to become more fluent in their reading. Each book should be reread two times before the next book is introduced.

Pepin, son of Charles Martel, and called "the Short" due to his small stature, was the king of the Franks (French) in the latter half of the 700's, an office which he had usurped from the rightful king, King Childeric. Through the use of accumulated power, he had King Childeric placed in a monastery and convinced the Pope that the title of king should be bestowed on the one who holds the king's power—namely, Pepin himself. This essentially set the stage for the struggle between the papacy and civil authority during the Middle Ages by setting a precedent for the Pope's "right" to give and take away kingdoms.

The following vocabulary and expressions are used in this story:

> of tip to top—from head to toe (or toe to head!)
> tag—name
> sag—bend or break at the center
> was a pig—ate a lot
> rid the map—did away with
> top man—king
> fit—competent, able (note that this word was used differently
>   in Book 3)
> dim dip—unintelligent, silly person
> set to get—ready to obtain
> sit with men of God—go into a monastery
> bid—desired, ordered
> set in pen—wrote down

Worksheet 70B: Read the instructions aloud. Assist the children to interpret and number the events in the order they are presented in the story. Have them place small numerals in the upper right corner of the pictures and then cut them out. This will help when they reassemble the pictures in the blocks.

LESSON 71
REVIEW

 Play the Museum Song for the children encouraging them to sing along while pointing to the corresponding letters on the flashcards.

ACTIVITY 1: HEARING AND SEEING

Have the children generate a list of as many words which begin with short A as they can think of in a brief period of time (2-3 minutes). Write the words on the board as they say them—this could get hectic for you, but fun for them! When time is up, read all the words back, checking to see if they really do begin with short A. You can have students come up and circle the A in each word. Make sure you capitalize proper names!

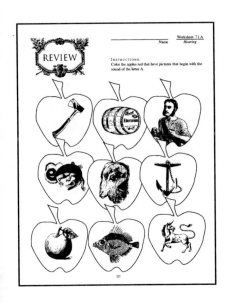

Worksheet 71A: Read the instructions aloud and monitor their progress as they work independently. Remind them that they will be listening only for beginning short A sounds and that this sheet can be tricky! Assist with labeling as necessary but do not give any further clues.

> Row 1: ax, barrel, man
> Row 2: alligator, ram, anchor
> Row 3: apple, fish, unicorn

ACTIVITY 2: WRITING

Write the following words on the board: be, in, it. Draw lines beside each word and invite students to come up and copy the words in their best writing. Recite the words several times for reinforcement.

Worksheet 71B: Read the instructions aloud and assist the students to complete the worksheet as directed.

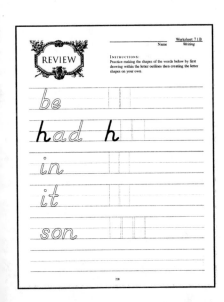

 Archives: Picture/Initial Sounds
Use only cards with pictures that begin with the sound of the letters: A, E, I, O, U, S, M, F, R, G, N, B, T, and L.

LESSON 72
REVIEW AND READING

ACTIVITY 1: HEARING AND SEEING REVIEW

Draw three circles on the board in a vertical column. To the right of each circle write one of the following letters: b, p, t. Tell the children that they must be careful listeners today. You will be saying a word which will begin with one of the letter sounds on the board. Say the word "boat." Call on a student to come to the board and fill in the circle beside the correct letter. Change the letters to three others which have been taught so far this year. You may mix consonants and vowels among the choices. Say a word each time which begins with one of the letter sounds and repeat this activity until you are confident of the children's ability to do this with ease.

Worksheet 72A: Read the instructions aloud. Assist the children to label if necessary and monitor their work.

   Row 1: pear, ostrich, donkey
   Row 2: sun, monkey, feet
   Row 3: elephant, ink, top
   Row 4: rabbit, octopus, goat

ACTIVITY 2: READING REVIEW

Divide the board into two sections. In one section write the following: the, on, his. On the other section write the following: Ben, Tom, set, pet, log. Challenge the children to read the words as you point to them randomly. Ask why they think you have divided the words into groups (one group are Special Exhibits, the other group are words that can be sounded out).

Repeat the little grammar lesson here! Remind them that words have different jobs in sentences. Ask the children if they can find the word on the board which tells what someone does (set). The other three words in that group (Ben, Tom, pet, mat) all name things. Remind them that Special Exhibits are extra helpers to make the sentences sound right.

Rearrange the words on the board to make the sentence: Ben set Tom, his pet, on the mat. Have the children echo the sentence several times, and then read it independently.

Worksheet 72B: Read the instructions and encourage the children to be neat and creative as they draw.

Ben set Tom, his pet, on the mat.

LESSON 73
REVIEW AND ALPHABETIC ORDER

ACTIVITY 1: READING REVIEW

Write the following words on the board: bat, bed, fan, dog, pet. Guide the children through the sounding out of each word and elicit sentences using each one.

Ask the children which two words begin with the same letter/sound (bat, bed). Ask them which have the same middle sounds (bat/fan, bed/pet). Ask them which two have the same ending sound (bat, pet). Praise them for their careful listening and reading.

Worksheet 73A: Read the instructions aloud. Call on children to read the words and then find the picture which best matches the word. Be careful with the pictures for "dog" and "pet," the latter is the one with the boy and the dog together. Monitor their work as they respond as directed.

ACTIVITY 2: ALPHABETICAL ORDER

 Sing the Alphabet Song again with enthusiasm, pointing to the stimulus pictures in order and having another student display the flashcards in order as you sing. If doing this at home, have your child flip through the cards. Praise their efforts!

On the board draw 10 to 12 dots in a simple pattern. Label each with a letter of the alphabet in the order in which you wish the picture to be formed. Have the students call out the letter names in order as you connect them on the board.

Worksheet 73B: Read the instructions aloud and monitor their progress as they work independently.

LESSON 74
HEARING AND WRITING REVIEW

ACTIVITY 1: HEARING AND WRITING

Write the following lower case letters on the board: B, D, F, P. Review the name and sound of each letter. Tell the children that you will be reading a list of words which will each start with one of these letter sounds. You will be calling on volunteers to come to the board, point to, and then copy the correct beginning letter for each word.

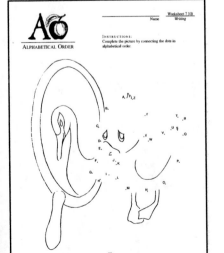

pot	bed	fox	dog	big	fix
den	pig	doll	bag	pat	fun

Leave the four letters on the board for reference.

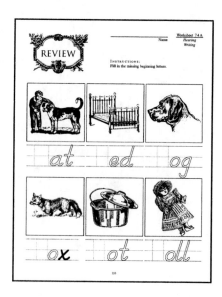

Worksheet 74A: Read the instructions aloud. Call on students to label the pictures. Monitor their progress as they independently decide which letter makes the beginning sound and write them in the spaces provided.

ACTIVITY 2: WRITING

Call on students to come to the board and make the shapes for all the lower case letters taught so far, in groups of three or four.

 Remind about the "FOUR P's," stroke direction and order.

Worksheet 74B: Read the instructions aloud and monitor their progress as they work independently.

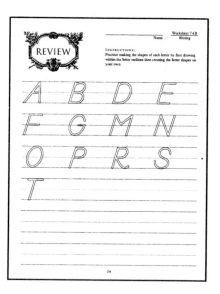

Worksheet 74C: Test. This test is optional and is added to evaluate your students if you feel it is necessary at this time. The answers are worth 2 points each.

LESSON 75
REVIEW OF SHORT I AND O

ACTIVITY 1: READING

 Play the Alphabet Song for the children encouraging them to sing along while pointing to the corresponding letters on the flashcards.

Write the words from Worksheet 75A on the board in columns just as they are presented on the worksheet. Have the children echo the words as you point to them. Discuss any words whose meanings may be unclear. Use the words in familiar sentences and elicit sentence ideas from the children.

Worksheet 75A: Read the instructions aloud. Assist the children to read the words from top to bottom of each column, following along on the worksheet as you point to the corresponding written word on the board. Repeat the activity going from bottom to top of each column. Finally, point randomly to the words on the columns and call on students to read them.

bog   bib
dog   big
dot   dig
fog   fig
God   fit

 Use any of the previous alternative ideas for reinforcing the printed to written type and encourage fluent blending. You may also want to categorize the words based on beginning, middle, or ending sounds as in previous lessons.

ACTIVITY 2: WRITING

Worksheet 75B: Instruct the students to write their names neatly on the lines provided.

LESSON 76
TARGET SOUND: SHORT U
(AS IN "UMBRELLA")

ACTIVITY 1: HEARING

 Play the Museum Song for the children encouraging them to sing along while pointing to the corresponding letters on the flashcards.

 Show the children the flashcard with the letter U on it. Have them hear the sound of short U as in "umbrella."

Challenge them to "catch" the short U in the following list of sounds:
   i, u, a, e, u, u, o, e, u, a, u, i, i, u, a, e, u, u, i, o, u, i, u

 Here is the sound for which raising the hand "UP" is a perfect indicator!

 Give your students the reproduction of the *Lady in a Meadow* and allow them to hang it in the museum. Talk to them about the story *The Alphabet Quest* and give them their museum bag. Allow them time to go through the house and collect items that begin with the sound of U to make their own museum. If you are teaching in a school setting, instruct the children to take the bag home and bring in objects the following day.

ACTIVITY 2: SEEING

Tell the children that the letter which makes the short U sound is the letter "U,u." Draw attention to the stimulus picture on the wall and display the flashcard. Point out the features of the letter (both cases are formed the same way, a "horseshoe" with the open end UP; they only differ in size).

Mix the printed upper case U card with the other upper case letter cards which have been studied so far. Present these to the children in random order, instructing them to indicate when they see the target letter U.

Repeat this activity with the lower case letters, then with both upper and lower case combined.

On the board, write the written upper and lower case letters for U, describing and numbering your strokes as you do so. Compare and contrast the printed letters and the written letters. Leave both the printed and written letters on display as you present the worksheet.

 As you are doing the above activity and the following worksheet, carefully watch for discrimination between the letters U and N. They are vertical reversals of each other and can be confusing to children who are prone to perceptual errors.

Worksheet 76A: Read the instructions aloud and monitor their progress as they work independently.

ACTIVITY 2: WRITING

Place guidelines and perimeter lines on the board. Call on students to come to the board and make the upper and lower case letter U.

 Remind about stroke direction.

Worksheet 76B: Read the instructions aloud and monitor their progress as they work independently.

 You may want to give the students the coloring page along with the flashcard. Read the information about the artist to your students before they color the picture.

LESSON 77
TARGET SOUND: SHORT U

ACTIVITY 1: HEARING

Tell the children that the short U sound is going to be the "leader" in a list of new words today and that they must continue to listen carefully for it at the beginning:

ugly	animal	exit	igloo	under
ox	umbrella	apples	up	Emily
olives	Adam	uncle	elephant	usher
Indian	inside	unwrap	alligator	understand

Worksheet 77A: Read the instructions aloud to the children. Tell them that you will name the pictures for them while they respond independently on their own papers.

Row 1: anchor, orange, umpire
Row 2: vase, umbrella, plane
Row 3: nest, up, turkey

ACTIVITY 2: READING SYLLABLES

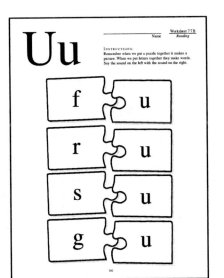

 Present the puzzle pieces for these letters: F, R, S, G. Review the letter names and sounds. Pair the piece for U with each of the preceding consonants and assist the children to sound out each syllable which is formed.

Worksheet 77B: Read the instructions aloud and assist the children to read them in order from top to bottom. You may number them and call on students to read the syllable beside the number you designate, or use a board display of written syllables to reinforce written to printed type.

ACTIVITY 3: READING WORDS

Take away the syllable "fu." Present the puzzle piece for final N and review the letter name and sound with the children. Link the piece with each of the syllables in turn and assist the children to sound out the word which is formed. Use each word in an original sentence.

Worksheet 77C: Read the instructions aloud and assist the children to read the words fluently. Any of the previous variations for practicing and reinforcing may be used here also (written to printed, number designations, etc.)

LESSON 78
TARGET SOUND: SHORT U AND SPECIAL EXHIBITS

ACTIVITY 1: HEARING AND WRITING

 Play the Short Vowels Song for the children encouraging them to sing along while pointing to the corresponding letters on the flashcards.

Remind the children how the vowel sounds—short A, E, I, O, and now U—all like to be in the middle of words. They love to change places and change the meanings of many little words. Read the following word pairs aloud and discuss how the meaning of the words changes with different middle vowels:

Ben, bun   fan, fun   sin, sun   bed, bud

Challenge them to listen only for the sound of short U in the middle of the following words and indicate when they hear it:

lobster	ring	sun	lock	boat
bike	cup	ram	golf	gorilla
gun	pizza	nut	gate	vest
pen	happy	butter	run	Dan

Remind about stroke direction.

Worksheet 78A: Read the instructions aloud. Allow them to follow the first letter maze at the upper left. Label the pictures across the row and monitor as they respond as directed. Continue in the same manner with the rest of the sheet.

Row 1: lobster, ring, sun, lock
Row 2: boat, bike, cup, ram
Row 3: golf, gorilla, gun, pizza
Row 4: nut, gate, vest, pen

ACTIVITY 2: SEEING AND READING

Write the words on Worksheet 78B on the board in a column just as they are presented on the worksheet. Ask the students if they can figure out what is the same in each of the words (the middle U). Call on students to come to the board and circle each one of these.

Starting at the top of the list, have the children sound out and echo the words. Point to them randomly and call on students to read them aloud.

ACTIVITY 3: SPECIAL EXHIBITS

In a few days the children will be reading a new book *The Rig Ran On*. This book will utilize the words on Worksheet 78C. Present these words to the children at this time. Draw attention to similarities with words previously taught. Of particular interest on this list are the words "Ma" and "Pa." Although they have A in them, it is not the sound of short A, but the sound "ah." Most children will not have any difficulty remembering this.

LESSON 79
READING AND COMPREHENSION

ACTIVITY 1: READING

This is a story about a family's trip west during the westward expansion. The following vocabulary and language expressions are used in this story:

bit—piece that goes in the horse's mouth to direct it
nag—old horse
dim—not bright
sob—cry
red man—American Indian
rig—a horse-drawn wagon (note that this word was used differently in Book 3)

Introduce the book *The Rig Ran On*. Guide the children through "round robin" reading, as a class or in small groups. Discuss the pictures and events as you proceed through the book. Encourage the children to read with fluency as much as possible. You may want to have them read sentences a second time, after the initial decoding is done, to reinforce this. Have the student reread the book aloud in order to become more fluent in their reading. Each book should be reread two times before the next book is introduced.

You may want to discuss Ma's attitude at the end of the story. Her character is full of faith. Is this something to be admired? Why or why not?

ACTIVITY 2: READING COMPREHENSION

Worksheet 79A: Read the instructions aloud and help the children to number the events in the order in which they occurred in the story. Allow them to cut out the pictures and paste them in order as directed.

LESSON 80
REVIEW AND READING

ACTIVITY 1: HEARING AND SEEING REVIEW OF BEGINNING VOWEL SOUNDS

 Before you begin this activity, make copies for your students of Appendix 1. Put 20 Cheerios in cups for each of your students.

Give each student a copy of the 5-section paper which you have prepared. Divide the board into five sections as shown on the paper. At the top of each section write one of the five vowels in lower case: a, e, i, o, u. Direct the children to copy the letters on their papers in the same sections just as you have shown. Monitor their work.

Pass out little cups containing 20 Cheerios. Remind them not to eat them yet—they will have a chance to do that after the game is over!

When they are all ready, tell them you will be reading some words aloud and they should listen carefully for the sound at the beginning of the word. It will be their job to tell you if the word starts with short A, E, I, O, or U and then place a Cheerio in the correct column. When all the Cheerios have been placed properly, they will be permitted to eat them.

Read the following list of words and guide the children to determine beginning sound and place the Cheerio in the correct column. This is a group activity, not a competition. When they have made the correct determination, write the word on the board, highlighting or circling the beginning sound and drawing attention to the matching letter at the top of the column. Tell them that there will not be the same amount of Cheerios in each column.

up	at	end	in	off	odd
ask	under	ugly	exit	on	ill
if	us	olive	umpire	it	enter
office	unhappy				

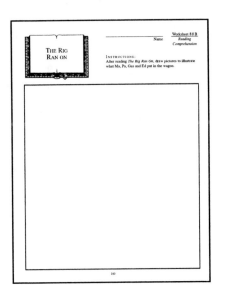

 There are two A words, three E words, four I words, five O words, and six U words in the above list, so there should be that number of Cheerios in each column on each paper.

Check the papers for the correct number of Cheerios in each column. Praise their listening and tell them to "eat them up!"

Worksheet 80A: Read the instructions aloud. Assist them to label the pictures and determine the beginning sound. Do not help them to determine the letter which makes the sound. You may direct their attention to the board if necessary—there is a small word in each column which they should be able to decode in order to confirm their letter/sound association.

> Row 1: umbrella, eggs, Indian
> Row 2: elephant, ink, ostrich
> Row 3: ax, otter, anchor

ACTIVITY 2: READING COMPREHENSION

Do a brief review of yesterday's story. On the board, list the names of the items the family puts in the rig. Have the children read the list in unison as you point randomly to each word. Review word meanings and have students put the words in original sentences.

Worksheet 80B: Read the instructions aloud and encourage detail and color in their drawing.

LESSON 81
TARGET SOUND: L (AS IN "LION")

ACTIVITY 1: HEARING

 Play the Museum Song for the children encouraging them to sing along while pointing to the corresponding letters on the flashcards.

Tell the children that it is time for a new consonant sound! This will help them to read and write many more new words.
Show the children the flashcard with the letter L on it. Have them hear the sound of L as in "lion."

Have them echo the word "lion" several times, then ask them to "hold" the first sound—L. Their tongue is stuck right behind their top teeth, just like with the T, but it stays there to make the L. This is the "singing" sound, because we use it all the time when we don't know the words to songs—"La, la, la, la, la...!"

This is another one of those sounds which may be late developing in some children. The most common substitution/distortions which you will see will be the use of W or Y. The error here is the neglect of the use of the tongue. In a very small percentage of children, structural or musculature problems in the tongue prevent it from lifting to articulate clearly. If you suspect this in any student, alert the parent for a more thorough examination. In most cases, however, the sound is just slow to develop due to differences in maturation. Emphasis on how the sound is produced may encourage this process, just like with the R sound. Remind the students that we do not use our lips to make this sound (as in W) or the back of our tongues (as in Y).

Challenge them to be good listeners and find the L sound as it plays "hide-and-seek" in the following list:

An idea for an indication gesture would be to use another sign language finger spelling letter. The letter L is formed by the LEFT hand (starts with L also!) using the thumb and index finger. This can also be a way of reminding children of the difference between their right and left hands.

m, b, l, p, t, l, l, f, r, s, l, d, a, l, w, l, y, l, e, m, n, l, s, l, l

Praise their fine listening. Now direct them that they will listen for the L sound as the "leader" in words:

lion	leader	bat	man	ox
deer	watch	yard	lace	gorilla
lemon	lightbulb	wagon	yes	whale

Worksheet 81A: Read the instructions aloud. Call on students to label the pictures and direct them to place small dots of red in the corners of the ones which begin with L. They may then go back and color in the correct boxes.

Row 1: ox, whale, lightbulb
Row 2: gorilla, lace, bat
Row 3: lemon, deer, man

Give your students the reproduction of *The Christian Martyr's Last Prayer* and allow them to hang it in the museum. Talk to them about the story *The Alphabet Quest* and give them their museum bag. Allow them time to go through the house and collect items that begin with the sound of L to make their own museum. If you are

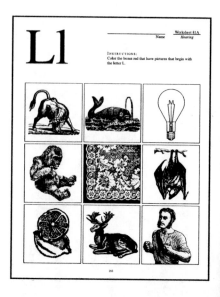

teaching in a school setting, instruct the children to take the bag home and bring in objects the following day.

ACTIVITY 2: SEEING

Tell the children that the letter which makes the L sound is the letter "L,l." Draw attention once again to the stimulus picture on the wall and display the flashcard. Point out the features of the letter (the upper case is one vertical and one horizontal line, the lower case is a single vertical line, etc.)

 Mix the printed upper case L card with the other upper case letter cards which have been studied so far. Present these to the children in random order, instructing them to indicate when they see the target letter L.

Repeat this activity with the lower case letters, then with both upper and lower case combined.

 Watch carefully for the discrimination of upper case I (as in Indian) and lower case L (as in lion)—they are almost identical in the printed form. You may want to remove the upper case I at first, and then present only these two as an activity to promote finer discrimination.

On the board, write the written upper and lower case letters for L, describing and numbering your strokes as you do so. Compare and contrast the printed letters and the written letters. Leave both the printed and written letters on display as you present the worksheet.

Worksheet 81B: Read the instructions aloud and monitor their progress as they work independently.

ACTIVITY 3: WRITING

Place guidelines and perimeter lines on the board. Call on students to come to the board and make the upper and lower case letter L.

 Remind about stroke direction and order.

Worksheet 81C: Read the instructions aloud and monitor their progress as they work independently.

 You may want to give the students the coloring page along with the flashcard. Read the information about the artist to your students before they color the picture.

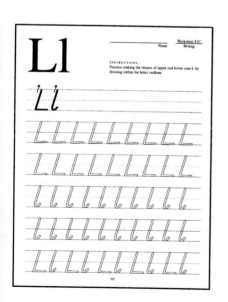

LESSON 82
TARGET SOUND L

ACTIVITY 1: HEARING AND WRITING

Tell the children that the L sound is going to be the "leader" in a list of new words today and that they must continue to listen carefully for it at the beginning of the following list of words:

lobster	ring	sun	lock	lemon
bike	cup	lantern	golf	lion
lace	pizza	goat	gate	lamb
lighthouse	yam	wind	want	yawn

Worksheet 82A: Read the instructions aloud to the children. Tell them that you will name the pictures for them while they respond independently on their own papers.

Row 1: lobster, ring, sun, lock
Row 2: lemon, bike, cup, light
Row 3: golf, lion, lace, pizza
Row 4: goat, gate, lamb, lighthouse

ACTIVITY 2: WRITING

Write the following words on the board: Leo, the, lion.

 Because the letter H has not yet been taught, do not require students to copy it. Place perimeter and guidelines on the board beside each word. Call on students to come to the board and copy the words on the lines provided. Monitor their stroke direction and order.

Worksheet 82B: Read the instructions aloud and monitor their progress as they work independently.

Archives: Picture/Initial Sounds
Use only cards with pictures that begin with the sound of the letters: A, E, I, O, U, S, M, F, R, G, N, B, T, P, L, and D

LESSON 83
TARGET SOUND: L

 You may want to do the painting for Activity 2 first, then use Activity 1 to fill the time it takes for the plates to dry. You can then return to the gluing and finishing of the lion face.

ACTIVITY 1: HEARING AND SEEING

Brainstorm with the children to come up with words which begin with the L sound. You may select categories, or place the words in categories after they are suggested. Write the words on the board, highlighting or having students come up and circle the L in each one.

ACTIVITY 2: ART ACTIVITY

Worksheet 83A : Prepare an example of the lion face as directed. Describe the steps for making the face. Prepare a work table with yellow paint, paper plates, and brushes. Students may paint at the work table, then go to their seats to cut out the lion face on their worksheets. When their plates are dry, they may glue the face to the plate.

LESSON 84
TARGET SOUND: L

ACTIVITY 1:HEARING

Praise the children for coming up with so many L words in yesterday's hearing activity. Remind them of some of those words. Challenge them to indicate to you when they hear the L in a list of new words today:

leash	bug	love	win	Lynn	lady
wax	listen	rope	yawn	lawn	yes
room	loom	last	low	row	yet

Worksheet 84A: Read the directions aloud. Name or have students name the pictures in order, putting a small dot of color in those which begin with L. They may go back and color in the entire picture afterwards.

Row 1: lion, pear, lemon
Row 2: leg, lips, sun
Row 3: lobster, pen, lamb

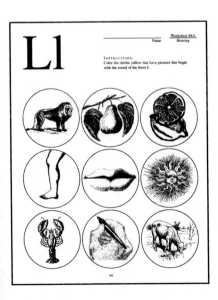

ACTIVITY 2: READING

Remind the children that the letter which makes the L sound is the letter "L,l." Write the letter in both upper and lower case on the board and display the printed letters using the flashcards.

 Display the L puzzle piece. Have the children echo it several times. Present the puzzle pieces for each of the short vowel sounds in this order: U, O, I, E, A. Have the children echo them for you, then say them independently as you display or point to them randomly.

Place the U to the right of the L and assist the children to sound out the syllable which is formed. Continue in the same way with the rest of the vowels, linking them to the L sound.

Worksheet 84B: Read the directions aloud. Direct the children to read the syllables in various ways: in order, randomly, pointing to them as you say them randomly, etc.

Point out the upper case L in the first syllable. Ask why it is okay to do this and what reason would make it necessary (if these were the first two letters of a proper name).

ACTIVITY 3: READING WORDS

Ask students to think of words which may begin with the syllables listed on Worksheet 84B. Write these on the board, circling or highlighting the two beginning sounds.

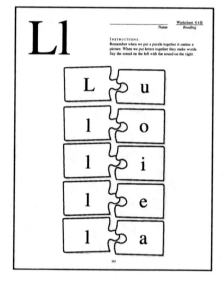

 Tell the students that you are now going to add another sound to the syllables to form words. Present the pieces for T and G.

Place the T to the right of the syllable "lo." Assist the children to read the word formed (lot). Move the T to the syllable "le." Read the word "let." Place the G beside the syllable "la" to form the word "lag" and have them read it.

 You may want to discuss briefly what the word "lag" means. Generating sentences with all words formed is always a good idea also.

Explain to the children that L doesn't like to be alone at the end of the line of sounds in many of our words, so it brings its twin brother along to keep it company. They will often see two "l's" at the end of words, but they will always only make one sound of L.

Display the letter pieces for B and S. Place the E beside the B and sound out the syllable. Place the "ll" piece at the end and read the word formed.

Now link the E and "ll" pieces to the initial S piece. Assist the children to sound out the new word formed. Draw attention to the rhyming nature of the two words. Tell them that there are many other words which would rhyme also (fell, tell, dell, etc.) Take away the initial puzzle piece and write in the beginning letters for these words before the "ell" and have them read each one. Praise their great reading!

Put the puzzle word "bell" back together. Take away the E and replace it with I. Challenge the children to read the new word formed. Ask them what they would have to change if this were a person's name (replace the lower case with upper case).

Worksheet 84C: Read the instructions aloud. Use any of the previous techniques for eliciting reading or word identification from the students.

To continue to encourage the matching of the written letters with the printed ones, you may want to write the words on the board as a stimulus display. Pointing to words randomly on the board and having students indicate the corresponding word on the worksheet isolates the visual discrimination task and turns this into a "seeing" activity.

LESSON 85
TARGET SOUND: L AND REVIEW

ACTIVITY 1: REVIEW

Play the Museum Song for the children encouraging them to sing along while pointing to the corresponding letters on the flashcards.

Do a class review of all the sounds studied so far: m, b, p, t, d, n, g, s, f, r, l, and the short vowels (a,e,i,o,u). Remind them of the indication gestures you may have used for these sounds, match their letter names with sounds, and discuss the stimulus pictures on display. Call on children to give you spontaneous examples of words which begin with each of the sounds, call attention to children's names which may begin with the sounds, etc.

One by one, show the picture flashcards again. Say the stimulus words and call on students to come to the board and write the letter which makes each initial sound.

Leave the display of both the printed and written letters for reference. Tell the children that you will be reading a list of words and that they will be called upon to come to the board, indicate the letter which makes each word's beginning sound, and then write it again on the board. Read the following list, calling on students to do as instructed:

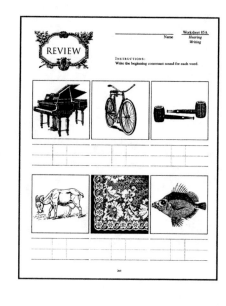

palace	lost	family	mustard
butter	doll	nose	sun
rabbit	toe	gate	alley
edge	up	office	inside

Worksheet 85A: Read the instructions aloud. Tell the children that you will be doing this page together. Read the label for each picture, eliciting responses for beginning sound and letter. Monitor as they write the chosen letter in the spaces provided.

Row 1: piano, bike, pipe
Row 2: goat, lace, fish

ACTIVITY 2: READING

Write the words on Worksheet 85B on the board in columns just as they are presented on the worksheet. Remind them about the "twin 'l'" rule. Discuss the meanings of any of the words and use in sentences as necessary to clarify.

Worksheet 85B: Read the instructions aloud. Assist the children to read the words from top to bottom of each column, following along on the worksheet as you point to the corresponding written word on the board. Repeat the activity going from bottom to top of each column. Finally, point randomly to the words on the columns and call on students to read them.

An additional way to use this sheet for further reinforcement is to erase the words from the board and then have students point to or circle the correct word as you randomly say them. You may want to do this on an individual or small group basis to more carefully monitor their responses.

Worksheet 85C: Read the instructions aloud. Monitor as they work independently.

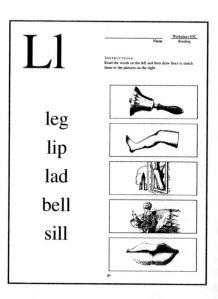

LESSON 86
TARGET SOUND: H

ACTIVITY 1: HEARING

 Play the Museum Song for the children encouraging them to sing along while pointing to the corresponding letters on the flashcards.

Tell the children that today's sound is the "laughing" sound. Tell the children to echo after you: "ha, ha, ha," "ho, ho, ho" (like Santa), "hee, hee, hee." Ask if they can tell you what sound is in each of those types of laughter (they all start with H).

 Show the children the flashcard with the letter H on it. Have them hear the sound of H as in "hat."

Have them echo the H sound several times. Remind them that H is a quiet sound and that they must listen very carefully for it in the following list of sounds:

 An indication gesture for this may be to place one hand (starts with H) over their heart (also starts with H) when they hear the sound.

m, p, h, r, a, h, u, s, e, h, h, d, h, i, o, h, t, n, h, g, h, h, h

Praise their careful listening. Now challenge them to indicate when they hear H at the beginning of these words:

hear	hanger	bird	heart	guitar
cow	apples	pig	horse	house
hook	under	end	holly	lift
mud	dim	hug	goose	hope

Worksheet 86A: Read the instructions aloud. Label the pictures, having students place dots of red in the corners of the H words. They may return to those pictures to color in after all the pictures have been labeled.

Row 1: hanger, guitar, bird
Row 2: apples, hook, cow
Row 3: house, pig, horse

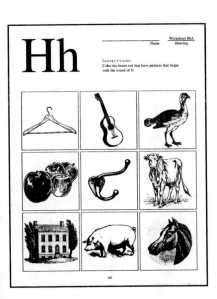

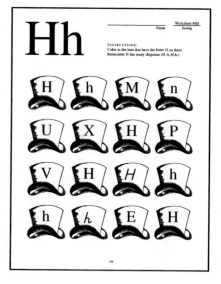

Give your students the reproduction of *Girl Reading* and allow them to hang it in the museum. Talk to them about the story *The Alphabet Quest* and give them their museum bag. Allow them time to go through the house and collect items that begin with the sound of H to make their own museum. If you are teaching in a school setting, instruct the children to take the bag home and bring in objects the following day.

ACTIVITY 2: SEEING

Tell the children that the letter which makes the H sound is the letter "H,h." Draw attention to the stimulus picture on the flash-card. Point out the features of the letter (the upper case has two vertical lines with a horizontal line connecting the two like the rung of a ladder, the lower case is like a little chair when viewed from the side). Show them a chair and draw attention to the similarity to lower case H.

Mix the printed upper case H card with the other upper case letter cards which have been studied so far. Present these to the children in random order, instructing them to indicate when they see the target letter H. Repeat this activity with the lower case letters, then with both upper and lower case combined.

On the board, write the written upper and lower case letters for "H,h," describing and numbering your strokes as you do so. Compare and contrast the printed letters and the written letters. Leave both the printed and written letters on display as you present the worksheet.

Worksheet 86B: Read the instructions aloud. Monitor as they work independently.

ACTIVITY 3: WRITING

Place guidelines and perimeter lines on the board. Call on students to come to the board and make the upper and lower case letter H.

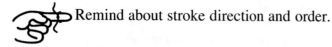Remind about stroke direction and order.

Worksheet 86C: Read the instructions aloud and monitor their progress as they work independently.

You may want to give the students the coloring page along with the flashcard. Read the information about the artist to your students before they color the picture.

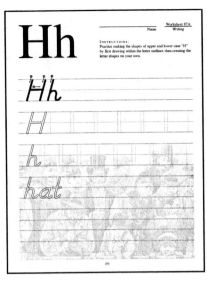

LESSON 87
TARGET SOUND: H AND REVIEW

ACTIVITY 1: WRITING

Review the writing of both upper and lower case "H,h," using independent board writing.

Have students write the word "hat" on the board. Make sure all students are able to read this with ease.

Worksheet 87A: Read the instructions aloud and monitor their progress as they work independently. Have them write the word "hat" at least three times on the lines at the bottom of the sheet. Give direction for letter and word spacing as needed.

ACTIVITY 2: REVIEW

Do another class review of all the sounds studied so far: m, b, p, t, d, n, g, s, f, r, l, and the short vowels (a,e,i,o,u). Remind them of the indication gestures you may have used for these sounds, match their letter names with sounds, and discuss the stimulus pictures on display. Call on children to give you spontaneous examples of words which begin with each of the sounds, call attention to children's names which may begin with the sounds, etc.

 One by one, show the picture flashcards again. Say the stimulus words and call on students to come to the board and write the letter which makes each initial sound.

Leave the display of both the printed and written letters for reference. Tell the children that you will be reading a list of words and that they will be called upon to come to the board, indicate the letter which makes each word's beginning sound, and then write it again on the board. Read the following list, calling on students to do as instructed:

roof	ten	muffin	igloo	understand
opposite	dandy	puppy	animal	gum
fudge	soda	nasty	run	elephant

Worksheet 87B: Read the instructions aloud. Tell the children that you will be doing this page together. Read the label for each picture, eliciting responses for beginning sound and letter. Monitor as they write the chosen letter in the spaces provided.

Row 1: umbrellas, rabbit, turtle
Row 2: mittens, Indian, octopus

LESSON 88
TARGET SOUND: H

ACTIVITY 1: READING

 Play the Short Vowel Song for the children encouraging them to sing along while pointing to the corresponding letters on the flashcards.

Remind the children that the letter which makes the H sound is the letter "H,h." Write the letter in both upper and lower case on the board and display the printed letters using the flashcards.

Display the H puzzle piece. Have the children echo it several times. Present the puzzle pieces for each of the short vowel sounds in this order: U, O, I, E, A. Have the children echo them for you, then say them independently as you display or point to them randomly.

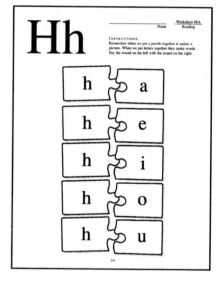

Place the U to the right of the H and assist the children to sound out the syllable which is formed. Continue in the same way with the rest of the vowels, linking them to the H sound.

Worksheet 88A: Read the directions aloud. Direct the children to read the syllables in various ways: in order, randomly, pointing to them as you say them randomly, etc.

ACTIVITY 2: READING WORDS

Ask students to think of words which may begin with the syllables listed on Worksheet 88A. Write these on the board, circling or highlighting the two beginning sounds.

Tell the students that you are now going to add another sound to the syllables to form words. Then present the pieces for T, N, P, and M. Review the sounds made by each of these. Link the T as an ending sound for "ha," forming the word "hat." Help the children to read this word and echo it once or twice. Move the T to the syllable "hi," forming the word "hit" and challenge the children to read this aloud.

Continue with linking N to "he," forming "hen"; linking P to "ho," forming "hop"; linking M to "hu," forming "hum."

Write these words on the board in random order: hen, hop, hum, hat, hit. Read and echo them several times.

Worksheet 88B: Read the instructions aloud. Use any of the previous techniques for eliciting student response, including sight matching (written board to printed worksheet).

Another idea with these sheets at this point would be to play an informal riddle game: give clues which help define the words and have students tell and show you which one is meant.

For example, you may ask for this worksheet, "I am thinking of something which keeps the rain off your head (that girls wear on Easter, etc.). There are many kinds of these. You can sometimes tell what job a person has by this." This reinforces vocabulary while practicing the reading and discrimination of the words.

ACTIVITY 3: ART ACTIVITY

Worksheet 88C: Prepare an example of the crazy top hat described. Carefully go through the steps needed to make the hat and call attention to the numbering and ordering of the tasks. Prepare a worktable for the painting and assist students as needed.

LESSON 89
TARGET SOUND H AND REVIEW

ACTIVITY 1: READING

Play the Museum Song for the children encouraging them to sing along while pointing to the corresponding letters on the flashcards.

Write the words on Worksheet 89A on the board in columns just as they are presented on the worksheet.

Worksheet 89A: Read the instructions aloud. Assist the children to read the words from top to bottom of each column, following along on the worksheet as you point to the corresponding written word on the board. Repeat the activity going from bottom to top of each column. Then point randomly to the words on the columns and call on students to read them.

An additional way to use this sheet for further reinforcement is to erase the words from the board and then have students point to or circle the correct word as you randomly say them. You may want to do this on an individual or small group basis to more carefully monitor their responses. Also, any of the previous techniques for eliciting student response (written to printed recognition, riddles, etc.) would be helpful.

ACTIVITY 2: REVIEW

Do a class review of all the sounds studied so far: m, b, p, t, d, n, g, s, f, r, l, h, and the short vowels (a,e,i,o,u). Remind them of the indication gestures you may have used for these sounds, match their letter names with sounds, and discuss the stimulus pictures on display. Call on children to give you spontaneous examples of words which begin with each of the sounds, call attention to children's names which may begin with the sounds, etc.

Praise their work, then erase the board. Write the letters L and H on the board. Say the word "lady." Call on a student to come to the board and point to the written letter which begins the word "lady." Ask the student what the letter name is and what sound it makes. Continue in the same manner with the following words, providing a written choice on the board of two different letters each time (similar to what is on Worksheet 89B):

lace	happy	exit	pony	table
bug	family	David	mask	bone
Adam	note	it	olive	up

Worksheet 89B: Read the instructions aloud. Do the worksheet together, labeling the pictures and eliciting responses. Monitor their progress as they work.

Row 1: lips, house, elephant, pizza
Row 2: tent, basket, fence, dog
Row 3: moon, bell, anchor, nest

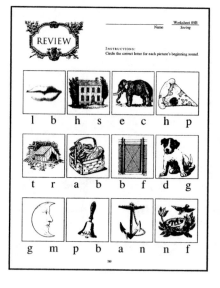

ACTIVITY 3: WRITING

Write the following words on the board in random order: ran, sad, The, dog. Challenge the children to rearrange the words to make a sentence and lead them through this activity. Point out that the word "The" uses an upper case T as its first letter. Ask what that tells them (it should be the first word in the sentence). Continue to assemble the sentence and rewrite it in its proper order on the board.

Tell them that they know how to make all the letters of all the words in this sentence now! Call on volunteers to come to the board and copy complete words of the sentence under the examples.

Worksheet 89C: Read the instructions aloud and monitor their progress as they work independently.

LESSON 90
SPECIAL EXHIBITS AND READING

ACTIVITY 1: SPECIAL EXHIBITS

Write the Special Exhibits from Worksheet 90A on the board. Review them with the children, using in original sentences and eliciting sentences from the children.

Worksheet 90A: Read the Special Exhibit words aloud.

 Before you present *The Dog, the Hog, the Rat, the Ram, the Hen and the Big Big Din* to the children, there are some "language twists" in this story which should be brought to your attention.
    The following vocabulary and phrases may need to be explained to the children as the story is read:

    din—loud noise, commotion
    nag—old horse
    fig—sweet fruit (remind them of Fig Newtons!)
    ham—meaty part of a hog's leg
    "red hot"—angry
    "mad fit"—temper tantrum
    mob—group
    "got rid of"—threw off
    lob—to throw
    "dug in"—pinched with claws, or pecked at
    lad—small boy
    nip—bite
    hem—bottom edge of garment
    "the log ran"—it slid
    tug—a boat
    "that they were from"—that came from their home

 The previously taught Special Exhibits used in this story are listed under Book 6 in Appendix 6. It would be a good idea to go over these as well before reading the story.

Lead the children in reading the story "round robin" style, as a class or in small groups. Guide them as needed with the vocabulary and phrases. Encourage fluency. Repeat sentences for students, using appropriate expression to aid comprehension. Have the student reread the book aloud in order to become more fluent in their reading. Each book should be reread two times before the next book is introduced.

Worksheet 90B: Read the instructions aloud. Allow several students to read the sentence for the class. Monitor as they work independently. Encourage neat and careful work. Remind children to take their time and do their best.

Worksheet 90C: Read the instructions aloud. Call on students to read the sentences and each of the word choices. Assist them to choose the correct answer and respond as indicated.

 Worksheet 90D: Test. This test is optional and is added to evaluate your students if you feel it is necessary at this time. The answers are worth 2 points each.

 Archives: Picture/Initial Sounds
Use only cards with pictures that begin with the sound of the letters: A, E, I, O, U, S, M, F, R, G, N, B, T, P, L, and D

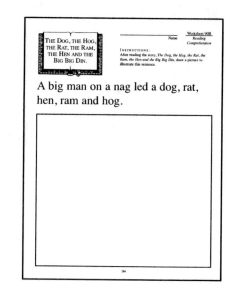

A big man on a nag led a dog, rat, hen, ram and hog.

LESSON 91
TARGET SOUND: HARD C (AS IN "CAT")

ACTIVITY 1

 Play the Museum Song for the children encouraging them to sing along while pointing to the corresponding letters on the flashcards.

Show the children the flashcard with the letter C on it. Have them hear the sound of C as in "cow."

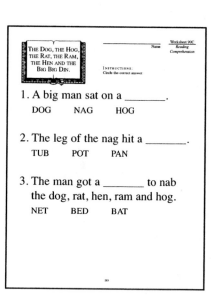

INSTRUCTIONS:
Circle the correct answer.

1. A big man sat on a _____.
DOG   NAG   HOG

2. The leg of the nag hit a _____.
TUB   POT   PAN

3. The man got a _____ to nab the dog, rat, hen, ram and hog.
NET   BED   BAT

Say the sound of hard C several times and have the children echo it. Just like all the other sounds, C likes to play "hide and seek." Challenge them to "find" the C sound among the other sounds in this list and indicate when they hear it.

The indication gesture may be the formation of a "cup" with one hand—fingers together and hand slightly curved, as if to be used to scoop up water from a stream. Another option is to use the fingerspelling sign for C, using the left hand for proper orientation of the letter.

a, c, e, i, c, o, c, u, m, c, c, t, d, c, s, c, p, b, c, c, c

Tell the children that the C sound is going to be the "leader" in the words on the list today and that they must continue to listen carefully for it at the beginning of the following list of words:

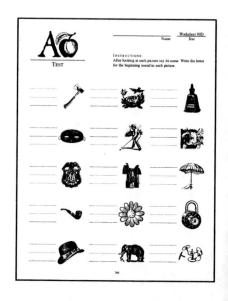

Veritas Press PHONICS MUSEUM *Kindergarten Teacher's Manual* | 128

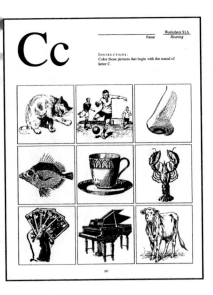

cat	cup	nose	lobster	fish
cards	piano	tap	cap	pan
can	dove	cover	cone	band
hope	comb	fame	came	cut

Worksheet 91A: Read the instructions aloud to the children. Tell them that you will name the pictures for them while they respond independently on their own papers.

Row 1: cat, soccer, nose
Row 2: fish, cup, lobster
Row 3: cards, piano, cow

Give your students the reproduction of *The Latest News* and allow them to hang it in the museum. Talk to them about the story *The Alphabet Quest* and give them their museum bag. Allow them time to go through the house and collect items that begin with the sound of C to make their own museum. If you are teaching in a school setting, instruct the children to take the bag home and bring in objects the following day.

ACTIVITY 2: WRITING

Tell the children that the letter which makes the C sound is the letter "C,c." Draw attention to the stimulus picture on the flashcard. Ask if they can tell you what letter they have already studied which is almost the same (o). What is different between the O and the C? Tell them that a C is made exactly the same way as an O, except that the circle is not completed on the right side.

On the board, write the written upper and lower case letters for C, describing your stroke as you do so. Place guidelines and perimeter lines on the board. Call on students to come to the board and make the upper and lower case letter C.

Remind about stroke direction.

Worksheet 91B: Read the instructions aloud and monitor their progress as they work independently.

Remind them about the "FOUR P's!"

ACTIVITY 3: WRITING WORDS

Write the word "cat" on the board and invite students to come up and copy the word on the lines provided. Praise their work.

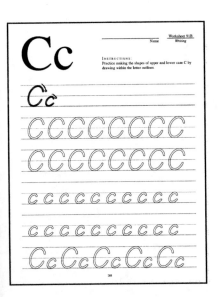

Worksheet 91C: Read the instructions aloud and monitor their progress as they work independently. Watch letter spacing carefully and correct as needed.

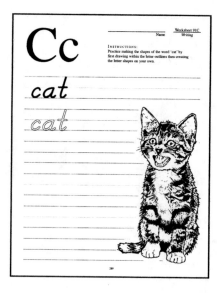

 You may want to give the students the coloring page along with the flashcard. Read the information about the artist to your students before they color the picture.

LESSON 92
TARGET SOUND: K

ACTIVITY 1: HEARING

 Play the Museum Song for the children encouraging them to sing along while pointing to the corresponding letters on the flashcards.

Ask the children if any of them have little brothers or sisters who like to follow them around and do everything they do. Tell them that C has a friend like that, the letter K. In fact, the letter K even sounds just like C, although it looks very different. Draw attention to the flashcard and stimulus pictures for K and say the sound several times, with students echoing.

Remind them that sometimes their little brothers and sisters use their "big kid" ideas when they play with their friends and K does the same thing. It makes the same sound as C when it is the leader in a line of sounds to form words. So even though some words may sound like they start with C, the letter K is really the leader.

 Show the children the flashcard with the letter K on it. Have them hear the sound of K as in "kangaroo."

Tell them that the words which you will read today which have the K sound at the beginning are spelled with the letter K. Ask them to indicate to you when they hear K at the beginning of the following words:

 The indication gesture may be sliding one hand into the other, like a pocket of a kangaroo. If you want to get a little more active, allow them to jump slightly in their seats, like kangaroos.

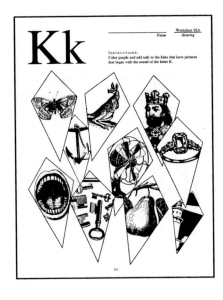

butterfly	king	pear	keys	lighthouse
anchor	fan	ring	goose	kangaroo
penny	keep	game	kin	tin
tame	kit	done	race	kitchen

Worksheet 92A: Read the instructions aloud. Label each picture and allow students to respond independently.

Row 1: butterfly, kangaroo, king
Row 2: anchor, fan, ring
Row 3: mouth, keys, pear, lighthouse

Give your students the reproduction of the *"Good Gracious, Matilda—You Too?"* and allow them to hang it in the museum. Talk to them about the story *The Alphabet Quest* and give them their museum bag. Allow them time to go through the house and collect items that begin with the sound of K to make their own museum. If you are teaching in a school setting, instruct the children to take the bag home and bring in objects the following day.

ACTIVITY 2: SEEING

Draw attention to the stimulus picture on the wall and display the flashcard for "K,k." Point out that even though this letter makes the same sound as C, it looks very different. Draw attention to the features of the letter (single vertical line with two shorter lines forming a point which touches the vertical line almost in the center).

Mix the printed upper case K card with the other upper case letter cards which have been studied so far. Present these to the children in random order, instructing them to indicate when they see the target letter K.

Repeat this activity with the lower case letters, then with both upper and lower case combined.
On the board, write the written upper and lower case letters for "K,k," describing and numbering your strokes as you do so. Compare and contrast the printed letters and the written letters. Leave both the printed and written letters on display as you present the worksheet.

Worksheet 92B: Read the directions aloud and monitor their progress as they work independently.

ACTIVITY 3: WRITING

Place guidelines and perimeter lines on the board. Call on students to come to the board and make the upper and lower case letter K.

Remind about stroke direction and order.

Worksheet 92C: Read the instructions aloud and monitor their progress as they work independently.

 Remind them about the "FOUR P's!"

 You may want to give the students the coloring page along with the flashcard. Read the information about the artist to your students before they color the picture.

LESSON 93
TARGET SOUNDS: C AND K AND REVIEW

ACTIVITY 1: HEARING, SEEING, AND WRITING

 Play the Alphabet Song for the children encouraging them to sing along while pointing to the corresponding letters on the flashcards.

Invite children to brainstorm with you to come up with words which begin with the K or C sound. Write these on the board as they are suggested.

 What will happen here is that you will get a combination of words which begin with both letters C and K, depending upon their spelling. That is fine, in fact, it illustrates the point of the lesson: C and K make the same sound. This is a better way to do it than the other way around (soliciting words which start with the letter C) since some words beginning with C utilize the sound of S rather than K (Cindy, cents, etc.) and that will not be taught yet.

The children will notice that the words begin with both C and K. Ask them why this is so (they sound alike) and tell them that spelling rules and customs determine which letter is used. Highlight the C and K in each word, or have children come to the board and circle those beginning letters.

Place guidelines and perimeter lines on the board. Call on students to come to the board and make the upper and lower case letters C and K. Remind them about stroke direction and order.

Worksheet 93A: Read the instructions aloud. Tell them that since the sound is the same, the letter which is used to begin the C or K words in that row is given at the beginning of each row. They don't need to know how to spell the word to pick the correct ones.

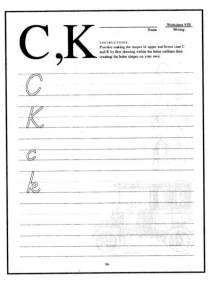

Have the students do the letter maze for C on the top row. Label the pictures for them and monitor as they respond on their papers. Complete the rest of the page in the same manner.

Row 1: camel, rooster, cat, bear
Row 2: king, parasol, duck, kite
Row 3: cup, rabbit, cow, barrel
Row 4: sun, kangaroo, keys, elephant

Worksheet 93B: Read the instructions aloud and monitor their progress as they work independently. Watch letter spacing.

ACTIVITY 2: READING REVIEW

Before doing this activity, you may want to do a quick review of all the letters and sounds studied so far to reinforce letter/sound association.

Write the words on Worksheet 93C on the board in columns just as they are presented on the worksheet.

Worksheet 93C: Read the instructions aloud. Assist the children to read the words from top to bottom of each column, following along on the worksheet as you point to the corresponding written word on the board. Repeat the activity going from bottom to top of each column. Finally, point randomly to the words on the columns and call on students to read them.

An additional way to use this sheet for further reinforcement is to erase the words from the board and then have students point to or circle the correct word as you randomly say them. You may want to do this on an individual or small group basis to more carefully monitor their responses.

LESSON 94
TARGET LETTER COMBINATION CK

ACTIVITY 1: HEARING AND SEEING

Write the letters C and K on the board and ask the children what sound is made by each one. Put the two letters together and ask if they can guess what sound they make if they are side by side. Praise correct answers and affirm to them that when these two "brothers" stand together in line in a word they make one sound (hard) C or K.

Remind them that the same thing happened with "ll." Ask if anyone remembers whether the "ll" comes at the beginning or ending of words (ending). Affirm that they will only find "ll" at the end of words and that CK is like that too. They will only be standing together to make one sound K at the end of words.

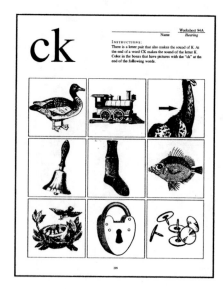

Write the following words on the board, highlighting the CK letter pairs:

    duck   neck   lock   sock   tack

Assist the children to sound out the words and praise their terrific reading. Leave the words on the board for display.

Worksheet 94A: Read the instructions aloud and label the pictures for the children as they respond as indicated.

    Row 1: duck, train, neck
    Row 2: bell, sock, fish
    Row 3: nest, lock, tack

For further reinforcement, you may have students come to the board and point out the words for the pictures whose labels end in CK.

ACTIVITY 2: SEEING

Add two or three of the words which are listed on Worksheet 94B on the board with the others on display. Have student volunteers come up and circle the CK combination at the end of each. Erase the board.

Worksheet 94B: Read the instructions aloud and monitor their progress as they work independently.

This sheet may be used in a variety of ways. Have students read through the list of words. Define them as needed, use them in original sentences. Write the words on the board and have students match the written to the printed. Play the riddle game. You may even have some students try to write the word on the board from the printed example—this would be a good measure of how well they are making the transference of printed lettering to written lettering without a model.

ACTIVITY 3: ART ACTIVITY

Draw the artist's palette on the board and place the following color "splotches" on it: yellow, red, blue, brown, orange. Beside or on each color place either the printed or written letter as indicated by the key on Worksheet 94C.

Worksheet 94C: Read the directions aloud and monitor their progress as they work independently.

LESSON 95
TARGET LETTERS C AND K

ACTIVITY 1: READING SYLLABLES

 Remind the children that the letter which makes the C sound is the letter "C,c." Write the letter in both upper and lower case on the board and display the printed letters using the cards.

 Display the C puzzle piece. Have the children echo it several times. Present the puzzle pieces for each of the following short vowel sounds in this order: U, O, A. Have the children echo them for you, then say them independently as you display or point to them randomly.

Place the U to the right of the C and assist the children to sound out the syllable which is formed. Continue in the same way with the rest of the vowels, linking them to the beginning C sound.

Worksheet 95A: Read the directions aloud. Direct the children to read the syllables in various ways: in order, randomly, pointing to them as you say them randomly, etc.

ACTIVITY 2: READING WORDS

Ask students to think of words which may begin with the syllables listed on Worksheet 95A. Write these on the board, circling or highlighting the two beginning sounds.

 Tell the students that you are now going to add another sound to the syllables to form words. Then present the pieces for T and P. Review the sounds of each of these letters.

Place the piece for P beside the "ca" syllable, forming the word "cap." Guide the children to read it aloud. Replace it with T to form the word "cat" and read aloud. Do the same with the syllables "cu" and "co."

Present the puzzle pieces for K and middle I. Sound out the syllable formed. Present the pieces for D and N. Link each of these to the "ki" syllable, forming the words "kid" and "kin." Discuss the meanings of any of the words formed as needed.

Worksheet 95B: Read the instructions aloud and assist the children to read the words in various ways. Use any of the previous techniques for eliciting student response and vary the activity to reinforce different skills.

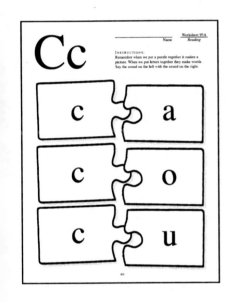

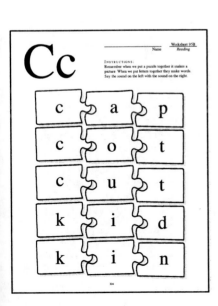

LESSON 96
REVIEW

ACTIVITY 1: HEARING AND SEEING

 Play the Museum Song for the children encouraging them to sing along while pointing to the corresponding letters on the flashcards.

Aa Using the written lower case short vowel cards: a, e, i, o, u, review the letters and sounds with them through your presentation of the following (In each case, students should respond by raising their hand and answering when called upon—or if using at home, the student should answer):

Present the printed lower case letters, one at a time, asking the question: "What sound does this make?"

Present the written upper case letters, asking the question: "What letter is this?" Write simple words beginning with each of the letters on the board and have them find the same beginning letter in their set. (Do not read them aloud.)

Say words beginning with each sound, without providing a visual display of any kind.

Worksheet 96A: Read the instructions aloud. Call on students to label the pictures and monitor as the children indicate their responses as directed.

    Row 1: eggs, apples, octopus
    Row 2: umbrella, ax, Indian

ACTIVITY 2: ART ACTIVITY

Draw the artist's palette on the board. Place and label the "paint splotches" on it according to the key on Worksheet 96B.

Worksheet 96B: Read the instructions aloud and monitor their progress as they work independently.

LESSON 97
REVIEW DAY

ACTIVITY 1

 Play the Short Vowels Song for the children encouraging them to sing along while pointing to the corresponding letters on the flashcards.

Write the words on Worksheet 97A on the board in columns just as they are presented on the worksheet.

Worksheet 97A: Read the instructions aloud. Assist the children to read the words from top to bottom of each column, following along on the worksheet as you point to the corresponding written word on the board. Repeat the activity going from bottom to top of each column. Finally, point randomly to the words on the columns and call on students to read them.

You may use any of the previous ideas or variations for reviewing these words: printed to written, reading aloud and matching, categorizing according to beginning, middle, or ending sounds, etc.

 Several words on this list will require special attention for either decoding and/or defining: cuff, combat, kin, puck, ransack, attack, lack. This may be a good time to introduce the idea of syllabication, since two two-syllable words are included here. Clapping out each syllable to emphasize that the word has "two beats" is a good way to start.

Worksheet 97B: Read the instructions aloud and monitor their progress as they work independently.

Row 1: man, bear, pear
Row 2: tent, duck, nut

ACTIVITY 2: GAME

 Archives: The Medial Vowel Edition

LESSON 98
REVIEW

ACTIVITY 1: HEARING AND WRITING

Aa Praise the children for knowing so many words and letters now! Present the lower case cards for the following: m, b, p, t, d, n, g, s, f, r, i, c. Call on students to name these letters, give their sounds, and think of one word which begins with that sound. Write their words on the board, omitting the beginning letter. Allow students to come up to the board and fill in the missing letter for the appropriate sound. Leave the letters on display as you present the worksheets.

 Remind them of correct stroke direction and order!

Worksheet 98A: Present the worksheet, read the instructions aloud and monitor their progress as they work independently. Draw their attention to the "Indian" and ask what kind of letter this word will need and why (upper case, because it is a proper name).

Row 1: goat, sun, fan
Row 2: rat, Indian, cat

Worksheet 98B: Present the worksheet, read the instructions aloud and monitor their progress as they work independently.

Percival's Pairs: Using A, M, B, P, T, D, N, G, S, F, R, E, I, O, U, L, H and C, and K

LESSON 99
READING AND ALPHABETICAL ORDER

ACTIVITY 1: SPECIAL EXHIBITS

 Play the Alphabet Song for the children encouraging them to sing along while pointing to the corresponding letters on the flashcards.

Worksheet 99A: Present the worksheet, read the instructions aloud and monitor their progress as they work independently.

Write the Special Exhibits from Worksheet 99A on the board.

Draw attention to the similarity between "me" and the previously introduced Special Exhibits "he" (from Book 6) and "be" (from Book 4). Do the same with "or" and "for" (also from Book 6), "call" and "all" (from List 3). "has" and "had" (from Book 4). Write the words under each other and have students describe the differences and similarities.

The last five words (been, has, me, are, call) will not be found in Story 7 (*Ben and His Pen*) but will be in Story 8 (*Dan of the Den*). They are introduced here in order to lessen the number of new Special Exhibits presented right before Story 8 is read. For the reading of Story 7, emphasize "by" and "or." You should also review the words previously introduced before reading the story.

 This story is about Ben Franklin. In addition please note the following vocabulary and expressions which may require further definition and explanation:

Pap—affectionate nickname for father
mess with—play with, experiment, pick a fight
putt—golf term, get the ball in the cup
puck—hockey term, get it in the net
cuff—part of shirt around the wrist
mad huff—angry attitude
men in red—British
put in pen—write down
bill—document of law
by and by—eventually
ransack—attack, loot
all mad—very angry
hot in his cap—anger that makes you hot
put a lid on it—stopped
combat—fight
mull—think about
lack—be without
benefit—good result
kin—relatives, countrymen

Also, please note the use of America and American. You will need to supply these when the students come to them in the text.

ACTIVITY 2: READING

Lead the children through the reading of *Ben and His Pen* "round robin" style. Point out the vocabulary and language as you go along to aid comprehension. Encourage fluency. Have the student reread the book aloud in order to become more fluent in their reading. Each book should be reread two times before the next book is introduced.

Worksheet 99B: Read the instructions aloud. Monitor as they work independently. Draw attention to the word "Ben" and ask why the first letter is in upper case.

ACTIVITY 3: ALPHABETICAL ORDER

If you have not listened to the Alphabet Song in a while, now is the time to do so! Point to the stimulus pictures as you sing along.

Worksheet 99C: Read the directions aloud and monitor their progress as they work independently. If time permits, allow them to color the picture after you have checked it.

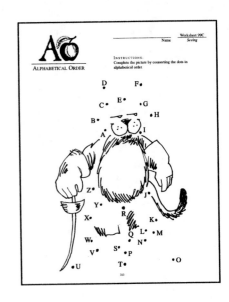

LESSON 100
READING COMPREHENSION

ACTIVITY 1: REVIEW

Play the Alphabet Song for the children encouraging them to sing along while pointing to the corresponding letters on the flashcards.

Briefly discuss yesterday's story. Help the students to place the events in order as they retell it to you. Go over vocabulary and expressions as needed.

Worksheet 100A/B: Read the directions aloud. Go through the worksheet as a class, calling on students to read the response choices for questions 1 and 3 and make suggestions for question 2. Students should be able to read questions 1 and 3 on their own, but you will need to read question 2 aloud to them.

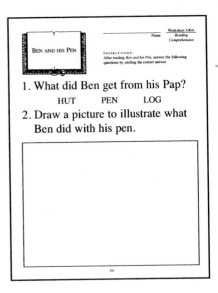

LESSON 101
TARGET SOUND: J (AS IN "JAR")

ACTIVITY 1: HEARING

Play the Museum Song for the children encouraging them to sing along while pointing to the corresponding letters on the flashcards.

Show the children the flashcard with the letter J on it. Have them hear the sound of J as in "jar."

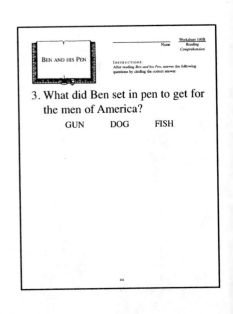

Tell them that J starts the word "jump" and the indication gesture for it will be holding both hands out to the side and making small circles as if holding and rotating a jump rope. Have them use this gesture when they hear the J sound in the following sound list:

g, j, j, k, l, d, t, j, g, j, m, a, j, i, j, j, j, k, g, j, j

Praise their careful listening. Now tell the children that the J sound is going to be the "leader" in a list of new words today and that they must continue to listen carefully for it at the beginning of the following list of words:

jar	ark	thimble	whistle	jumping
jewelry	squirrel	jaguar	juice	goose
Kelly	jelly	ill	Jill	Jim
Tim	jam	ham	jealous	sell

Worksheet 101A: Read the instructions aloud to the children. Tell them that you will name the pictures for them while they respond independently on their own papers.

Row 1: jar, ark, thimble
Row 2: whistle, jumping, jug
Row 3: jewelry, squirrel, jaguar

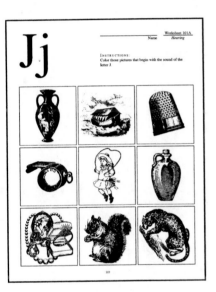

Give your students the reproduction of the Etruscan Jar and allow them to hang it in the museum. Talk to them about the story *The Alphabet Quest* and give them their museum bag. Allow them time to go through the house and collect items that begin with the sound of J to make their own museum. If you are teaching in a school setting, instruct the children to take the bag home and bring in objects the following day.

ACTIVITY 2: SEEING

Tell the children that the letter which makes the J sound is the letter "J,j." Draw attention to the stimulus picture on the flashcard. Point out the features of the letter (both upper and lower cases look like hooks, the lower case extends below the line, etc.)

Mix the printed upper case J card with the other upper case letter cards which have been studied so far. Present these to the children in random order, instructing them to indicate when they see the target letter J.

Repeat this activity with the lower case letters, then with both upper and lower case combined.

On the board, write the written upper and lower case letters for J, describing your strokes as you do so. Compare and contrast the printed letters and the written letters. Leave both the printed and written letters on display as you present the worksheet.

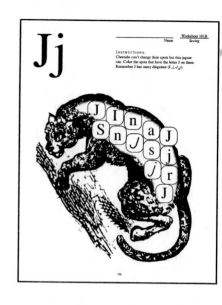

Worksheet 101B: Read the directions aloud. Students may select their own color to use for this sheet. Monitor as they work independently.

ACTIVITY 3: WRITING

Place guidelines and perimeter lines on the board. Call on students to come to the board and make the upper and lower case letter J.

Remind about stroke direction.

Worksheet 101C: Read the instructions aloud and monitor their progress as they work independently.

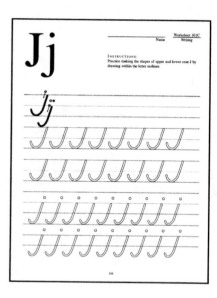

Remind them about the "FOUR P's" and about the importance of following all the mazes first before making the letter on their own on the top line.

LESSON 102
TARGET SOUND: J

ACTIVITY 1: HEARING

Play the Short Vowels Song for the children encouraging them to sing along while pointing to the corresponding letters on the flashcards.

Tell the children that the J sound is going to be the "leader" in another list of words today and that they must continue to listen carefully for it at the beginning of the following list of words:

jump	dice	man	apples	fish
rat	jug	jewelry	deer	Indian
razor	lock	jacks	roller	skate
jig	fig	Jenny	penny	ten

Worksheet 102A: Read the instructions aloud to the children. Tell them that you will name the pictures for them while they respond independently on their own papers.

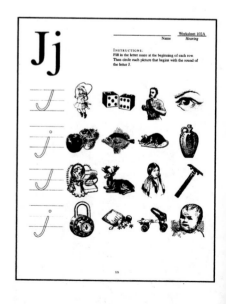

Row 1: jump, dice, man, eye
Row 2: apples, fish, rat, jug
Row 3: jewelry, deer, Indian, razor
Row 4: lock, jacks, roller skate, baby

ACTIVITY 2: ART ACTIVITY

Worksheet 102B: Follow instructions to make a yarn covered jar.

LESSON 103
TARGET SOUND: J

ACTIVITY 1: READING SYLLABLES

 Play the Museum Song for the children encouraging them to sing along while pointing to the corresponding letters on the flashcards.

Remind the children that the letter which makes the J sound is the letter "J,j." Write the letter in both upper and lower case on the board and display the printed letters using the cards.

 Display the J puzzle piece. Have the children echo it several times. Present the puzzle pieces for each of the short vowel sounds in this order: U, O, I, E, A. Have the children echo them for you, then say them independently as you display or point to them randomly.

Place the U to the right of the J and assist the children to sound out the syllable which is formed. Continue in the same way with the rest of the vowels, linking them to the J sound.

Worksheet 103A: Read the directions aloud. Direct the children to read the syllables in various ways: in order, randomly, pointing to them as you say them randomly, etc. Use any of the previous techniques and variations for eliciting student response and varying the task.

ACTIVITY 2: READING WORDS

Ask students to think of words which may begin with the syllables listed on Worksheet 103A. Write these on the board, circling or highlighting the two beginning sounds.

Tell the students that you are now going to add another sound to the syllables to form words. Then present the pieces for G.

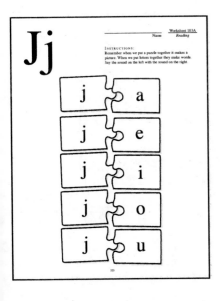

Place the G beside the "ju" syllable. Assist the students to decode the word "jug." Continue in the same manner with "jog," "jig," and "jag" (do not use "je" with this final consonant). Briefly discuss the meanings of the words which are formed and use them in sentences.

Worksheet 103B: Read the instructions aloud. Assist the children to decode the words formed.

Praise their wonderful reading!

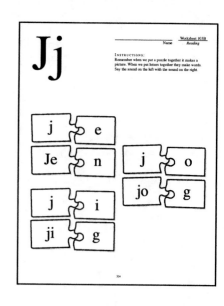

LESSON 104
TARGET SOUND J, SPECIAL EXHIBITS, AND REVIEW

ACTIVITY 1: READING WORDS

 Play the Alphabet Song for the children encouraging them to sing along while pointing to the corresponding letters on the flashcards.

Remind the students of yesterday's activity with the beginning J words. Challenge them to remember what some of those words were. Write the words on the board: jag, Jed, jig, jog, jug. Read through them several times, pointing at them randomly to elicit student responses.

Erase the final consonant sounds. After the syllable "ja" write the consonant M, forming the word "jam." Have the children decode it, then briefly discuss its meaning(s) and use(s) in sentences. Erase the M and write G in its place. Discuss as above. Erase the G and write CK in its place. Challenge the children to remember what single sound is made by these two letters when they are together (k). Assist them to decode the word formed. Since this word "jack" can be a proper name, ask what you must do to make it correct (replace the lower case with upper case). Demonstrate that on the board.

Worksheet 104A: Read the instructions aloud. Elicit reading from the children using any of the previous techniques. Match the printed words with the written words on the board for further visual discrimination practice.

ACTIVITY 2: READING MORE WORDS

Write the words on Worksheet 104B on the board in columns just as they are presented on the worksheet.

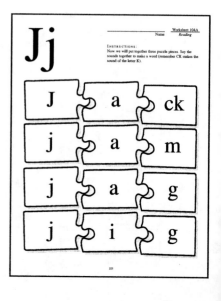

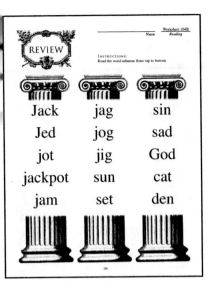

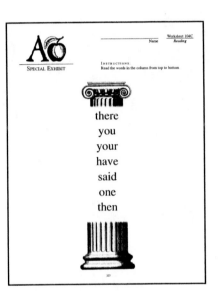

Worksheet 104B: Read the instructions aloud. Assist the children to read the words from top to bottom of each column, following along on the worksheet as you point to the corresponding written word on the board. Repeat the activity going from bottom to top of each column. Finally, point randomly to the words on the columns and call on students to read them.

ACTIVITY 3: SPECIAL EXHIBITS

Write the *Dan of the Dan* Special Exhibit words on the board.

Point out the similarities between "you" and "your," "there" and "then." Compare the last two with the previously learned word "them."

Write the word "has" on the board. Remind them that this word was given to them before. Compare and contrast it with the new word "have."

Worksheet 104C: Read the instructions aloud. Assist the children to echo the words in order and randomly. Have them match the printed words on the sheet with the written words on the board. Have them point to the correct words on their sheets as you read them randomly. Challenge them to read them independently as you point to the board display words randomly.

The following words from previous Special Exhibits lists are also found in the upcoming story *Dan of the Den:*

no, be, when, them, he, put, for, or

You may want to review these briefly for the children before reading the book.

LESSON 105
READING *DAN OF THE DEN*

ACTIVITY 1: READING ALOUD

Vocabulary words and creative expressions used in this story are as follows:

sun-up, mid-sun, sun-set—various times in the day
with God—in prayer to the true God
top job—important position
dig up—find
jot—little bit, any
pin on—place blame for
set—determined, ready
hit the jackpot—found a way to get what is wanted
tactic—idea, way

rat—tattle, tell on
in a jam—in trouble
big cat—lion
rip or nip—claw at or bite
gag—God shut the lions' mouths
jag—jaguar, wild beast
jig is up—the truth is known

Ask if any of the children can tell you where to find the story of Daniel (in the Bible). Affirm that it is found in the book of Daniel and that this particular story which they will read today is in Daniel 3. Because this is from the word of God, it is a true story and a powerful testimony of God's sovereign power and control over all of life. [Westminster Confession of Faith, Chapter 2, Section 2 (abridged): "God...hath most sovereign dominion over them (all creatures), to do by them, for them, and upon them, whatsoever himself pleaseth."]

 Lead the children in the round robin reading of this story. Call attention to the pictures, order of events, motives of the characters, etc. Have the students reread the book aloud in order to become more fluent in their reading. Each book should be reread two times before the next book is introduced.

Worksheet 105A: Read the instructions aloud. Assist the children to decode the words and respond as directed.

Worksheet 105B: Read the instructions aloud. Call on students to read the sentences in each of the boxes. Monitor their progress as they work independently.

LESSON 106
TARGET SOUND: Z

ACTIVITY 1: HEARING

 Play the Museum Song for the children encouraging them to sing along while pointing to the corresponding letters on the flashcards.

 Show the children the flashcard with the letter Z on it. Have them hear the sound of Z as in "zebra."

Give your students the reproduction of the Zebra chromo and allow them to hang it in the museum. Talk to them about the story *The Alphabet Quest* and give them their museum bag. Allow them time to go through the house and collect items that begin with the sound of Z to make their own museum. If you a teaching in a school setting, instruct the children to take the bag home and bring in objects the following day.

ACTIVITY 2: SEEING

Draw attention to the stimulus picture on the wall and display the flashcard for "Z, z." Point out that even though this letter makes the same sound as C, it looks very different. Draw attention to the features of the letter (single vertical line with two shorter lines forming a point which touches the vertical line almost in the center).

On the board, write the written upper and lower case letters for "Z, z," describing and numbering your strokes as you do so. Compare and contrast the printed letters and the written letters. Leave both the printed and written letters on display as you present the worksheet.

Worksheet 106A: Read the directions aloud and monitor their progress as they work independently.

ACTIVITY 3: WRITING

Place guidelines and perimeter lines on the board. Call on students to come to the board and make the upper and lower case letter Z.

Remind about stroke direction and order.

Worksheet 106B: Read the instructions aloud and monitor their progress as they work independently.

You may want to give the students the coloring page along with the flashcard. Read the information about the artist to your students before they color the picture.

LESSON 107
TARGET SOUND: Z AND REVIEW

ACTIVITY 1: HEARING AND WRITING

 Play the Museum Song for the children encouraging them to sing along while pointing to the corresponding letters on the flashcards.

Ask the children if they can be a hive of bees today and make the Z sound for you. Play the riddle game with them, giving them clues to elicit the following Z words: zebra, zipper, zoo, zero. For instance, the clues for "zoo" might be: this is a place where lots of animals are kept; we like to go there in the summer during vacation; etc.

Ask for a volunteer to come to the board and make the letter Z in both cases. Watch their stroke direction and order. Allow several other students to write the letters on the board also.

Tell them they are such good listeners and writers that they may go right into doing the worksheet.

Worksheet 107A: Read the directions aloud. Label the pictures or call on students to do so. Monitor their work. They may proceed directly to the writing portion after finishing the top part.

Row 1: gorilla, dart, zebra
Row 2: zipper, pirates, tie

ACTIVITY 2: REVIEW OF MEDIAL VOWELS

Aa Do a class review of all the short vowels (a,e,i,o,u). Match their letter names with sounds. Call on children to give you spontaneous examples of words which begin with each of the sounds, call attention to children's names which may begin with the sounds, etc.

Remind the children that the vowels are also found in the middle of many words. Write the following on the board in a vertical column, lining up the middle A: pal, bat, man. Ask what letter and sound they all have in common. Have a student come up and circle the A in each word.

Do the same activity with consonant-vowel-consonant (CVC) words containing the other short vowels in the middle position. Stick to words which use consonants the children have already studied.

Write the lower case vowel at the top of each column of words as a reference model. Then, erase the middle vowels of all the A words and have students fill them in independently. Do the same with the rest of the words, one vowel group at a time.

Leave written letters for reference, but erase the words. Tell the children you will be reading a list of words and asking them to tell you which vowel sound they hear in the middle of each word. They will respond by both the letter name and sound.

Read a list of simple CVC words randomly. You may use the same words that were used for the board activity, or generate new ones. Call on students to identify the vowel used in each one. Point to the written vowel on the board after each response for reinforcement.

Worksheet 107B: Read the instructions aloud. Label the pictures or call on students to do so and assist children to determine the middle vowels and write them in the spaces provided. Encourage careful letter spacing and neatness.

Row 1: nut, pin, fox
Row 2: pan, dog, bed

LESSON 108
TARGET SOUND: Y (AS IN "YELLOW")

ACTIVITY 1: HEARING

Play the Museum Song for the children encouraging them to sing along while pointing to the corresponding letters on the flashcards.

Play a variation on the game of "I Spy": ask the children to name as many things as they can see in the classroom which are yellow. You may have some brief discussions on the various shades of yellow as a result of this activity, but that's fine! Tell them that artists see many variations of colors and they use them in their art. Draw attention to the stimulus picture for the letter/sound "Y,y" and briefly discuss the artist's use of yellow.

Show the children the flashcard with the letter Y on it. Have them hear the sound of Y as in "yellow."

This sound is made with the back of the tongue, not the tip. A few children may persist with substituting L for Y in some instances. Calling attention to tongue placement may be helpful here. The word "yellow" tends to be more difficult for some children for this reason. Help them to feel the "rocking" of the tongue in the mouth from the Y to L in this word. For other children, the difficulty may be the confusion of Y and W. As before, remind them that the Y sound does not use the lips. Show that you can "smile" when you say Y!

Give each child a piece of yellow construction paper and give them a few minutes to cut a flower out of it. Challenge them to find the Y sound in the following list of sounds, indicating by holding up their flowers:

h, s, j, y, l, y, i, o, y, y, r, t, y, a, y, l, y, j, h, y, y, y

Praise their listening and challenge them to find Y when it is the leader in any of these words:

less	yes	yawn	lawn	jump	joke
yolk	igloo	up	yum	soap	you
year	wet	yet	yell	well	watch
your	young	window	last	juice	off

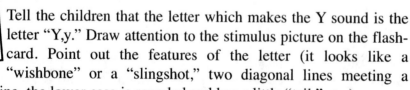 Give your students the reproduction of the *Sunflowers* and allow them to hang it in the museum. Talk to them about the story *The Alphabet Quest* and give them their museum bag. Allow them time to go through the house and collect items that begin with the sound of Y to make their own museum. If you are teaching in a school setting, instruct the children to take the bag home and bring in objects the following day.

ACTIVITY 2: SEEING

Tell the children that the letter which makes the Y sound is the letter "Y,y." Draw attention to the stimulus picture on the flashcard. Point out the features of the letter (it looks like a "wishbone" or a "slingshot," two diagonal lines meeting a vertical line, the lower case is rounded and has a little "tail," etc.)

Mix the letters with the other letters studied so far, upper case first, then lower, then both cases. Present to the children and ask for their response when they see the "Y,y."

On the board, write the written upper and lower case letters for "Y,y," describing and numbering your strokes as you do so. Compare and contrast the printed letters and the written letters. Leave both the printed and written letters on display as you present the worksheet.

Worksheet 108A: Read the instructions aloud and monitor their progress as they work independently.

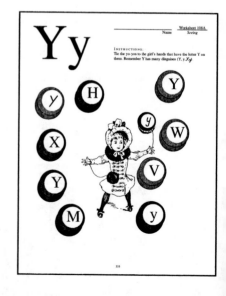

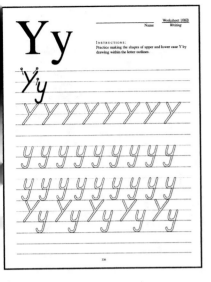

ACTIVITY 3: WRITING

Place guidelines and perimeter lines on the board. Call on students to come to the board and make the upper and lower case letter Y.

Remind them about stroke direction and order.

Worksheet 108B: Read the instructions aloud and monitor their progress as they work independently.

Remind them about the "FOUR P's!"

You may want to give the students the coloring page along with the flashcard. Read the information about the artist to your studentss as they color the picture.

LESSON 109
TARGET SOUNDS: Z AND Y AND REVIEW

ACTIVITY 1: HEARING AND WRITING

Play the Alphabet Song for the children encouraging them to sing along while pointing to the corresponding letters on the flashcards.

Put the letter mazes for Z and Y on the board. Read the following words one at a time and call on students to come to the board and fill in the correct letter which makes the beginning sound of each word:

zipper	zebra	yard	zoom	yellow
yo-yo	zoo	yarn	yum	yesterday
zinnia	year	zip	zebra	yet

Worksheet 109A: Read the instructions aloud. Start by filling in the top letter maze for upper case Z. Label the pictures for the children and monitor as they respond as indicated.

Row 1: bell, zebra, tiger, umbrellas
Row 2: yo-yo, cup, hanger, man
Row 3: deer, zipper, bed, skate
Row 4: wagon, yarn, turkey, jewelry

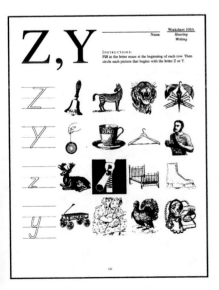

ACTIVITY 2: HEARING AND SEEING REVIEW

Write on the board any two of the letters the children have studied so far. Elicit the names and sounds of each letter. Say a word which begins with one of the letter sounds and call on volunteers to come to the board and circle the letter which corresponds with the beginning sound of that word.

 You may also use the cards for this activity, matching the printed letter with the written to reinforce both.

Worksheet 109B: Read the instructions aloud. Draw attention to the fact that this page is full of animals and is like a Z word (zoo). Praise them for being able to identify the beginning letters and sounds of all of the animals in this zoo! Call on students to label the pictures. Monitor as they work independently on identifying the letter which makes the initial sound.

Row 1: zebra, alligator, elephant, horse
Row 2: goat, jaguar, fish, dog
Row 3: cat, kangaroo, monkey, bear

LESSON 110
TARGET SOUND: Y AND REVIEW

ACTIVITY 1: READING SYLLABLES AND WORDS

Remind the children that the letter which makes the Y sound is the letter "Y,y." Write the letter in both upper and lower case on the board and display the printed letters using the flashcards.

Display the Y puzzle piece. Have the children echo it several times. Present the puzzle pieces for each of the short vowel sounds in random order. Have the children echo them for you, then say them independently as you display or point to them randomly. Place the U to the right of the Y and assist the children to sound out the syllable which is formed. Continue in the same way with the rest of the vowels, linking them to the Y sound.

Tell the students that you are now going to add another sound to the syllables to form words. Ask them to tell you what you must change about the puzzle pieces first. Do this, then present the piece for P.

Form the words "yap" and "yip." Assist the children to decode these words and discuss their meanings.

Present the piece for S and form the word "yes."

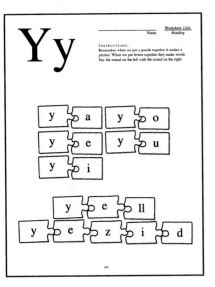

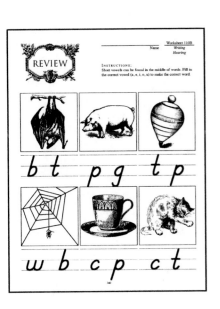

Present the piece for "ll." Ask if anyone remembers what single sound is made by these two twin letters (l). Form the word "yell" and assist the children to decode it.

Now tell them you will be giving them a real challenge. Using the pieces for Z, I, and D, form the word "Yezid." Assist the children to decode this word and ask if they have ever heard of this. Explain to them that this is the name of the main character in the next story they will read!

Worksheet 110A: Read the instructions aloud and use any of the previous techniques for eliciting student response.

ACTIVITY 2: HEARING AND WRITING

 Do a class review of all the short vowels (a,e,i,o,u). Match their letter names with sounds.

Remind the children that the vowels are often found in the middle of words. Write three words using middle A on the board in a vertical column, labeling the top of the column with the letter A and lining up the middle A in all the words. Ask what letter and sound they all have in common. Have a student come up and circle the A in each word. Continue in the same manner with the other short vowel sounds and letters. Leave the letter labels on the board for reference.

Worksheet 110B: Read the instructions aloud and monitor their progress as they work independently. Assist any students who may have difficulty labeling.

Row 1: bat, pig, top
Row 3: web, cup, cat

ACTIVITY 3: READING REVIEW

Draw three circles on the board in a vertical column. To the right of each circle write one of the following words: rack, tack, pack. Tell the children that they must be careful listeners and readers today. You will be reading one of the words on the board and they must choose which word is the one you have read. Read the word "pack." Call on a student to come to the board and fill in the circle beside the correct word. After the correct response is completed, have students read the other words also to reinforce reading skills.

You may want to point out the small differences in the words, reminding them of past lessons when they learned that just one letter can change the entire meaning of a word. Using the words as they are presented on Worksheet 110C, continue this activity.

Worksheet 110C: Read the instructions aloud and monitor their progress as they work independently.

Left: tacks, bed, gun, pig
Right: sun, fan, lock, bell

 Percival's Pairs: Using A, M, B, P, T, D, N, G, S, F, R, E, I, O, U, L, H and C, K, J, Z, and Y

LESSON 111
TARGET SOUND: W

ACTIVITY 1: HEARING

Play the Museum Song for the children encouraging them to sing along while pointing to the corresponding letters on the flashcards.

 Bring a candle to class today. Light it and gently blow it out, rounding your lips as you do so. Describe that today's sound is as soft as the "wind" you used to blow out the candle. In fact, it starts the word "wind." Make the W several times and have the children echo it after you.

 Show the children the flashcard with the letter W on it. Have them hear the sound of W as in "windmill."

Because it is "like the wind" it is hard to catch! Challenge them to find it in this list of sounds, indicating by blowing gently when they hear it:

l, r, w, w, o, a, i, w, y, w, l, y, y, r, u, e, w, l, w, w, y, w, o, a, w, w

Now challenge them to find the W when it plays "follow the leader" in these words:

dice	zebra	wolf	wink	alligator
wagon	turkey	walrus	camel	wonderful
wicked	window	Lynn	win	read
weed	yes	Wes	was	wow

Worksheet 111A: Read the instructions aloud and monitor as they respond as indicated. Label or call on students to label the pictures as needed.

Row 1: dice, alligator, wink
Row 2: walrus, zebra, wolf
Row 3: wagon, turkey, camel

 Give your students the reproduction of the *Landscape* and allow them to hang it in the museum. Talk to them about the story *The Alphabet Quest* and give them their museum bag. Allow them time to go through the house and collect items that begin with the sound of W to make their own museum. If you are teaching in a school setting, instruct the children to take the bag home and bring in objects the following day.

ACTIVITY 2: SEEING

 Tell the children that the letter which makes the W sound is the letter "W,w." Draw attention to the stimulus picture on the flashcard. Point out the features of the letter (two mountains, upside down! or two valleys and one mountain in the middle, etc.)

Mix the letters with the other letters studied so far, upper case first, then lower, then both cases. Present to the children and ask for their response when they see the "W,w."

On the board, write the written upper and lower case letters for "W,w," describing and numbering your strokes as you do so. Compare and contrast the printed letters and the written letters. Leave both the printed and written letters on display as you present the worksheet.

Worksheet 111B: Read the instructions aloud and monitor their progress as they work.

ACTIVITY 3: WRITING

Place guidelines and perimeter lines on the board. Call on students to come to the board and make the upper and lower case letter W.

 Remind them about stroke direction and order.

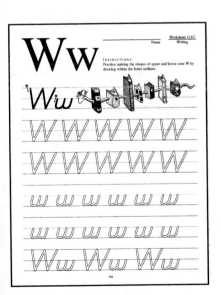

Worksheet 111C: Read the instructions aloud and monitor their progress as they work independently.

 You may want to give the students the coloring page along with the flashcard. Read the information about the artist to your students before they color the picture.

LESSON 112
TARGET SOUND W

ACTIVITY 1: READING SYLLABLES AND WORDS

Remind the children that the letter which makes the W sound is the letter "W,w." Write the letter in both upper and lower case on the board and display the printed letters using the flashcards.

 Display the W puzzle piece. Have the children echo it several times. Present the puzzle pieces for these short vowels: I, E, A. Have the children echo them for you, then say them independently as you display or point to them randomly.

Place the I to the right of the W and assist the children to sound out the syllable which is formed. Continue in the same way with the rest of the vowels, linking them to the W sound.

Ask students to think of words which may begin with the syllables listed. Write these on the board, circling or highlighting the two beginning sounds.

Tell the students that you are now going to add another sound to the syllables to form words. Take away the "wa" syllable, but keep the other two on display. Then present the pieces for "ll" and T.

Form the words "will" and then "well" with the puzzle pieces. Assist the children to decode and read them. Discuss their meanings and use them in sentences.

Form the words "wet" and "wit" and continue as above.

Worksheet 112A: Read the instructions aloud and use various techniques for eliciting and reinforcing student response and skill.

Worksheet 112B: Read the instructions aloud and monitor their progress as they work independently.

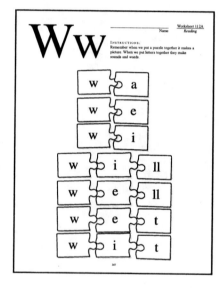

LESSON 113
TARGET SOUND: Q (AS IN "QUEEN")

ACTIVITY 1: HEARING AND SEEING

 Play the Museum Song for the children encouraging them to sing along while pointing to the corresponding letters on the flashcards.

Today's sound is one that never, never stands alone in our language. It always has another sound with it, the same sound every time.

 Show the children the flashcard with the letter Q on it. Have them hear the sound of Q as in "queen."

Ask them if they hear the "buddy sound" when they say Q. The children may think that the buddy sound is W. Acknowledge that it does sound like W, but the letter is actually a U. Write the word "queen" on the board and highlight the "qu." Tell them the Q and U run together to make a sound much like "kw."

 Don't go into too much detail or devote too much time to this. It will be clearer as they see "qu" occurring regularly in their reading.

Tell the children that they must listen carefully for the Q sound in the following list:

 They may indicate this sound by placing both hands at the sides of their heads, fingers separated and extended beyond the tops of their heads like the points of a queen's crown. (Reassure the boys that they can consider themselves "kings" rather than "queens!")

g, k, q, y, w, q, q, k, l, y, u, q, w, q, q, q, k, q, g, l, q, q

Praise their very careful listening! Now challenge them to find the Q at the beginning of the following words:

quit	keys	watch	quiz	quilt
kitten	yell	quail	weather	window
quiet	lose	offer	question	quick
water	quiver	wax	quack	kind

 Give your students the reproduction of *Anne of Cleves* and allow them to hang it in the museum. Talk to them about the story *The Alphabet Quest* and give them their museum bag. Allow them time to go through the house and collect items that begin with the sound of Q to make their own museum. If you are teaching in a school setting, instruct the children to take the bag home and bring in objects the following day.

ACTIVITY 2: SEEING

 Tell the children that the letter which makes the Q sound is the letter "Q,q." Draw attention to the picture on the flashcard. Point out the features of the letter (a circle with a tail, the lower case extends its tail beyond the lower line and it curls to the right, etc.)

 Mix the letters with the other letters studied so far, upper case first, then lower, then both cases. Present to the children and ask for their response when they see the "Q,q."

Pay particular attention to the discrimination between upper case O and Q. You may want to remove O at first and then present it just with Q for a finer discrimination activity. The same thing may occur with lower case Q and G, especially with the written letters. Separate them out if necessary and discuss the similarities and differences in detail before doing the discrimination activity.

On the board, write the written upper and lower case letters for "Q,q," describing and numbering your strokes as you do so. Compare and contrast the printed letters and the written letters.

Draw the artist's palette on the board and label the color splotches as indicated on the worksheet. Leave on display for reference.

Worksheet 113A: Read the instructions aloud and monitor their progress as they work independently.

ACTIVITY 3: WRITING

Place guidelines and perimeter lines on the board. Call on students to come to the board and make the upper and lower case letter Q.

 Remind them about stroke direction and order.

Worksheet 113B: Read the instructions aloud and monitor their progress as they work independently.

 Remind them about the "FOUR P's!"

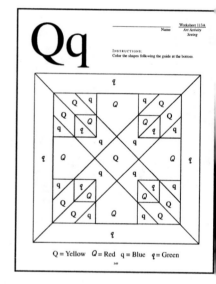

LESSON 114
TARGET SOUND: Q

ACTIVITY 1: HEARING AND WRITING

 Play the Short Vowels Song for the children encouraging them to sing along while pointing to the corresponding letters on the flashcards.

Tell the children that the Q sound is going to be at the beginning of words in a new list today and that they must continue to listen carefully:

quarter	guitar	quilt	fish	windmill
rabbit	candle	quill	cookie	willow
lost	quench	young	lobster	quest

Place guidelines and perimeter lines on the board. Call on students to come to the board and make the upper and lower case letter Q.

Worksheet 114A: Read the instructions aloud to the children. Monitor as they respond independently on their own papers, assisting them to label as needed.

Row 1: queen, gorilla, saddle, guitar
Row 2: windmill, candle, quilt, fish
Row 3: quarter, lobster, rabbit, scale
Row 4: whale, elf, umbrella, quill

ACTIVITY 2: ART ACTIVITY

Worksheet 114B: Read the instructions aloud. Provide a worktable with assorted art supplies: paints, watercolor crayons, markers, swatches of wallpaper or fabric, scissors, glue, etc. Allow students to choose a medium in which to create their quilt square and monitor their progress as they work.

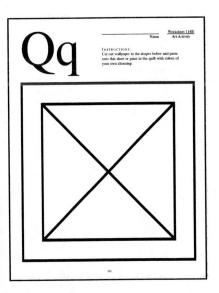

It would probably be a good idea to make a few patterns of the shapes on the quilt square for children to use when cutting. You can show them how to trace the shape outline on the fabric (wallpaper, etc.), cut it out on the lines, and then place it in one of the sections of their quilt square.

LESSON 115
TARGET SOUND: Q

ACTIVITY 1: READING WORDS

 Present the puzzle pieces for QU and I. Have the students make the letter sounds, then link them to form the syllable QUI.

Discuss with the students that the piece with Q on it also has the U on it because Q is never, never found without its buddy. Sometimes U goes off by itself, but never Q!

Display the puzzle pieces for T, Z, and CK. Review the sound made by each. Link each in turn to the QUI pieces, forming the words "quit," "quiz," and "quick." Discuss the meanings of each word and use in original sentences.

Worksheet 115A: Read the instructions aloud and elicit responses in various ways: riddles, written to printed, pointing to correct word when it is read, etc.

ACTIVITY 2: READING SENTENCES

Write the following on the board: The cat was quick. Assist the children to decode each word and read the sentence aloud. Write the next sentence on the board: "The dog quit." Help the children read it and discuss what this means.

Write the following question on the board: Will the yak get wet? Remind them about the use of question marks. Assist the reading of the sentence and briefly discuss.

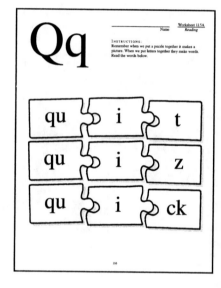

You will want to display a picture of a yak for the students. It's not a common animal!

Worksheet 115B: Read the instructions aloud and monitor their progress as they work.

Archives: Picture/Initial Sounds
Use only cards with pictures that begin with the sound of the letters: A, M, B, P, T, D, N, G, S, F, R, E, I, O, U, L, H and C, K, J, Z, Y, Q, V and W

LESSON 116
TARGET SOUND: V

ACTIVITY 1: HEARING

 Play the Museum Song for the children encouraging them to sing along while pointing to the corresponding letters on the flashcards.

Remind the children of all the pairs of sounds they have had so far which are different only because one uses the voice and the other doesn't. Write the letters on the board as you review them: p/b, t/d, k/g, s/z. Reinforce the difference between them by having them make the sound pairs alternately, with their hands on their throats to feel the vibration with the voiced sounds.

Now have them echo the F sound. Tell them to add their voices and what do they get? (v) Tell them that V is the sound of the day!

 Show the children the flashcard with the letter V on it. Have them hear the sound of V as in "violin."

Make the finger spelling gesture for V: index and middle fingers extended to form the letter V (like the "victory" sign). Tell them this will be the indication gesture when they hear V in the following list:

d, g, v, d, f, v, f, m, t, v, b, v, v, d, v, g, f, v, b, v, v, v

Now challenge them to find it in the following list, at the beginning of the word:

violin	bird	face	vase	vise	xylophone
vest	best	bull	fudge	visor	village
dust	vote	valley	ball	ban	van

Worksheet 116A : Read the instructions carefully. Label the pictures for the children and monitor as they respond as indicated.

Row 1: vest, baby, vise
Row 2: bike, vase, xylophone
Row 3: violin, bull, bird

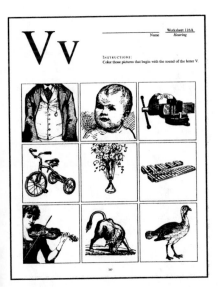

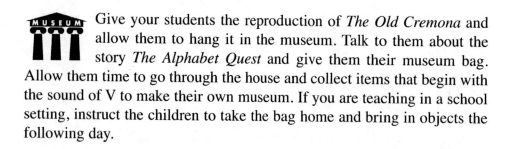 Give your students the reproduction of *The Old Cremona* and allow them to hang it in the museum. Talk to them about the story *The Alphabet Quest* and give them their museum bag. Allow them time to go through the house and collect items that begin with the sound of V to make their own museum. If you are teaching in a school setting, instruct the children to take the bag home and bring in objects the following day.

ACTIVITY 2: SEEING

Tell the children that the letter which makes the V sound is the letter "V,v." Draw attention to the picture on the flashcard. Point out the features of the letter (an upside-down teepee, a valley, point at the bottom, etc.)

 Mix the letters with the other letters studied so far, upper case first, then lower, then both cases. Present to the children and ask for their response when they see the "V,v."

 Pay particular attention to the discrimination between V, Y, and U. Point out the similarities and differences between these letters as needed.

On the board, write the written upper and lower case letters for "V,v," describing and numbering your strokes as you do so. Compare and contrast the printed letters and the written letters. Leave both the printed and written letters on display as you present the worksheet.

Worksheet 116B: Read the instructions aloud and monitor their work.

ACTIVITY 3: WRITING

Place guidelines and perimeter lines on the board. Call on students to come to the board and make the upper and lower case letter V.

Worksheet 116C: Read the instructions aloud and monitor their progress as they work independently.

 Remind about the "FOUR P's!"

 You may want to give the students the coloring page along with the flashcard. Read the information about the artist to your students before they color the picture.

LESSON 117
TARGET SOUND V

ACTIVITY 1: HEARING AND SEEING

Brainstorm with the children to come up with a list of words which begin with V. Write these on the board, have students come up and circle the V in each one. You may stimulate responses by using riddles, categories (names, places, etc.).

Erase the V in several of the easier words and have students rewrite it in the spaces.

 Display the puzzle pieces for V, A and E. Assist students to sound out the syllables "va" and "ve." Present the pieces for T. Link to the syllables, forming the words "vat" and "vet." Define and discuss each word. Use them in original sentences.

Praise their great reading!

ACTIVITY 2: ART ACTIVITY

Worksheet 117A: Read the instructions aloud and monitor their work.

LESSON 118
TARGET SOUND X

ACTIVITY 1: HEARING AND SEEING

 Play the Museum Song for the children encouraging them to sing along while pointing to the corresponding letters on the flashcards.

Draw a big tic-tac-toe design on the board. Ask a student to come up and play with you, assigning them to be O and you will be X. Play the game through (it doesn't matter who wins!)

Tell them to look carefully at the board and see if they can tell you what today's new letter might be. (X) Lead them as necessary (we've already had O...) Praise correct responses.

 Show the children the flashcard with the letter X on it. Have them hear the sound of X as in "boxing."

Affirm that today's letter is X. It makes the sound "ks" and that it is a very strange letter. It doesn't like to be the leader in words at all—in fact, it prefers to be at the end! So they won't be listening for any words which begin with this sound, only words which end with it!

First, ask them to indicate to you when they hear it in the following list of sounds:

An indication gesture might be to form an X with both index fingers or forearms.

g, k, x, a, x, k, x, s, z, x, x, i, t, g, x, s, x, x, x, g, x

Now ask them to listen for it at the end of the following words:

| box | pick | mix | fox | lock | lost |
| boss | ox | puck | fax | fix | pack |

Draw attention to the picture on the flashcard for "X,x. Since most children have probably made this letter many times before, it will not be necessary to go into too much detail on its features.

 Give your students the reproduction of *Dempsey and Firpo* and allow them to hang it in the museum. Talk to them about the story *The Alphabet Quest* and give them their museum bag. Allow them time to go through the house and collect items that begin with the sound of X to make their own museum. If you are teaching in a school setting, instruct the children to take the bag home and bring in objects the following day.

Mix the letters with the other letters studied so far, upper case first, then lower, then both cases. Present to the children and ask for their response when they see the "X,x."

On the board, write the written upper and lower case letters for "X,x," describing and numbering your strokes as you do so. Compare and contrast the printed letters and the written letters. Leave both the printed and written letters on display as you present the worksheet.

Worksheet 118A: Read the instructions aloud and monitor their progress as they work.

ACTIVITY 3: WRITING

Place guidelines and perimeter lines on the board. Call on students to come to the board and make the upper and lower case letter X.

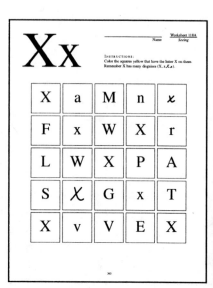

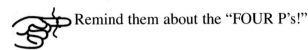Remind them about stroke direction and order.

Worksheet 118B: Read the instructions aloud and monitor their progress as they work independently.

Remind them about the "FOUR P's!"

You may want to give the students the coloring page along with the flashcard. Read the information about the artist to your students before they color the picture.

LESSON 119
TARGET SOUND X AND REVIEW

ACTIVITY 1: HEARING AND SEEING

Play the Museum Song for the children encouraging them to sing along while pointing to the corresponding letters on the flashcards.

Ask the children if they remember where X likes to be in a word (at the end). Affirm this and ask them to listen again to the following words:

fix   mix   vex   Rex   tax

Write the words on the board and have students come up and circle the final X in each one. Briefly discuss their meanings and use in original sentences. Remind them about the use of the upper case with the proper name "Rex."

Worksheet 119A: Read the instructions aloud. Label the pictures or call on students to label them. Monitor as they respond as indicated.

Row 1: ax, fox, lace
Row 2: sled, box, spider
Row 3: six, pot, chair

ACTIVITY 2: READING WORDS

 Present the V puzzle piece to the children and have them identify the sound. Present A and E and identify the sounds. Link the V with each vowel in turn, decoding the syllables formed. Present the pieces for N and T. Use both of these with the syllable "va," forming "vat" and "van." Discuss the meaning of each and use in sentences. Link the T with "ve," forming "vet." Discuss and use this word also.

Present the puzzle pieces for B, S, O and I. Identify the sounds made by each of these letters. Form the syllables "bo" and "si" with the pieces and decode. Present the piece for X. Link with each syllable to form the words "box" and "six." Use in sentences.

Worksheet 119B: Read the instructions aloud. Use any of the previously described techniques for eliciting student response.

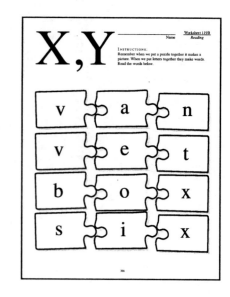

LESSON 120
REVIEW AND ALPHABETICAL ORDER

ACTIVITY 1: HEARING

 Play the Alphabet Song for the children encouraging them to sing along while pointing to the corresponding letters on the flashcards.

Do a class review of all the sounds studied so far: m, b, p, t, d, n, g, s, f, r, l, h, c, k, j, z, y, w, q, x, v, and the short vowels (a,e,i,o,u). Remind them of the indication gestures you may have used for these sounds, match their letter names with sounds. Call on children to give you spontaneous examples of words which begin (or end, in the case of X) with each of the sounds, call attention to children's names which may begin with the sounds, etc.

One by one, show the picture flashcards again. Say the words and call on students to come to the board and write the letter which makes each initial sound.

Draw three circles on the board in a vertical column. To the right of each circle write one of the letters they have studied. Tell the children that they must be careful listeners today. You will be saying words and they must choose which letter represents the beginning sound of each word. Say a word which begins with one of the letter sounds you have written on the board. Call on a student to come to the board and fill in the circle beside the correct letter. They may also copy the letter beside the one on the board for further writing reinforcement.

Row 1: lightbulb, turtle, zipper
Row 2: rabbit, wagon, quilt
Row 3: cow, monkey, apple
Row 4: hat, pizza, vase

ACTIVITY 2: ALPHABETICAL ORDER

 Sing the alphabet song a second time today, pointing to the pictures on the flashcards or having a student do so. After the song is finished, point to two letters at random and ask which one is "before" the other, or "after" the other. This will reinforce the language concept of position and ordering.

Worksheet 120B: Read the instructions aloud and monitor their progress as they work independently.

ACTIVITY 3: READING

Write the words on Worksheet 120C on the board in columns just as they are presented on the worksheet.

Worksheet 120C: Read the instructions aloud. Assist the children to read the words from top to bottom of each column, following along on the worksheet as you point to the corresponding written word on the board. Repeat the activity going from bottom to top of each column. Finally, point randomly to the words on the columns and call on students to read them.

Have students point to the word on their sheets which matches the word you point to on the board, without hearing it read.

Erase the words from the board and then have students point to or circle the correct word as you randomly say them. You may want to do this on an individual or small group basis to more carefully monitor their responses.

Discuss the meanings of any of the more uncommon words. Use the words in sentences.

You may have children come to the board and copy entire words from their sheets, further reinforcing writing skills.

Worksheet 120D: Test. This test is optional and is added to evaluate your students if you feel it is necessary at this time. The answers are worth 10 points each.

LESSON 121
PLURAL ENDINGS

ACTIVITY 1: HEARING, READING, AND WRITING

 Have two paper cups for display. Present one of them to the children and ask them what it is. Write "cup" on the board.

Now add the second one to the display. Ask the children what we would call the two of them together (cups). Ask them to listen carefully as you say the word "cups" several times. Challenge them to tell you what sound they hear at the end of this word (s). Praise correct responses.

Write the letter S in a different color at the end of "cup." Have the children read the word "cups" several times. Tell them that this is how we show when there are two or more things—we add the letter S to the end of the word. The words are then called "plurals."

Write the following on the board: top, duck, pin, dog, rat. Ask the children what you would add to each of these words if you had two or more of each of them. Allow students to come up and write the S after each of the words. Have the students read the plurals formed.

Some children may notice that the S sounds like Z at the end of some of these words. This occurs anytime there is a voiced sound preceding the final S. Acknowledge that this is true, but we use the S even though the sound may be slightly different. Remind them that Z is really just S with a voice.

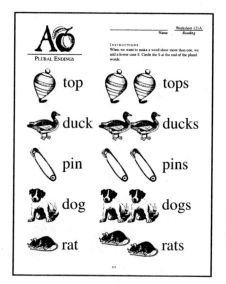

Very observant children with strong auditory skills may even realize that the "ks" at the end of "ducks" is the same sound as X. Acknowledge that this is indeed true and isn't it interesting that some letters "borrow" sounds from other letters? Call their attention to the spelling of the original singular word and that adding S is all we have to do, as opposed to replacing all three letters (cks) with X. Avoid further explanation of this phenomena at this time.

Worksheet 121A: Read the instructions aloud. Guide the children through the reading of the singulars and plurals. Have them circle the S at the end of the plural words.

Worksheet 121B: Read the instructions aloud. Have students read the word "gun" under the first picture pair. Ask them if this word means one of them or more than one. Monitor as they circle the correct picture. Have them complete the page independently.

 Archives: Medial Short Vowel

LESSON 122
PLURALS AND POSSESSIVES

ACTIVITY 1: READING AND WRITING

 Play the Museum Song for the children encouraging them to sing along while pointing to the corresponding letters on the flashcards.

Write the following words on the board: cup, pen, tack. As you do so, remind them of the stroke direction and order of each letter. Have children read the words aloud.

Ask if anyone remembers what we must add to each of these words if we have more than one of them. (s) Have students come to the board and write the S after each of the words and read the plural aloud.

Worksheet 122A: Read the instructions aloud. Permit them to complete the worksheet independently. Monitor stroke formation and order. Direct them to write each of the words on their own on the lines provided at the bottom of the page. Encourage neatness and careful letter spacing. Remind them to leave enough space between words.

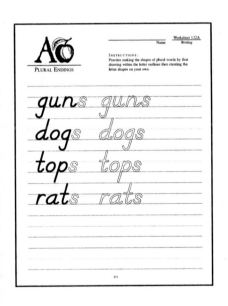

A helpful way to assist them to space words properly is to have them place their index finger as a spacing guide. Words should not be closer together than the width of their finger when using paper of this gauge.

ACTIVITY 2: POSSESSIVES

Walk around the room and indicate various items which belong to the students: desks, pencils, hair ribbons, bookbags, etc. (Avoid students whose names are the same—the reason for this will become clear later.) Ask "Whose ——- is this?" When the answers are given, write those children's names on the board, along with the word for the item.
Repeat their answers, emphasizing the S (or Z) sound at the end of each child's name. Write an S after each name, slightly apart from the rest of the word. Describe to the children that because you can hear this sound, it must be written down.

Now ask them "Does this S mean that there are two of each of these children in our room?" The answer should be no (since you have avoided those who are identically named). Tell them that this S at the end means "possession," that the next word is something that belongs to them.

When we use an ending S in this way, we must add a little mark, called an "apostrophe." Place apostrophes in a different color in the proper place in each of the words. By doing this we are showing that there are not more than one person, but that this person owns something. Point to the object word after each of the children's names and say "This ——— belongs to ————." Go down the list in this manner.

Worksheet 122B: Read the instructions aloud. Have the children place their finger on the second word in the first word pair (gun). Have someone read it aloud. Ask the children "Whose gun is it?" and call on someone to read the first word (Pam's). Proceed through the worksheet in the same manner.

You may also further reinforce this by asking questions such as: Does Pam own the cat? (Answer: No, it is Dan's cat.) Is it Ned's gun? (Answer: No, it is Pam's gun.)

LESSON 123
POSSESSIVES AND REVIEW

ACTIVITY 1: READING POSSESSIVES

Write the following on the board: Jim bat. Ask the children what you must add to the word "Jim" to show that the bat belongs to him. If the children answer S only, write it in and ask if that is the only thing which is necessary to show possession and prompt them to add the apostrophe also. If they respond immediately with apostrophe and S, add both and praise their good memories! Do this several more times as necessary to reinforce the concept.

Worksheet 123A: Read the instructions aloud. Remind them that when they read these statement pairs they will sound alike, but that something is different about them. Which one in each pair means possession? Acknowledge that you cannot "hear" the apostrophe, but you know it is there because of the meaning of the phrases.

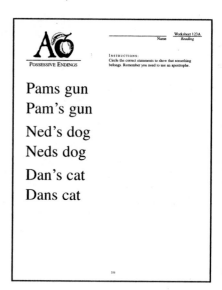

ACTIVITY 2: HEARING AND WRITING MIDDLE VOWELS

Review briefly the sounds of the short vowels. Write them across the top of the board and display the flashcards. Give examples or solicit examples of words which use each short vowel in the middle. Write the simpler ones (CVC) on the board, under the middle vowel letter examples.

Worksheet 123B: Read the instructions aloud. Label or have children label the pictures, but give no other clues regarding the sound or letter to be written in the middle spaces. Monitor their work. Present the next worksheet right away.

   Row 1: nut, fin, dog
   Row 2: hat, cup, pat

Worksheet 123C: Read the instructions aloud and proceed as above

   Row 1: ten, bell, bed
   Row 2: bat, pig, top

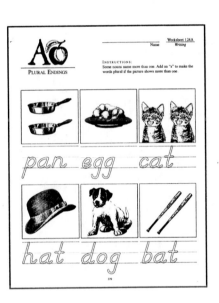

LESSON 124
PLURALS AND REVIEW

ACTIVITY 1: WRITING PLURALS

Play the Short Vowels Song for the children encouraging them to sing along while pointing to the corresponding letters on the flashcards.

Write the following words on the board: pen, mat, fin. Ask the children how many of these you are writing about if you use the words as they are written. (one)

Call on students to come to the board and add what is necessary to show more than one of each item. Do NOT say the words with the S—you want the children to add it without hearing it first!

Read the words when they are completed as plurals.

Worksheet 124A: Read the instructions aloud and monitor their progress as they work independently. Tell them to be careful—not all of the words need the S! Monitor stroke direction and order in all lettering. Remind them to keep the S close to the rest of the word.

ACTIVITY 2: HEARING AND WRITING

Call on students to come to the board and write the following letters as you make the letter sounds: d, p, g, z, w, m, l, f, s, h, v, r, e. They may refer to the stimulus pictures or flashcards for the printed model of the letter, but must recall the written letter on their own.

Ask students to give you an example of a word which starts with each of the letters on the board.

Leave the letters on display.

Worksheet 124B: Read the instructions aloud. Assist with labeling as necessary (a few of the pictures may be tricky). Do not offer further assistance with sounds or letters.

    Row 1: deer, pear
    Row 2: goat, fence
    Row 3: zebra, parasol
    Row 4: girl, walrus

Worksheet 124C: Read the instructions aloud and allow them to work independently, with minimal labelling help as needed.

Row 1: mittens, lace
Row 2: sun, horse
Row 3: monkey, violin
Row 4: elephant, ring

LESSON 125
SPECIAL EXHIBITS AND READING
IN A CAMEL'S EYE

ACTIVITY 1: SPECIAL EXHIBITS

Write the Special Exhibits *In a Camel's Eye* on the board. Draw attention to similarities with words previously taught. Have them echo the words after you, in order, then randomly. Have students read them independently as you point to them.

give   eye   love   visit   my   I

In addition, the following special names which cannot be decoded are used: Omar, Adulis

ACTIVITY 2: READING IN A CAMEL'S EYE

This story is set in the Arabian desert. The following vocabulary and language expressions are used:

caravan—travelers journeying together
sat a lot—tired easily, liked to take breaks!
all was not well—something was wrong
vex—upset, bother
duck—stoop quickly to hide
timid—shy
dim—hard to see

Draw attention to the use of plurals and possessives in this story as you go along! Guide the children through the round robin reading of this story. Continue to encourage fluency, expressiveness, and understanding. Pause throughout the story as necessary to discuss pictures or ideas. Possible discussion questions might be: What is a caravan and why do you think people traveled this way? Why was Yezid's way of scaring the bad men a clever one?

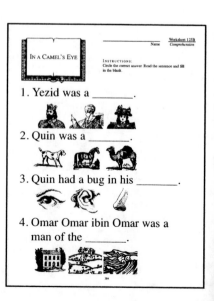

Worksheet 125A/B: Read the instructions aloud. Monitor their progress as they work independently.

LESSON 126
TARGET SOUND SH

ACTIVITY 1: HEARING

 Play the Consonant Digraphs Song for the children encouraging them to sing along while pointing to the corresponding letters on the flashcards.

Most of the remaining lessons this year will focus on consonant digraphs. Consonant Digraphs are two or more consonants combined to form one single simple elementary speech sound. SH as in "ship" will be the sound taught today.

Walk through the room with your index finger to your lips and say "shhh" six or seven times. Go to the front of the class and ask what they think today's sound is. If you do not get any responses, say "shhh" again. If you get an incorrect response, say "no" and then say "shhh." Repeat this until one of the students finally realizes that the sound is "shhh!"

Praise the correct response. Have the students make the sound several times, placing their index fingers to their lips. This gesture will be the indication gesture for this sound.

Again, you may notice some students who will demonstrate distortions of this sound. Do not be overly concerned at this point.

Make the SH sound alternately with S several times. Acknowledge that the two sounds are much alike, but emphasize that the lips are rounded for SH. Challenge them to listen carefully for SH in the following list of sounds:

t, d, s, sh, z, sh, r, k, sh, sh, s, sh, z, l, sh, s, sh, j, r, sh, sh, j, sh

Praise their listening. Now challenge them to indicate when they hear the SH sound at the beginning of any of these words:

sun	ship	jump	shout	soap	rope
sharp	zoo	shadow	lost	shake	soda
zinnia	shell	shape	sand	zipper	shoulder

Worksheet 126A: Read the instructions aloud. Assist the children to label as necessary and monitor their work.

Row 1: shoe, rooster, duck
Row 2: whale, shell, snake
Row 3: shirt, soldier, ship

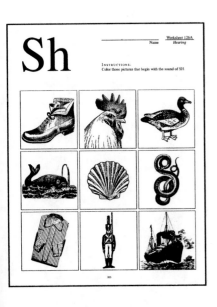

ACTIVITY 2: SEEING

Tell the children that we need two letters to write the sound of SH. Draw attention to the stimulus picture on the wall and display the flashcard. Both letters they have learned to make before.

Write S on the board and make the sound. Add the H to it and make the SH sound. Tell them that when S takes its buddy H along with it, the two of them make the SH sound together. Everytime you see them together, they will be making this sound.

Using index cards oriented lengthwise with the letters individually written on them, form the following words for the children and display them: sip, sell, sin. Have the children read them aloud and discuss their meanings.

Move the S to the left in the word "sip" and slip in the letter H, forming the word "ship." Help the children to decode it, then ask what it means. Discuss how the addition of the H and the change of sound changes the entire meaning of the word.

Do the same thing with the pairs: sell/shell, and sin/shin.

Worksheet 126B: Read the instructions aloud. Monitor as they work independently.

ACTIVITY 3: WRITING

Place guidelines and perimeter lines on the board. Call on students to come to the board and make the letters SH.

Worksheet 126C: Read the instructions aloud and monitor their progress as they work independently.

LESSON 127
TARGET SOUND SH

ACTIVITY 1: HEARING, SEEING, AND WRITING

 Play the Consonant Digraphs Song for the children encouraging them to sing along while pointing to the corresponding letters on the flashcards.

Brainstorm with the children to come up with more words beginning with the SH sound. Write them on the board. Use any of the previous techniques for enrichment and reinforcement. Play the riddle game, categorize in various ways, etc.

Have students come to the board and circle the SH in every word. Erase the SH and have students write it in independently.

Worksheet 127A: Read the instructions aloud. Label or have students label each of the pictures, row by row, after following the letter mazes. Monitor their responses.

    Row 1: shell, owl, gun, saw
    Row 2: snake, flag, hammer, shirt
    Row 3: ship, tacks, sheep, horse
    Row 4: sun, shoe, table, sailboat

ACTIVITY 2: WRITING WORDS

On the board, write each of the words found on Worksheet 127B. Have students come to the board and make the words. Remind them about stroke direction and order.

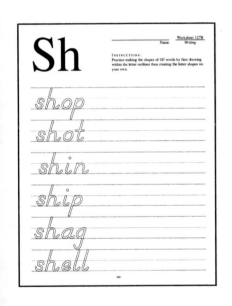

Worksheet 127B: Read the instructions aloud. Monitor as they work independently. Remind them about word and letter spacing.

LESSON 128
TARGET SOUND SH

ACTIVITY 1: READING SYLLABLES

 Play the Consonant Digraphs Song for the children encouraging them to sing along while pointing to the corresponding letters on the flashcards.

Remind the children that the letter pair which makes the SH sound is S plus H. Write the letter pair in lower case on the board and display the printed letters using the flashcards.

 Display the SH puzzle piece. Have the children echo it several times. Present the puzzle pieces for each of the short vowel sounds in this order: U, O, I, E, A. Have the children echo them for you, then say them independently as you display or point to them randomly.

Place the U to the right of the SH and assist the children to sound out the syllable which is formed. Continue in the same way with the rest of the vowels, linking them to the beginning SH sound.

Worksheet 128A: Read the instructions aloud. Have students read the syllables independently in order and randomly, using any of the previous techniques for eliciting student response.

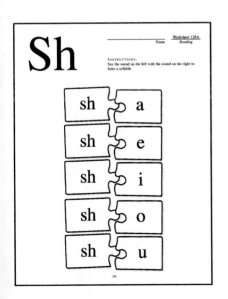

Review all the different techniques for eliciting student response at this time and use some of the ones you may not have used for a while!

ACTIVITY 2: READING WORDS

Ask students to think of words which may begin with the syllables listed on Worksheet 128A. Write these on the board.

Tell the students that you are now going to add another sound to the syllables to form words. Then present the pieces for G, "ll," P, and T. Review the sounds made by each of these.

Form the words found on Worksheet 128B with the puzzle pieces. Have students decode each of them, discuss their meanings and use in original sentences.

Worksheet 128B: Use any of the previous techniques for eliciting student response.

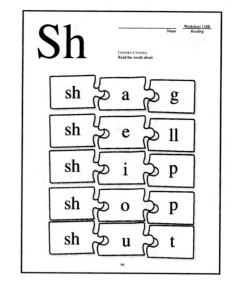

LESSON 129
TARGET SOUND SH

ACTIVITY 1: HEARING

 Play the Consonant Digraphs Song for the children encouraging them to sing along while pointing to the corresponding letters on the flashcards.

Today walk through the class and say "hush" several times, bringing your index finger to your lips only at the end of the word when the SH sound is made. Ask if anyone knows what the word "hush" means. (be quiet)

Ask what sound is heard at the end of the word "hush" (sh). Maybe the use of the sound SH is just a shortened version of the word "hush" since it means the same thing!

The SH sound also likes to come at the end of lots of words which do not mean "be quiet." Challenge the children to indicate when they hear SH at the end of the following words:

dish	pass	mush	mess	rush	dash
has	hash	fix	fish	rash	bush
fuss	last	lash	miss	cash	mix

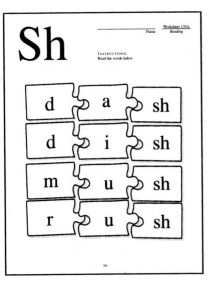

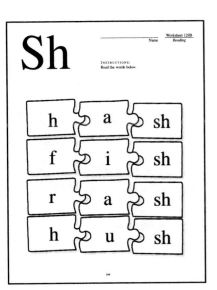

ACTIVITY 2: SEEING AND READING

Write some of the above words which end with SH on the board. Have students come up and circle the SH in each word. Erase the SH and have students fill it in different colors.

 Erase the board. Present the puzzle pieces for D, M, R, F, and H. Review the sounds made by each. Present the pieces for A, I and U. Review the sounds. Present SH. Keep the pieces in groups based on their positions in the words to be formed.

Challenge the children to pick out the pieces which will need to be linked to make the word "dash." Children may designate the letters by name, except for SH, which should be designated by sound. Link the letters together as they are suggested and confirm the correct formation of the word.

Continue in the same manner to form all of the words found on Worksheets 129A and B. Discuss the meanings of the words and use in original sentences.

Worksheets 129A/B: Read the instructions aloud. Elicit responses from the children in any of the suggested ways.

ACTIVITY 3: ART ACTIVITY

Worksheet 129C: Make a display model of the completed sheep. Prepare a worktable with the supplies needed. Demonstrate the steps carefully and assist as necessary.

LESSON 130
TARGET SOUND SH AND REVIEW

ACTIVITY 1: READING

 Play the Consonant Digraphs Song for the children encouraging them to sing along while pointing to the corresponding letters on the flashcards.

Write the following words on the board: shop, shut, shack, shed. Assist the children to decode each word.

Play a riddle game. Ask which of these words means a place to buy things, or going out to buy things. (shop) Ask which one means a place to keep tools or garden equipment. (shed) Which one means to close? (shut) Then ask what the last one means. (a small, broken-down house) Use each word in a sentence and allow students to create original sentences.

Do the same thing with the following words: dish, cash, rush.

 Try to encourage the use of interrogative and exclamatory sentences. Model this by changing declarative sentences into each style. For instance, if a child suggests "The old man lives in a shack in the woods," you can modify it as a question: "Where is the old man's shack?" or an exclamatory sentence, with the proper expression, "The old man lives in a shack in the woods!"

Worksheet 130A: Read the instructions aloud. Assist students to decode as needed and monitor their work.

The students are able to form all of the letters for both the board activities and on the worksheet. You may want students to copy some of these words on the board for further writing practice and reinforcement.

ACTIVITY 2: REVIEW

Challenge the children to give you an example of a word which begins with each of the following letters, using the letter name(s), not the sound: r, d, c, z, b, l, f, g, and the letter pair SH. Write the words on the board, leaving out the beginning letter. Have students come to the board and write the proper letter in the beginning space for each word.

Worksheet 130B: Read the instructions aloud. Assist students to label the pictures as necessary, but do not give any other sound or letter cues. Monitor their work.

Row 1: rabbit, dog, camel
Row 2: zebra, bat, sheep
Row 3: lion, fox, goat

LESSON 131
TARGET SOUND CH

ACTIVITY 1: HEARING

Play the Consonant Digraphs Song for the children encouraging them to sing along while pointing to the corresponding letters on the flashcards.

Assemble the children into a train today, hands on each other's waists, with you in the lead. "Chug" once around the room, making the CH sound over and over, in imitation of a train engine. When you have completed the "trip," blow the whistle once and have everyone "disembark" and return to their seats. Homeschoolers can and should enjoy this creative introduction to this sound. There is no reason the train has to have any more than one car!

Ask what they think today's sound might be. Affirm correct answers. If no one can guess correctly, make the CH sound several more times.

 Show the children the flashcard with the CH on it. Have them hear the sound of CH as in "chicken."

Describe today's sound as the "chugging" sound. It is very much like SH, but harder. The tongue actually has to stick to the top of the mouth in the T position to start the sound. It is actually produced as "tsh." Have students say both sounds one after the other several times: sh, ch, sh, ch. Call attention to the use of the tongue in CH.

It is also the unvoiced equivalent of J. Teaching it from this angle is probably not as efficient, however, you may have a student or two who can produce J, but stumble on CH. Try having them "turn off" their voices and make J—what they will have is CH!

 This is another hard-to-produce, later developing sound for any child who struggles with "sibilant sounds" (such as S, Z, SH, etc.) These are high frequency sounds which require careful tongue placement and precise air flow to produce accurately. Their absence is noticeable in the speech of hearing impaired individuals; the high frequency sounds are simply not heard. If you have a student who shows a marked inability to discriminate or produce these types of sounds, a hearing test may be in order.

Challenge them to listen carefully for this sound among its buddies, who are very much alike!

s, ch, ch, z, t, ch, j, sh, ch, s, z, ch, ch, ch, sh, t, j, ch, s, ch, ch

Tell the children that the CH sound is going to be the "leader" in words (like the engine of a train!) and that they must continue to listen carefully for it at the beginning:

chair	frog	thumb	chicks	chest
web	church	shirt	chum	chart
shin	chin	jam	Sam	chap
tap	chase	lace	shoe	chew

Worksheet 131A: Read the instructions aloud to the children. Label the pictures or call on students to do so.

Row 1: chair, web, frog
Row 2: fish, church, shirt
Row 3: chest, thumb, chicks

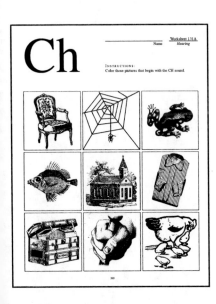

ACTIVITY 2: SEEING

Tell the children that the CH sound is written with a pair of letters, just like the SH they just studied. Write SH on the board. Tell them that in order to write CH we remove the S and replace it with C. Do this on the board.

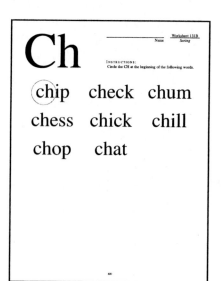

Draw attention to the picture on the flashcard.

Write the following words on the board: chin, chap, chug. Have students come to the board and circle the CH in each one. Assist students to decode the words, discuss the meanings and use in original sentences.

Worksheet 131B: Read the instructions aloud and monitor their progress as they work independently.

ACTIVITY 3: WRITING

Place guidelines and perimeter lines on the board. Call on students to come to the board and make the letters CH.

Remind them about stroke direction and order.

Worksheet 131C: Read the instructions aloud and monitor their progress as they work independently.

Remind them to space the letter pairs as if they were full words, using the index finger as their guide.

LESSON 132
TARGET SOUND CH

ACTIVITY 1: HEARING, SEEING, AND WRITING

Play the Consonant Digraphs Song for the children encouraging them to sing along while pointing to the corresponding letters on the flashcards.

Remind them about stroke direction and order.

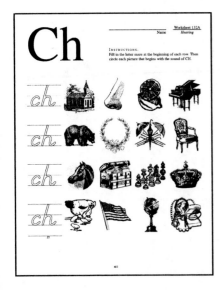

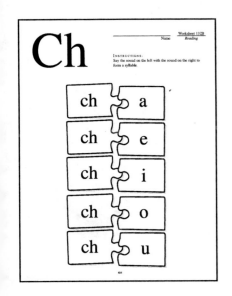

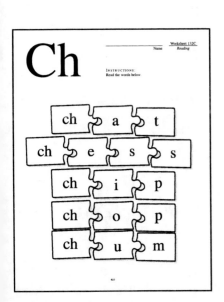

Worksheet 132A: Read the instructions aloud. Tell them that you will name the pictures for them while they respond independently on their own papers, following in the letter mazes before each line first:

Row 1: church, nose, lemon, piano
Row 2: bear, wreath, umbrellas, chair
Row 3: horse, chest, chess, crown
Row 4: chicks, flag, globe, jewelry

ACTIVITY 2: READING SYLLABLES

Write CH on the board.

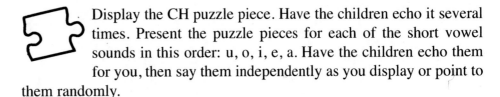 Display the CH puzzle piece. Have the children echo it several times. Present the puzzle pieces for each of the short vowel sounds in this order: u, o, i, e, a. Have the children echo them for you, then say them independently as you display or point to them randomly.

Place the U to the right of the CH and assist the children to sound out the syllable which is formed. Continue in the same way with the rest of the vowels, linking them to the CH sound.

Write the syllables on the board as they are shown on Worksheet 132A.

Worksheet 132B/C: Read the instructions aloud. Use any of the previous techniques for eliciting student response, using the board display or numbering the syllables to prompt responses.

ACTIVITY 3: READING WORDS

Ask students to think of words which may begin with the syllables listed on Worksheet 132B. Write these on the board, circling or highlighting the two beginning sounds.

 Tell the students that you are now going to add another sound to the syllables to form words. Then present the pieces for T, S, P, and M. Review the sounds made by these letters.

Use these pieces to form the words on Worksheet 132C. Write them on the board also. Discuss their meanings and use them in original sentences.

Tell the children that the CH sound is going to be the "engine" for new words today and that they must continue to listen carefully for it at the beginning:

chain	shame	chore	shore	joke
choke	chan	sink	cat	chat
Jill	chill	check	show	Joe
chatter	sat	zoo	chew	chip

Remind the children that the letter pair which makes the CH sound is "CH." Draw attention to the stimulus picture on the wall and display the flashcard.

On the board, write the lower case letter pair for CH, describing and numbering your strokes as you do so. Call on students to come to the board and make the letters. You may make any of these words plural when appropriate, to reinforce the pluralization concept.

LESSON 133
TARGET SOUND CH, TCH AND NCH

ACTIVITY 1: HEARING AND SEEING

 Play the Consonant Digraphs Song for the children encouraging them to sing along while pointing to the corresponding letters on the flashcards.

Discuss the fact that trains have engines at the front and something else at the end. (caboose) Tell them that sometimes the CH sound likes to be the caboose in words. When it does this it often takes another letter along.

Remind them of the first day you studied this sound and the instruction about their tongues sticking to the top of their mouths to start CH. This is what makes CH different from SH. That sound was a T. Tell them that at the end of words, CH often likes to take the T along.

Write the following words on the board: patch, catch, batch, hatch. Make the initial two letters in one color, the T in another color, and the CH in a third color. Decode the words for the children and have them echo them. Have students come up and circle the entire "tch" group at the end of each word.

Write the following on the board: hitch, pitch, ditch, botch. Use the color coding as above and proceed in the same manner.

Discuss the meaning of the words and use in original sentences.

Worksheet 133A: Read the instructions aloud. Tell the children to only circle the "tch" groups at this time. Monitor their work.

Ch

Worksheet 133A
INSTRUCTIONS: Name   Seeing
CH can also be heard at the end of a word. Sometimes it takes the letter T along. First circle all the letter groups TCH at the end with a red crayon. Sometimes it comes after the letter N. Circle all the letter groups NCH with a green crayon.

punch	patch	lunch
hitch	bunch	hunch
pinch	pitch	catch
bench	ditch	botch
hatch	quench	batch

ACTIVITY 2: HEARING AND SEEING N + CH

Tell the children that sometimes CH likes to take N along also. Write the following words on the board: punch, lunch, hunch. Write the N in one color and CH in another. Have students come up and circle the entire "nch" letter group. Read the words and have the children echo them.

Repeat with the following words: bench, pinch, quench. Proceed in the same manner as above.

Worksheet 133A: Now instruct the children to finish the sheet according to the directions, circling all the "nch" groups with green crayon. Reinforce all the words by having students find and read the printed words as you point to the written example on the board, use the riddle game, create original sentences with them, etc.

LESSON 134
TARGET SOUND CH, TCH AND NCH

ACTIVITY 1: READING SYLLABLES

 Play the Consonant Digraphs Song for the children encouraging them to sing along while pointing to the corresponding letters on the flashcards.

Divide the board in half. At the top of one half write "tch" in red. At the top of the other half, write "nch" in green. Remind students of stroke direction and order for each letter. Have the students echo the letter group sounds several times.

Under the heading "tch" write "ma," "ba," "di," "la." Under the heading "nch" write "be," "lu," "bu."

Call on students to sound out the syllables under each heading. Write the "tch" after the first syllable "ma," forming the word "match." Assist students to decode it. Invite students to the board to write "tch" after the other two syllables and decode them. Discuss the meanings of the words and use in original sentences.

Proceed in the same manner with the syllables under "nch."

Present the puzzle pieces which are necessary to form these words (also found on Worksheet 134A). Prompt the formation of the words with the pieces according to the riddle game. For instance, say "I am thinking of something which you bring to school to eat at noon when you are hungry. Can you solve this riddle by forming the answer with the puzzle pieces?" Guide and direct as necessary.

Worksheet 134A/B: Read the instructions aloud. Use any of the previous prompting techniques for eliciting student response. Monitor as they work independently.

 Archives: Medial Short Vowel

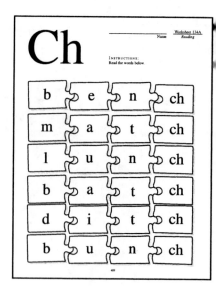

Lesson 135
Target Sound CH

 Play the Consonant Digraphs Song for the children encouraging them to sing along while pointing to the corresponding letters on the flashcards.

 Put or draw pictures of an engine and a caboose on the board, the engine on the left side in green and the caboose on the right in red. Write the letters CH under the engine and the letters CH, "tch," and "nch" under the caboose.

Green and red were chosen specifically. You can tell children that the engine is green because it makes the train "go" and the caboose is red because it signals the end of the train and the "stopping" of the word.

Give each child two pieces of paper, one green for the engine and one red for the caboose.

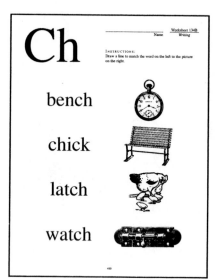

Tell the children that they are so good at listening that you are going to really challenge them today. You will be reading a list of words which may have CH at the beginning or at the end. They must listen carefully to hear if CH is the "engine" or the "caboose" in each word. Then they must hold up the corresponding color paper.

Remind them that the CH at the end may have T or N with it, but that won't change the sound of final CH.

Read the following list, watching carefully for student response:

bunch	champ	child	inch	rich
such	chime	munch	ranch	chunk
choose	charm	much	choke	branch

Praise their wonderful listening and tell them they are all "CHamps!"

Ch

ACTIVITY 2: ART ACTIVITY

Have a model of the finished project on Worksheet 135A for student reference. Prepare a table with the art supplies available and assist children as necessary to complete the project.

Worksheet 135A: Read the instructions aloud and go through the steps carefully. Draw attention to the order of the steps to reinforce this concept.

LESSON 136
TARGET SOUND TH

ACTIVITY 1: HEARING

Play the Consonant Digraphs Song for the children encouraging them to sing along.

Tell the children that this time you will be starting the lesson a little differently. Instead of telling them what the sound is, they will have to be "detectives" and figure it out for themselves. You will be reading a little paragraph to help them; it will be full of today's sound.

The "th" sounds in this story will be both voiced and unvoiced. The differentiation will not be important for the purposes of general discrimination. Students will intuitively recognize the sounds as having commonality.

Read the following:

The third or fourth Thursday in November is Thanksgiving Day. On that Thursday, we think upon and thank God for all the thousands of things He provides to us. Through thick and thin He is faithful to those He loves; His thoughts are with us then and now. We are thankful He sent Jesus to die for us, with thorns on His head and two thieves on three crosses. We are thankful He rose on the third day and now sits with God the Father. We thank Him that those who hunger and thirst for Him will never be thirsty again. That's why every day should be Thanksgiving Day!

Challenge them to deduce the target sound from the abundance of "th" words in the paragraph. You may read it a second time, emphasizing the "th" if necessary. Either the voiced or unvoiced sound is acceptable as a response.

Praise correct responses. Have the children echo the sound as an unvoiced sound first, then as a voiced sound. Tell them that with this sound, the same letter pair makes both sounds. Tell them their voices will automatically turn on in the right words.

This is another slow-to-develop sound. The most common errors are the substitution of S or T. The S has a similar airflow pattern, T is close in tongue placement. Prompting children to move the tongue forward to actually touch the bottom of the top teeth and then force air through may be enough to correct either error.

Tell the children that "th" can sometimes be mixed up with similar sounds like S and Z. Ask them to indicate to you when they hear "th" at the beginning of any of the following words:

An indication gesture here may be to place the tongue between the teeth and lightly "bite" on it. This will be the only time they will ever be permitted to "stick their tongues out" at the teacher!

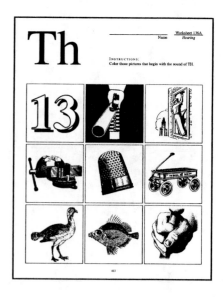

thirteen	zipper	window	vise
thimble	wagon	bird	fish
thumb	thank	tank	sing
thing	these	zebra	them

Worksheet 136A: Read the instructions aloud. Assist students to label the pictures and monitor their work.

Row 1: thirteen, zipper, window
Row 2: vise, thimble, wagon
Row 3: bird, fish, thumb

ACTIVITY 2: SEEING AND READING

Tell the children that this is another sound which requires a letter pair in order to write it. Draw attention to the stimulus picture on the wall and display the flashcard. Write "th" on the board, describing and numbering your strokes as you do so.

Write three or four of the words found on Worksheet 136B on the board. Circle the "th" in one of them, then call on students to come up and circle it in the other words.

Worksheet 136B: Read the instructions aloud. Monitor as they work independently. After they are done, assist them to read each word. Discuss the meanings of the words and use in original sentences.

ACTIVITY 3: WRITING

Place guidelines and perimeter lines on the board. Call on students to come to the board and make the letters TH. Remind them about stroke direction and order.

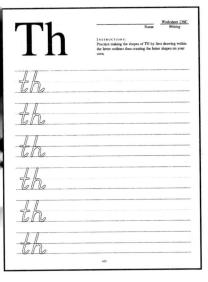

Worksheet 136C: Read the instructions aloud and monitor their progress as they work.

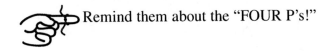Remind them about the "FOUR P's!"

LESSON 137
TARGET SOUND "TH"

ACTIVITY 1: READING SYLLABLES

Play the Consonant Digraphs Song for the children encouraging them to sing along while pointing to the corresponding letters on the flashcards.

Remind the children that the letter pair which makes the "th" sound is T + H. Write the letter in lower case on the board and display the printed letter pair using the flashcards.

Display the "th" puzzle piece. Have the children echo it several times as an unvoiced sound. Present the puzzle pieces for each of the short vowel sounds in this order: U, O, I, E, A. Have the children echo them for you, then say them independently as you display or point to them randomly.

Place the U to the right of the "th" and assist the children to sound out the syllable which is formed, using unvoiced "th." Continue in the same way with the rest of the vowels, linking them to the beginning "th" sound.

You may repeat the list using voiced "th." Reassure them that when they begin to make words with this sound, their voices will turn on when necessary.

Worksheet 137A: Read the instructions aloud. Use any of the previous techniques to elicit student response.

ACTIVITY 3: READING WORDS

Isolate the "thi" syllable from the rest. Present two final sounds: N, CK. Ask the children which one of these is needed to form the word "thin." Have a student link it with the "thi" syllable to form the word.

Remove the N and replace it with CK. Decode the word "thick."

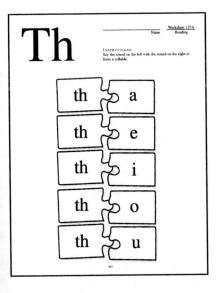

A side lesson here may be to point out that changing this single final sound turns one word into its opposite!

Present the "thu" syllable and the final sounds G and D. Say the word "thud" and ask a student to place the correct final sound on the syllable to form that word. Remove the D and add G. Decode the new word formed.

The words formed so far have all used the unvoiced "th" in speech. The next words formed will utilize voiced "th."

Present the pieces for "the." Remind them that this is a syllable with a short vowel sound (not the Special Exhibits "the"). Proceed to form the words "them" and "then" in the manner used above.

Repeat for "this," "that," and "thus."

Worksheet 137B: Read the instructions aloud. Use any of the previous techniques for eliciting student response. Discuss the meanings of the words and use in original sentences.

LESSON 138
TARGET SOUND TH

ACTIVITY 1: SEEING, WRITING, AND READING

Play the Consonant Digraphs Song for the children encouraging them to sing along while pointing to the corresponding letters on the flashcards.

Write the words found on Worksheet 138A on the board. Do this slowly and carefully, numbering and describing your strokes for each letter. Place lines after each word.

Invite children to come to the board and copy the words you have written.

Decode the words with the children. Review their meanings and use them in original sentences. Encourage children to make up their own sentences also.

Worksheet 138A: Read the instructions aloud and monitor their progress as they work. Remind them about letter and word spacing.

ACTIVITY 2: REVIEW

Write SH, CH, and TH on the board. Ask students what they see which is the same in each of the letter pairs (h). Ask them what is different.

 Give each child SH, CH, and TH puzzle pieces. Tell them you will be reading a list of words and they are to show you the letter pair which makes the beginning sound of each word.

church	shirt	thimble	thumb
shoe	chair	sheep	chicks
shell	chew	think	thousand
child	ship	thunder	cherry

Praise their careful listening! That was tricky!

Worksheet 138B: Read the instructions aloud. Assist children with labeling as necessary. Monitor their work.

LESSON 139
REVIEW

ACTIVITY 1: HEARING AND WRITING

Ask who can remember how to write the SH sound. Invite a student to come to the board and write the letter pair SH. Do the same with CH and TH, putting each one on a separate section of the board. Brainstorm with the children to come up with words which begin with each sound. Write these on the board surrounding the appropriate letter pair, highlighting the targeted letter pair in each word.

Play the riddle game with the words or create sentences which use one of the words on the board, but leave the word out for the children to supply. For instance, if one of the words is "ship," you could say the following sentence: The early Pilgrims came to America on a sailing _____. This is called "oral fill-in-the-blanks." Children can then come up and point to the proper word and read it aloud.

Worksheet 139A: Read the instructions aloud. Have them follow the maze at the beginning of each row, then assist them to label the pictures. Monitor as they respond independently. Remind them there may be more than one picture to circle in any given row.

Row 1: necklace, octopus, globe, sheep
Row 2: bear, church, ram, chair
Row 3: horse, shirt, apples, ship
Row 4: gorilla, thimble, Indian, mask

ACTIVITY 2: HEARING ENDING SH, CH, TH

Have the children get out the three index cards with the three letter pairs SH, CH, and TH which they made yesterday. Tell them that today they must listen to these sounds at the end of words. They must decide which sound they hear and hold it up.

rich	rash	path	patch	with	match
mash	math	dish	ditch	cash	catch
much	mush	Beth	fish	touch	such
church	shirt	thimble	thumb	shoe	chair
sheep	chicks	shell	chew	think	thousand

Praise their careful listening! That was tricky!

LESSON 140
REVIEW

ACTIVITY 1: REVIEW

Make this a "Reading Fair" Day!

Take time today to go over all of the letters, letter pairs, letter groups, and sounds which they have learned so far this year. Spend extra time playing any of the games included with the curriculum, or any of the suggested games for eliciting student responses or encouraging review.

 Invite children to do individual recitations of any of the songs or chants.

Review the stories you have read, allow students to reread them aloud or silently (they may be surprised how easy they are now!) Encourage students to retell the stories in their own words, paying careful attention to the order of events.

Get out some of the art supplies and encourage them to make letters and words (perhaps their own names) in different media.

This day will give you extra time for informal assessment and observation of skills.

Worksheet 140A: Read the instructions aloud. Draw an artist's palette on the board and label the paint splotches with the letters shown on the key. Monitor their work.

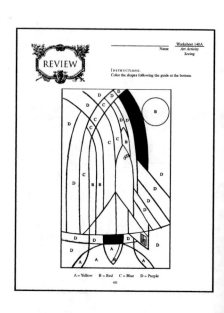

LESSON 141
TARGET SOUND WH

ACTIVITY 1: HEARING AND SEEING

 Play the Consonant Digraphs Song for the children encouraging them to sing along while pointing to the corresponding letters on the flashcards.

Write a lower case W on the board. Ask if anyone remembers what sound is made by this letter. Tell them that today's sound is very, very much like W. It is the sound WH. Make this sound with a slight breathiness.

 Show the children the flashcard with the WH on it. Have them hear the sound of WH as in "white."

These sounds are virtually identical except for this additional airflow which accompanies the WH. Sometimes it is phonetically written as "hw" to denote this. In spontaneous speech, the difference is hardly detectable. It is primarily in the spelling of words that they are distinguished.

Write the letter pairs SH, CH, and TH on the board. Ask what is the same about all three pairs (h). Challenge them to tell you what they think W will take along with it to make the WH sound. Praise and affirm the correct answer and write H beside the W on the board. Tell them that this letter pair makes the WH sound.

Remind them of the gesture for the W sound—blowing gently, like the wind. Allow them to use the same gesture for WH since the sounds are so similar. Tell them to listen for it at the beginning of the following words and indicate when it is heard:

whistle	shirt	whale	top	vest
moon	wheel	wheat	glasses	when
rabbit	race	yard	where	what

Worksheet 141A: Read the instructions aloud. Assist the children to label the pictures and monitor their progress as they work independently.

Row 1: whale, shirt, window
Row 2: top, moon, wheel
Row 3: vest, glasses, wheat

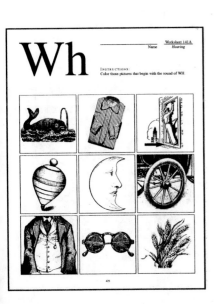

Worksheet 141B: Read the instructions aloud. Call attention to the WH on the board. Monitor as they work independently.

ACTIVITY 2: WRITING

Place guidelines and perimeter lines on the board. Call on students to come to the board and make the letters WH.

Worksheet 141C: Read the instructions aloud and monitor their progress as they work independently.

LESSON 142
TARGET SOUND WH

ACTIVITY 1: READING SYLLABLES

 Play the Consonant Digraphs Song for the children encouraging them to sing along while pointing to the corresponding letters on the flashcards.

Remind the children that the letter pair which makes the WH sound is W + H. Write the letter pair in lower case on the board and display the printed letters using the flashcards.

Connect the W, H puzzle pieces. Display these for the children and have them echo it several times. Present the puzzle pieces for each of the short vowel sounds in this order: u, o, i, e, a. Have the children echo them for you, then say them independently as you display or point to them randomly.

Place the U to the right of the WH and assist the children to sound out the syllable which is formed. Continue in the same way with the rest of the vowels, linking them to the beginning WH sound.

Write the syllables on the board.

Worksheet 142A: Read the instructions aloud and use any of the previous techniques for eliciting student response.

ACTIVITY 2: READING WORDS

Take away the "who" and "whu" syllables.

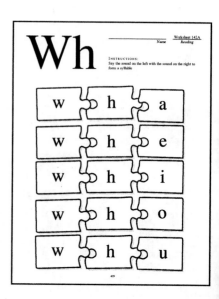

Present the following puzzle pieces: T, N, P, M, Z. Ask the children which piece you would need to add to which syllable to form the word "whet." Call on a student to add the correct piece to the correct syllable. Have the children echo the word several times.

Continue in the same manner for the words "when," "whip," "whim," and "whiz."

Discuss the meanings of each of the words formed and use in original sentences.

Write each of the words on the board.

Worksheet 142B: Use any of the previous techniques for eliciting student response. Challenge them to make up their own sentences using these words.

Since students are able to make all of the letters of these words, you may put guidelines on the board and allow children to come up and copy them independently for further reinforcement.

 Archives: Medial Short Vowel

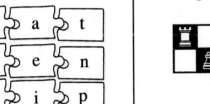

LESSON 143
REVIEW

ACTIVITY 1: HEARING, SEEING, AND WRITING INITIAL DIGRAPHS

 Play the Consonant Digraphs Song for the children encouraging them to sing along while pointing to the corresponding letters on the flashcards.

Give the children the WH, SH, CH, TH puzzle pieces

Tell them to listen carefully. You are going to say a list of sounds and they are to hold up the correct card with the letter pair which makes each sound. This is tricky, so give them plenty of response time!

Only present TH as an unvoiced sound in this exercise, since the others are unvoiced.

sh, ch, th, wh, wh, ch, th, sh, sh, ch, wh, th, th, ch, ch, sh, ch, th

Write each of the letter pairs in a separate section at the top of the board. Under each pair write three or four words which begin with each sound. Allow children to come to the board and circle the beginning letter pair in each word.

Erase the letter pairs and allow students to write them back in independently. Monitor their formation of the letters.

Worksheet 143A: Read the instructions. Assist the children to label each picture, but do not give any further clues. Monitor their work.

Row 1: whale, chest, sheep
Row 2: shirt, thimble, chess
Row 3: wheelbarrow, chair, thumb

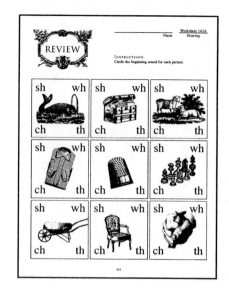

ACTIVITY 2: HEARING, SEEING, AND WRITING ENDING DIGRAPHS

Erase the words from the board, but leave the column headings. Under each letter pair, write three or four words which end with that sound. (You may use the lists from previous lessons.) Call students to the board to circle the letter pairs in each word.

Erase the letter pairs and allow students to write them in independently.

Worksheet 143B: Read the instructions aloud. Label the pictures for the children and monitor their lettering.

Row 1: fish, watch, bench
Row 3: dish, match, witch

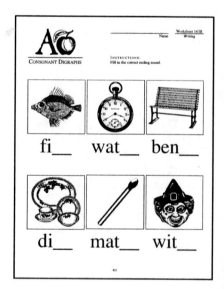

LESSON 144
SPECIAL EXHIBITS

ACTIVITY 1: SPECIAL EXHIBITS REVIEW

 Play the Consonant Digraphs Song for the children encouraging them to sing along while pointing to the corresponding letters on the flashcards.

Write on the board the previously taught Special Exhibits which will be used in the next story *Runs from Guns*. They are found after Book 10.

Review the words in various ways. Have students read them as you point randomly, play "Around the World" with them, use them in original sentences.

Students may be invited to come to the board and copy them, or copy them on lined paper at their desks.

ACTIVITY 2: NEW SPECIAL EXHIBITS

Write the Book 10 Special Exhibits on the board. Call attention to the similarity of "fall" and "wall" to the previously taught words "all" and "call." Some students may notice that "their" is spelled differently from "there," which they have already had. Affirm this and explain that the meanings are different. Use each in original sentences.

Worksheet 144A: Review the list using any of the previous techniques for eliciting student response.

LESSON 145
REVIEW AND ADDING "ES"

ACTIVITY 1: READING SH WORDS AND PLURALS

Play the Consonant Digraphs Song for the children encouraging them to sing along while pointing to the corresponding letters on the flashcards.

Write the following words on the board: cat, bug, pet. Ask if anyone remembers what you must add to these words if you have more than one of them. (s) Call on a student to come to the board and add the S to each word.

Say the word "cat" again. Clap one time while you say it to show that the word has only one beat. Say the word "cats." Clap one time to show that the plural word also has only one beat.

Now write the following on the board: ash, dish, inch. Ask how you would say the first word if there were more than one (ashes). Clap while you say it to show that this plural word has two beats. Have the children say it and clap also.

Explain to the children that each beat is called a syllable. All syllables have vowels in them. Because of this, we must add an E before the final S in the word "ashes" to make it plural.

Continue in the same way with the words "dishes" and "inches." Have students come to the board and circle the E which comes before each final S.

Tell the children that we never add just an S to words which end with SH; they will always see an E before the S.

Write the following words on the board: rushes, wishes, mashes. Remind them that these words are action words—they tell what something or someone is doing. Sometimes we need to add S to them to make them make sense in a sentence. Give the example: "I rush to the bus stop." and "He rushes to the bus stop." We say "rushes" when we talk about someone else who is not with us. When we read or write this, we must add "es" to the end of the action word "rush."

Write the words on Worksheet 145A on the board in columns just as they are presented on the worksheet.

Worksheet 145A: Read the instructions aloud. Assist the children to read the words from top to bottom of each column, following along on the worksheet as you point to the corresponding written word on the board. Repeat the activity going from bottom to top of each column. Finally, point randomly to the words on the columns and call on students to read them.

Pay particular attention to the words with "es" at the end.

Have students point to the word on their sheets which matches the word you point to on the board, without hearing it read.

Erase the words from the board and then have students point to or circle the correct word as you randomly say them. You may want to do this on an individual or small group basis to more carefully monitor their responses.

Discuss the meanings of any of the more uncommon words. Use the words in sentences. You may have children come to the board and copy entire words from their sheets for further reinforcement.

ACTIVITY 2: WRITING REVIEW

Go over the formation of any of the letters which need review or reinforcement.

Worksheet 145B: Read the instructions aloud and monitor their progress as they work independently.

LESSON 146
REVIEW AND ADDING "ES"

ACTIVITY 1: ADDING "ES" TO FINAL CH WORDS

 Play the Consonant Digraphs Song for the children encouraging them to sing along while pointing to the corresponding letters on the flashcards.

Remind the students about the rule for adding "es" when a word ends in SH. Write the following on the board: dash, wish. Call on students to come to the board and write "es" after each one. Assist the students to read the words formed and use in original sentences, with and without the "es" endings.

Now write the following on the board: patch, hitch, fetch. Ask the children what would have to be added if the first word was "patches" (es). Clap out the syllables with the children. Have a student come to the board and add "es" to the end of the word. Proceed in the same way with "hitch" and "fetch." Use each one in an original sentence, both with and without the "es" endings. So, the same rule applies with words which end with CH also (or "tch" or "nch"). We must always include the E with the final S.

Write the words from Worksheet 146A on the board in columns just as they are presented on the worksheet.

Worksheet 146A: Read the instructions aloud. Assist the children to read the words from top to bottom of each column, following along on the worksheet as you point to the corresponding written word on the board. Repeat the activity going from bottom to top of each column. Finally, point randomly to the words on the columns and call on students to read them.

Have students point to the word on their sheets which matches the word you point to on the board, without hearing it read.

Erase the words from the board and then have students point to or circle the correct word as you randomly say them. You may want to do this on an individual or small group basis to more carefully monitor their responses.

Discuss the meanings of any of the more uncommon words. Use the words in sentences.

You may have children come to the board and copy entire words from their sheets for further reinforcement.

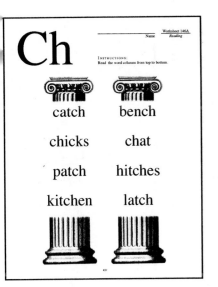

Ch

Worksheet 146A
Name _____ Reading

INSTRUCTIONS:
Read the word columns from top to bottom.

catch	bench
chicks	chat
patch	hitches
kitchen	latch

LESSON 147
REVIEW

ACTIVITY 1: REVIEW OF "TH" WORDS

 Play the Consonant Digraphs Song for the children encouraging them to sing along while pointing to the corresponding letters on the flashcards.

Write the words from Worksheet 147A on the board in columns just as they are presented on the worksheet.

Worksheet 147A: Read the instructions aloud. Assist the children to read the words from top to bottom of each column, following along on the worksheet as you point to the corresponding written word on the board. Repeat the activity going from bottom to top of each column. Finally, point randomly to the words on the columns and call on students to read them.

Some of the words on this sheet are previous Special Exhibits which the students are now able to decode.

Have students point to the word on their sheets which matches the word you point to on the board, without hearing it read.

Erase the words from the board and then have students point to or circle the correct word as you randomly say them. You may want to do this on an individual or small group basis to more carefully monitor their responses.

Discuss the meanings of any of the more uncommon words. Use the words in sentences.

You may have children come to the board and copy entire words from their sheets for further reinforcement.

ACTIVITY 2: WRITING REVIEW

Review any letters which have been more difficult for students to form. Verbally reinforce stroke direction and order.

Worksheet 147B: Read the instructions aloud. Monitor as they work independently.

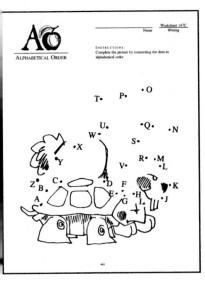

ACTIVITY 3: REVIEW OF ALPHABETICAL ORDER

 Play the Alphabet Song for the children encouraging them to sing along while pointing to the corresponding letters on the flashcards.

Call on several students to recite the Alphabet Song for the rest of the class. Ask several questions such as "Which comes first: A or X?" Ask for placement comparisons of letters which are far apart in the alphabet at this time.

 Another idea may be to start putting some things in alphabetical order. You may start with the children themselves, in groups of four or five. You may also try categories of objects: fruits, school supplies, subject names, etc.

Worksheet 147C: Read the instructions aloud. Monitor as they work independently.

LESSON 148
REVIEW

ACTIVITY 1: READING

 Play the Consonant Digraphs Song for the children encouraging them to sing along while pointing to the corresponding letters on the flashcards.

Write the words from Worksheet 148A on the board in columns just as they are presented on the worksheet.

Worksheet 148A: Read the instructions aloud. Assist the children to read the words from top to bottom of each column, following along on the worksheet as you point to the corresponding written word on the board. Repeat the activity going from bottom to top of each column. Finally, point randomly to the words on the columns and call on students to read them.

Call attention to the use of "es" after final SH and S after final P in the words "wishes" and "whips," respectively.

Have students point to the word on their sheets which matches the word you point to on the board, without hearing it read.

Erase the words from the board and then have students point to or circle the correct word as you randomly say them. You may want to do this on an individual or small group basis to more carefully monitor their responses.

Discuss the meanings of any of the more uncommon words. Use the words in sentences.

You may have children come to the board and copy entire words from their sheets for further reinforcement.

ACTIVITY 2: WRITING

Worksheet 148B: Read the instructions aloud. Monitor their progress as they work independently.

LESSON 149 TARGET: A AS "AH"

ACTIVITY 1: HEARING

Ask the children to give you several examples of words that use the short sound of A (like in "cat").

Now explain that the letter A has another sound which it will make in certain words. It is a "relaxing" sound, like a sigh when you settle into a soft chair after a long day—aaahhh! Make the sound slowly and gently and invite the children to echo it. This sound is almost identical to short "o"—the oral cavity is just slightly more open.

Tell them they have already used it several times. Write the following on the board: all, Ma, Pa, call, fall, wall (the last two are from Special Exhibits List 10). Invite children to read each one aloud, drawing out the "ah" sound in each word.

Challenge the children to be good listeners today and indicate to you when they hear "ah" in each of the following words. An indication gesture may be to lace their fingers behind their heads, as if they are reclining back in a chair or bed.

father	plate	sad	lake	mamma
water	watch	ball	tan	banana
salt	pale	papa	pan	spa

Praise their fine listening!

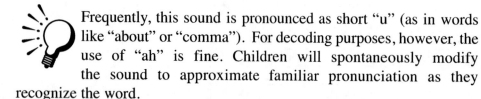 Frequently, this sound is pronounced as short "u" (as in words like "about" or "comma"). For decoding purposes, however, the use of "ah" is fine. Children will spontaneously modify the sound to approximate familiar pronunciation as they recognize the word.

(sidebar worksheet:)

Worksheet 148B
Name _____ Writing

A O
SPECIAL EXHIBIT

INSTRUCTIONS:
Copy the following words.

use
fall
wall
their
watch

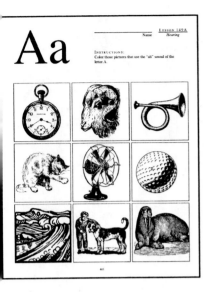

Row 1: watch, ram, horn
Row 2: cat, fan, ball
Row 3: water, pat, walrus

ACTIVITY 2: SPECIAL EXHIBITS AND VOCABULARY FOR RUNS FROM GUNS

Write the words found on Worksheet 149B on the board. Invite students to decode and read the words.

Define as necessary, using the definitions described in the next lesson. Use in original sentences. Invite students to come to the board to copy specified words.

Worksheet 149B: Read the instructions aloud. Use any of the previous techniques and variations for eliciting student responses.

Variations for prompting the reading of words on this sheet include: numbering the words and calling on students to read them by the designated number, verbal "fill-in-the-blanks," pointing to the written word on the board and having students point to the corresponding printed word on the sheet, riddle clues, categorizing on the basis of beginning sound, middle vowel, or ending letter group, etc.

LESSON 150
READING *RUNS FROM GUNS*

ACTIVITY 1: READING ALOUD

This story is set during the American War Between the States. The following vocabulary and expressions are used:

shell—bullet or casing
in shock—unbelieving, incredulous
as a rock wall—immovable
shucks—corn stalks
chap—fellow, man
gash—wound, deep cut
mush—hot cornmeal cereal
Will's lot—Will's piece of land
havoc—confusion
hitch—hook up
combat—fighting

bash—destroy, break down
mutt—dog
pen a bill—write an agreement
top men—the commanders of the army
call off—state their names
perish—die
sadness—sad, sorrowful
let up—slowed down, stopped
mull—think about
kick off—beginning

Special words:
Feds—Federal forces of the North
Rebs—Confederate forces of the South
Rockwall Jackson—Stonewall Jackson
Manassas
Appomattox

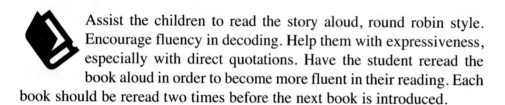 Assist the children to read the story aloud, round robin style. Encourage fluency in decoding. Help them with expressiveness, especially with direct quotations. Have the student reread the book aloud in order to become more fluent in their reading. Each book should be reread two times before the next book is introduced.

Some questions for comprehension may include: Who won the battle at Manassas? Why does Will want to move from that cabin? Where does he go and what happens there later on?

ACTIVITY 2: READING COMPREHENSION

Worksheet 150A: Read the instructions aloud. Assist the children to decode the words and monitor as they respond as directed.

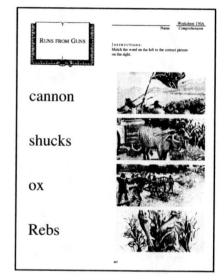

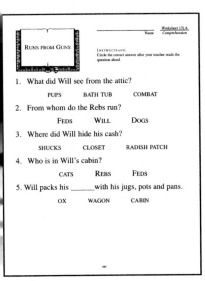

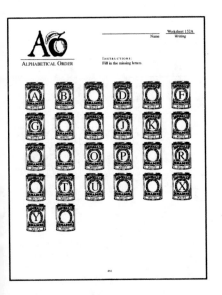

LESSON 151
READING COMPREHENSION

ACTIVITY 1: REVIEWING THE STORY

Lead the children in a review of yesterday's story. Discuss the order of the events, the characters, and the main ideas.

Worksheet 151A: Read the instructions aloud. Read the questions to the children one by one and monitor as they respond independently.

Worksheet 151B: Read the instructions aloud. Assist the children to interpret the pictures and assemble the events in order, numbering the pictures in the upper right hand corner of each. You may want to do this worksheet together to insure correctness.

 Archives: Medial Short Vowel

LESSON 152
REVIEW

ACTIVITY 1: ALPHABETICAL ORDER

 Play the Alphabet Song for the children encouraging them to sing along while pointing to the corresponding letters on the flashcards.

Write the alphabet on the board in lower case. Leave out random letters and call on students to come to the board and fill in the missing letters.

Worksheet 152A: Read the instructions aloud. Remind them that all these letters are in upper case and that they must write much smaller than usual. Monitor their work.

The following activities should require little to no formal instruction.

ACTIVITY 2: READING WORDS

Worksheet 152B: Read the instructions aloud. Monitor as they work independently.

ACTIVITY 3: READING SENTENCES

Worksheet 152C: Read the instructions aloud. Monitor as they work independently.

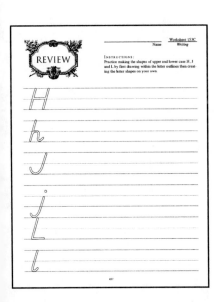

LESSON 153
REVIEW

ACTIVITY 1: READING WORDS

 Play the Museum Song for the children encouraging them to sing along while pointing to the corresponding letters on the flashcards.

The following activities should require little to no formal instruction.

Worksheet 153A: Read the instructions aloud. Monitor as they work independently. Assist any students who may have difficulty determining the labels for the pictures.

ACTIVITY 2: ALPHABETICAL ORDER

Worksheet 153B: Read the instructions aloud and monitor their work.

ACTIVITY 3: WRITING REVIEW

Invite students to the board to review the writing of the upper and lower case "H,h," "J,j," and "L,l."

Worksheet 153C: Read the instructions aloud and monitor their progress as they work. Remind them about letter spacing.

LESSON 154
REVIEW

ACTIVITY 1: HEARING AND SEEING

 Play the Consonant Digraphs Song for the children encouraging them to sing along while pointing to the corresponding letters on the flashcards.

Write on the board any four of the consonant sounds they have studied this year. Say a word which ends with one of the sounds. Challenge the children to tell you what letter on the board makes the ending sound of that word. Call on a student to come up and circle the correct letter.

Continue in the same manner, using all of the consonant sounds studied. Praise their careful listening!

Worksheet 154A: Read the instructions aloud. Assist the students to properly label each picture. Do not give any other clues about ending sounds or letters.

Row 1: hat, fox, bed
Row 2: pig, fan, sheep
Row 3: pan, cat, top

ACTIVITY 2: WRITING

Review any letters which have been more difficult for the children to form.

Worksheet 154B: Read the instructions aloud and monitor their work.

 Percival's Pairs

LESSON 155
REVIEW

ACTIVITY 1: WRITING

Worksheet 155A: Read the instructions aloud and monitor their work.

ACTIVITY 2: HEARING AND WRITING

Write the four digraphs SH, CH, TH and WH on the board. Under each one, write one word which begins and one word which ends with that letter pair. (The digraph WH will not have any examples of words which end with it.) Have a student come to the board and circle the letter pair in each word, wherever it occurs.

Leave the display on the board.

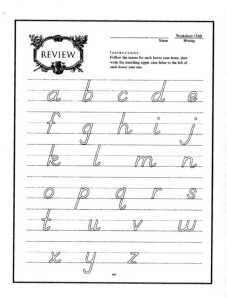

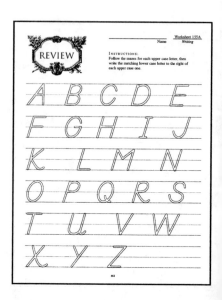

Worksheet 155B: Read the instructions aloud. Assist the children to label the pictures, but do not give any further sound or letter clues. Monitor their work.

Worksheet 155C/D: Cumulative Test.

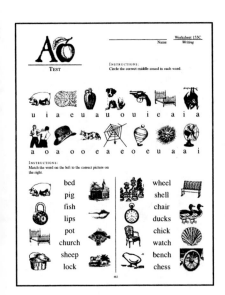

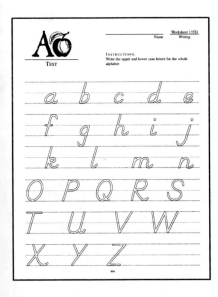

man

rat

ran

the

BINGO

You will need:
1 game board
25 game pieces per student

Object of the Game:
The winner is the first student to fill a row vertically, horizontally or diagonally and yell "Bingo!"

Set Up:
Photocopy this game board so each student gets a copy. Fill in the squares with the letters you have studied. Give each student enough game pieces to cover all the squares. Call out letters at random until there is a winner.

was

I

with

that

his

they

was

I

with

that

his

they

SPECIAL EXHIBIT LISTS

denotes words which are decodable by the end of the kindergarten year. ( ) denote words which were previously introduced as sight words but which are decodable at this point in the curriculum.

Book 1:
Pan and the Mad Man
a
is
the
to
on*
in*
this*
and

Book 2:
A Pet for Pat
that*
with*
they
his
was
of
not*
for
Previously introduced
BOOK 1:
is
and
the
to
a
in

Book 3:
The Rim of the Map
God
what
all
but*
were
as
no

Previously introduced:
BOOK 1:
a
and
on*
the
to
BOOK 2:
they
with*
not*
was
of
that*

Book 4:
Pepin the Not-Big
be
had*
can
son
Previously introduced:
BOOK 1:
to
(on)
(in)
BOOK 2:
was
of
with*
that*
his
(not)
BOOK 3:
as
what
all
were
(but)

Book 5:
The Rig Ran On
when*
from
them*
Ma
Pa
go

Previously introduced:
BOOK 1:
the
and
to
this*
BOOK 2:
was
they
with*
that*
his
BOOK 3:
all
were
as
BOOK 4:
had*

Book 6:
The Dog, the Hog, the Rat, the Ram, the Hen and the Big Big Din
he
put

Book 7:
Ben and His Pen
by
or
been
has
me
are
call

Previously introduced:
(Book 1 & 2 words no longer reviewed)
BOOK 3:
what*
were
all

Previously introduced:
(Book 1 words no longer reviewed)
BOOK 2:
they
of
with*
was
that*
his
BOOK 3:
all
were
as
what*
(but)
BOOK 5:
when*
from
(had)

BOOK 5
when*
from
BOOK 6
he
for
put

Book 8:
Dan and the Den
there
you
your
have
said
one
then*

Previously introduced
(Books 1, 2, & 3 not reviewed)
BOOK 4:
be
BOOK 5:
when*
them*
BOOK 6:
he
put
for
BOOK 7:
or

Book 9:
In a Camel's Eye
give
eye
love
visit
my
I

Previously introduced
(Books 1-4 not reviewed)
BOOK 5:
from
go
BOOK 6:
he
for
BOOK 7:
been
me
BOOK 8:
there
one
said
then*
you

Book 10:
Runs from Guns
use
fall
wall
their
watch

Previously introduced
(Books 1-5 not reviewed)
BOOK 6:
he
put
BOOK 7:
by
are
call
BOOK 8:
has
there
have
one
BOOK 9:
my
give
love
I

ARCHIVES GAME

You will need:
Game board
Die
Game cards

Object of the Game:
To reach the stack of paintings at the end of the path. The first player to reach the stack of paintings wins.

Set Up:
Each player chooses a game piece and places it on the first space. Place the game card deck on the card pile space on the game board.

Special Spaces on the board:
Roll Again:
If a player lands on one of these spaces, he rolls again and moves ahead that many spaces.
+3/-2:
If a player lands on one of these spaces, he moves forward or backward that many spaces.

Directions for game play:
Players roll the die and the player with the highest number goes first.

The first player draws a card from the card pile and reads it out loud.

PICTURE EDITION
If the student identifies the beginning letter sound correctly, he rolls the die and moves ahead that many spaces. After landing on the space, he must follow any direction printed there.

INITIAL SOUND EDITION
If the student identifies the beginning letter sound correctly, he rolls the die and moves ahead that many spaces. After landing on the space, he must follow any direction printed there.

MEDIAL VOWEL EDITION
The cards in this set feature two consonants and a blank (i.e. "b_d"). The student reads the card placing any vowel they wish in the middle of the word. If the word read by the student is really a word, he rolls the die and moves ahead that many spaces. After landing on the space, he must follow any direction printed there.

PERCIVAL'S PAIRS

You will need:
Playing card deck
  (using only letters prescribed in teacher's manual)

Object of the Game:
Collect the highest number pairs.

Set Up:
This game is best for 3-6 players, but it is possible for 2 to play. The dealer deals 5 cards to each player (7 each for 2 players). The remaining cards are placed face down to form a stock.

The player to dealer's left starts. A turn consists of asking a specific player for a specific letter. For example, if it is my turn I might say:
'Parker, would you please give me a letter F card?'. The player who asks must already hold at least one cards requested. If the player who was asked (Parker) has the card requested, he must give it to the player who asked for them. That player then gets another turn and may again ask any player for any other letter card already held by the asker.

If the person asked does not have any cards of the named, they say 'Pick a card'. The asker must then draw the top card of the undealt stock. If the drawn card is the letter asked for, the asker shows it and gets another turn. If the drawn card is not the rank asked for, the asker keeps it, but the turn now passes to the player who said 'Pick a card'.

The game continues until either someone has no cards left in their hand or the deck runs out. The winner is the player who then has the most pairs.

VARIATION: Instead of asking for a card by letter, the players request cards using the letter sounds.

[1] THE ALPHABET SONG *2:54*

[2] THE MUSEUM SONG *2:21*

[3] THE ALPHABET CHASE *2:09*

[4] SHORT VOWELS SONG *1:09*

[5] CHICKENS & SHEEP
(Consonant Digraphs) *1:36*

[6] THE ING ANG SONG *1:07*

[7] CRASH! SWING! SQUASH!
(Beginning Consonant Blends) *3:07*

[8] ACT LIKE A CLOWN
(Final Consonant Blends) *2:09*

[9] FUNNY BUTTERFLY (sounds of y) *1:01*

[10] THE E PARTNERSHIP (ea/ee) *0:49*

[11] PLAY EVERYDAY (ai/ay) *0:53*

[12] THE SOUTH SEA (oa/ow) *0:47*

[13] OYSTERS (oi/oy) *0:54*

[14] SHOUT (ou/ow) *1:00*

[15] THE BROAD-O SONG (au/aw/al) *1:27*

[16] MISSION TO THE MOON (sion/tion) *1:15*

[17] HOW MANY SOUNDS? (a/e/i/o/u/y) *3:40*

Tracks 18-34 are the previous songs without vocals. [18] *2:54* [19] *2:20* [20] *2:05* [21] *1:00* [22] *1:35* [23] *0:58* [24] *3:07* [25] *2:09* [26] *0:51* [27] *0:40* [28] *0:44* [29] *0:39* [30] *0:47* [31] *0:52* [32] *1:19* [33] *1:05* [34] *3:37*

THE MUSEUM SONG

Percival a knight in shining armor
And a boy who came to see the art
In a museum
They passed their time away
Looking at the paintings
Playing alphabetic games

Phonic sounds are simple
See the picture say the word
Just say it with a stutter and the phonic rule is heard
And with a little practice you'll be nimble you'll be quick
To say the sound of each that you have picked

A A Apples then M M Mummy B B Bull and
P P Pig then T T Table D D Dancer N N Nuts and G G Goat

S S Sun and F F Fan R R Rabbit and E E Egg
I I Indian and O O Ox U U Umbrella and L L Lion

CHORUS

H H Hat and C C Cow K K Kangaroo and J J Jar
Z Z Zebra then Y Y Yellow
Four more letters we will learn
So say them with each picture

W W Wind mill and Q Q Queen V V Vi o lin and X X Boxing
Twenty six letters in all Perhaps you'll try again
When you go to a museum
Try and play this phonic game

THE MUSEUM SONG

Veritas Press
Copyright 2000 Steve Scheffler

The Alphabet Song

The words we speak they come together
By using alphabetic letters;
And in this song we are going to teach you
The alphabet your gonna use.

Like a puzzle picture each jigsaw piece
Is like the letters in a word
And when they're put together in proper order
Then the sounds of each are heard.

Speak each letter they form the words
You can really do it if you try!

ABCDEFGHIJKLMNOPQRSTUVWXY and Z

Repeat

THE ALPHABET SONG

Veritas Press
Copyright Veritas Press

Joyful

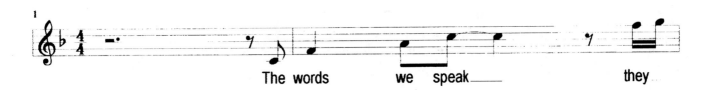

The words   we speak   they

come   to ge___ ther   by us ing al___ pha   be___ tic let___ ters; And

in   this   song___   we   are

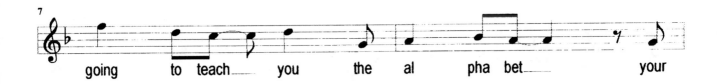

going   to teach___ you   the   al   pha bet___   your

gon___ na use.   Like   a   puz   zle pic___ ture   each

jig   zaw piece   is   like the   let   ters in___ a word;

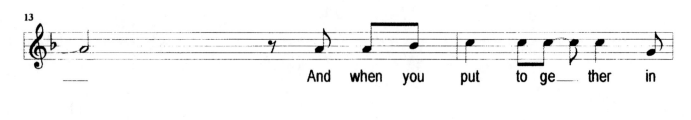

And when you put to ge ther in

pro per or der then the sounds of each are heard.

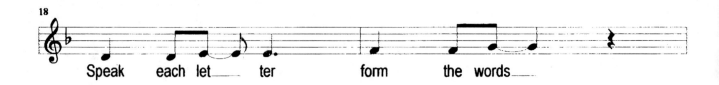

Speak each let ter form the words

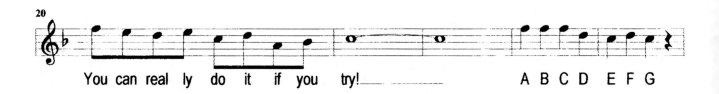

You can real ly do it if you try! A B C D E F G

H I J K L M N O P Q R S T U V W X

Y and Z

SHORT VOWELS SONG

A as in APPLE
E as in EGG
You can even say IT
Standing on your HEAD
And IF you were AN INDIAN
Short I is what you'd use
Just like using O in OX
Short O is what you'd choose

And finally now we introduce the one and only U
The SOUND when short comes OUT like the
UMBRELLA that we use in a rainstorm

A as in APPLE
E as in EGG
I as in INDIAN
And O as in OX
U as in UMBRELLA
There are five short vowels
They are A E I O U

SHORT VOWELS SONG

Veritas Press
Copyright Veritas Press

Lullabye

A   as in AP PLE   E   as in EGG

You can e ven say   IT   Stand ing   on   your HEAD   And

IF   you were AN IN DI AN Short   I   is what you'd use

Just like us ing O in OX Short O   is   what you'd choose   And

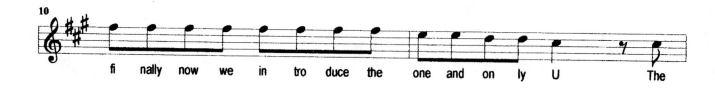

fi nally now we   in tro duce the   one and on ly   U   The

SOUND when short comes OUT like the UM BREL LA that we use   in a

CHICKENS & SHEEP
(Consonant Digraphs)

Consonant Digraphs there are five of them
C H S H are the first two
Then there are two of the same T H letters
Yet one is voiced and the other is not
And finally the letters W H
Concludes the list of these consonant sounds

C H is used in words like CHICKEN
CHURCH and CHALK and CHIMPANZEE
S H is used in SHEEP SHELL SHOWBOAT
and W H in WHITE and WHIPPO'WILL

Now the T H sound that is VOICED and heard
Is found in words like THIS and THAT

And don't forget at times that T H isn't voiced
As in words like THIN THICK THANK

Consonant Digraphs there are five of them
C H S H are the first two
Then there are two of the same T H letters
Yet one is voiced and the other is not

CHICKENS & SHEEP

Veritas Press
Copyright 2000 Veritas Press

Sing Song with Talk

The ING ANG ONG Song

There are many songs that have no rhyme or reason to sing em
So we change those sounds as we go a long
The same is said about times and the seasons
Describing them requires a different sound

Sing can be Sang and Sang can be Sung
Ring can be Rang and Rang can be Rung

ING ANG And ONG is just a way you may say it
When explaining the time it might have occurred

THE ING ANG ONG SONG

Veritas Press
Copyright Veritas Press

Jazz

There are ma ny_____ songs that have_____ no

rhyme or rea_____ son to sing_____ em_____

So we change those sounds as we go a

long_____ The_____ same_____ is

said_____ a_____ bout times_____ and_____ the

sea_____ sons_____ De scrib ing them_____ re

qui res a dif fer ent

CRASH! SWING! SQUASH!
Beginning Consonant Blends

Those consonant blends oh those consonant blends
Some have a family still some have none
But we will learn beginning consonant blends
Five categories each to attend

First the R family there's eight in the list
I'll teach you the blend a word I'll suggest
And then you will know the R family
Here we go do them accurately

B R as in BROKE
C R as in CRASH
D R as in DRAG
F R as in FRANK
G R as in GREAT
P R as in PRUNE
T R as in TRAIN
W R as in WRECK

Let's talk about that L family
Its really quite simple and easy you'll see
There's only the six that we have to know
Join with me and go with the flow

B L as in BLUE
C L as in CLAM
F L as in FLOOD
G L as in GLAD
P L as in PLAN
S L as in SLOSH

And for the letter the letter called S
No family here just seven on that list
Get yourself ready to repeat them out loud
Here we go again and I'll show you how

S C as in SCAT
S K as in SKATE
S M as in SMITTEN
S N as in SNAKE
S P as in SPOILED
S T as in STOP
S W as in SWING

And believe it or not S has a family too
Seven members make up this family and crew
Keep it in beat and you will learn all them well
Don't be afraid you are doing just swell

S C R for SCREAM
S Q U for SQUASHED
S T R for STRIK ING
S P R for SPRING ING
S P L for SPLIT TING
And S H R for SHRIEK
And S C H for SCHOOL

Finally there's one that has no family all
Its members are three, the list is quite small
But here is that list called the orphan Blends
Just three more till we come to the end

D W like in DWELL
T W like in TWIN KLE
T H R as in THREE

Well that's all of them
Surely the best of them
Those Beginning Consonant Blends

CRASH! SWING! SQUASH!

Veritas Press
Copyright Veritas Press

Broadway Musical

as   in THREE   Well thats   all___ of   them   Sure ly the best___ of them   Those Be gin   ning Con so nant

Blends

ACT LIKE A CLOWN
(Final Consonant Blends)

Final Consonant Blends we will try to attend
So come on say them out loud show everyone you know how

C T in ACT like a clown
F T in LIFT up your frown
L D as OLD as the hills
L T in SALT for the meal

Those Final Consonant Blends when said right they can make you grin
And if you say them out loud you'll make the teacher quite proud

M P in JUMP up and down
N C in SINCE we're a round
N D AND don't you forget
N K don't get INK on your pants

Final Consonant Blend's three more that we must attend
So that we can learn to say these Consonants Perfectly

N T in ANTS at the picnic
P T in KEPT them a way
Still I find it's not so easy
R D in HARD you might say

Final Consonant Blends we have one more list to attend
Join with me to say them out loud show everyone that you know how

R K in DARK as the night
R T in ART painted bright
S T in LEAST of them all
S K in RISK if you fall

These are the Consonant Blends that you will find in the end
Of words like the ones we just used say them again if you choose

ACT LIKE A CLOWN

Veritas Press
Copyright 2000 Veritas Press

FUNNY BUTTERFLY
(Two Y Sounds)

There are two sounds that the Y makes
Though its still the letter Y
Sometimes Y will sound like long E
Other times will sound like I

Words like SUNNY FUNNY PONY and the like
End with Y sounding like E
And in words like CRY TRY BUTTERFLY it is true
That the Y comes out sounding like I

There are two sounds that the Y makes
Though its still the letter Y
Sometimes Y will sound like long E
Other times will sound like I

FUNNY BUTTERFLY

Veritas Press
Copyright Veritas Press

Joyful

THE E PARTNERSHIP
(Phonics Rule EA & EE)

E A and E E
Operate a partnership
Though one might be silent
Said together they sound just the same
You find them sounding "E"
Like in SEED, FEED, EAT
They're GUARANTEED to always sound like "E"

So E A and E E
Operate their partnership
Though one might be silent
They always sound like "E"

THE E PARTNERSHIP

Veritas Press
Copyright Veritas Press

With Expression

PLAY EVERYDAY
(ai/ay)

A I and letters A Y
Put together make the sound of a LONG A
A I and A Y are in so many words
Such as PAID, AIDE, SAY, and HAY
Food the horses eat!

A I and also A Y when they're said correctly they say A
A I used in words such as RAIN, BRAIN, MAID
And A Y in some other words like DAY, WAY, PAY
And do not think it hard in words like RAID, PLAY, EVERYDAY
The Phonic rule for A I and A Y

PLAY EVERYDAY

Veritas Press
Veritas Press

Joyful

* A I and let ters A Y Put to

ge ther make the sound of a LONG

A A I and A Y are in so ma ny words Such as

PAID, AIDE, SAY, and HAY Food the hor ses eat!

A I and al so A Y when their

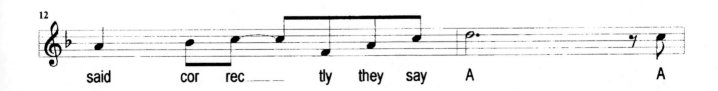

said cor rec tly they say A A

I used in words such as RAIN, BRAIN, MAID And

A Y in o ther words like DAY, WAY, PAY And

do not think it hard in words like

RAID, PLAY, E VERY DAY The

Pho nic rule for A I and A Y

THE SOUTH SEA
(oa/ow)

Off an island in the south sea
(Underneath men sing throughout entire song) O - A   O - W
On a BOAT in a nice breeze
We all do KNOW -
Where the south wind BLOWS — —

When we hear the sounds GROANING
We KNOW the letters O A
And O W - - -
Make the sound of "O"

THE SOUTH SEA

Veritas Press
Copyright Veritas Press

Hawaii Style

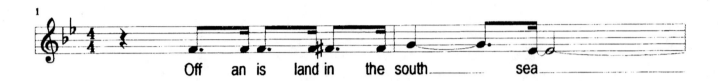

OYSTERS
(oi/oy)

I knew a BOY who loved to eat OYSTERS
He'd TOIL all day in the SOIL and then
He'd bring em home with JOY and excitement
Sit down to eat em then go diggin' again

And then one day while diggin' up OYSTERS
He swallowed one whole and his VOICE went a way
So when they asked him what was the trouble
OI OY OI OY was all he could say

Phonic rule O I
Phonic rule O Y
OI OY OI OY was all he could say

OYSTERS

Veritas Press
Copyright Veritas Press

Jazz

SHOUT
(ou/ow)

The Phonic rule for O U O W
They sound the same though
The spelling is different

Come sing with me and I will show you how
This Phonic rule applies

O U in words like out pout house snout and here about
When you see a mouse you shout

O W in how now brown cow let him pull the plow he likes it anyhow

The Phonic rule for O U O W
They sound the same though
The spelling is different

But now you know O U and O W
They make the sound of OW!

SHOUT

Veritas Press
Copyright Veritas Press

Bouncy

They make the sound of OW!

THE BROAD-O SONG

Ah
Ah
Ah
AH
The phonic rule BROAD O SOUND
Is made by A and L "like in CALL"
And if you see both A and W
It should sound so AWFUL

Sometimes you'll see A followed by U
And AUTOMATICALLY know
That you are using the Phonic rule
The Phonic Rule BROAD O

A W
A W
A U
A U
A L
A L

Ah
Ah
Ah
Ah
The phonic rule BROAD O SOUND
Is made by A and L "like in CALL"
And if you see both A and W
It should sound so AWFUL

Some times you'll see A followed by U
And AUTOMATICALLY know
That you are using the Phonic rule
The Phonic Rule BROAD O

THE BROAD-O SONG

Veritas Press
Copyright Veritas Press

Up Beat

MISSION TO THE MOON
(sion/tion)

A MISSION to the moon we all will take some ACTION
A NATION to the moon we'll build a real space STATION
And when we get all through we'll have the world's ATTENTION
The Phonic rule for S I O N is the same for T I O N
They may sound the same but still their spelling is quite different
They both sound like SHUN

A MISSION to the moon we all will take some ACTION
A NATION to the moon we'll build a real space STATION
And when we get all through we'll have the world's ATTENTION
The Phonic rule for S I O N is the same for T I O N
They may sound the same but still their spelling is quite different
They both sound like SHUN

MISSION TO THE MOON

Veritas Press
Copyright Veritas Press

Militant

A MIS SION to the moon _____ we

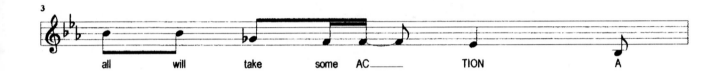

all will take some AC _____ TION A

NA TION to the moon _____ we'll

build a real _____ space STA TION And

when we get all through _____ we'll

have the world's AT TEN _____ TION The Pho nic rule for S I

O N is the same for T I O N They may sound the same but still their spel ling is quite dif fer

HOW MANY SOUNDS?
(a/e/i/o/u/y)

AEIOUY
AEIOUY

How many sounds does A make
A has three main sounds
Then let me hear the sound A makes
A it sounds like this

You got A as in FAT
A as in FATE
AHHH as in FATHER
How many sounds does A make
A has three main sounds

How many sounds does E make
E has two main sounds
Then let me hear the sound E makes
E it sounds like this

You got E as in MET
E as in ME
How many sounds does E make
E has two main sounds

How many sounds does I make
I has two main sounds
Then let me hear the sound I makes
I it sounds like this

You got I as in PIN
I as in PINE
How many sounds does I make
I has two main sounds

AEIOUY
AEIOUY

How many sounds does O make
O has three main sounds
Then let me hear the sound O makes
O it sounds like this

You got O as in NOT
O as in NO
OOO as in MOVE
How many sounds does O make
O has three main sounds

How many sounds does U make
U has two main sounds
Then let me hear the sound U makes
U it sounds like this

You got U as in TUB
U as in TUBE
How many sounds does U make
U has two main sounds

How many sounds does Y make
Y has two main sounds
Then let me hear the sound Y makes
Y it sounds like this

You got Y as in DU TY
Y as in SHY
How many sounds does Y make
Y has two main sounds

AEIOUY
AEIOUY

How Many Sounds?

Veritas Press
Copyright 2000 Veritas Press

Upbeat

91
make U has two main sounds
97
How ma ny sounds does Y make Y has two main sounds.
101
Then let me hear the sound Y makes
104
Y it sounds like this You got Y as in DU TY
107
Y as in SHY How ma ny sounds does Y make
111
Y has two main sounds A E I O U Y
115
A E I O U Y

THE ALPHABET CHASE

There was an A A A APPLE eaten by a M M MUMMY
Being chased from behind by a large B B B BULL

But then a big fat P P PIG jump up on the T T TABLE
And began to do a jig because he was a D D DANCER

And N N NUTS the G G GOAT went out in to the S S SUN
And got so hot they had to cool him off with a F F FAN

Now the R R RABBIT found the one and only colored E E EGG
While the I I INDIAN ran around his tent to get away
From the large O O OX

And when it started raining an U U UM BRELLA
Was used by L L LION and acted as his H H HAT
Who's heard of that a lion wearing a hat

You've heard of the C C COW who jumped over the moon
But a K K KANGAROO once flew in a balloon
You put flowers in a J J JAR see a Z Z ZEBRA at the zoo
And Y Y YELLOW is the color of the morning sun

A W W WIND MILL spins around creaking as it goes
A Q Q QUEEN sits down upon her high and lifted throne
And while the Jester sits and plays his V V VIOLIN
There's a X X BOXING match out in her court yard

TEACHER'S NOTE: This song may be sung as an alternative to singing *The Museum Song* for the sake of variety beginning in the second quarter.

THE ALPHABET CHASE

Veritas Press
Copyright 2000 Veritas Press

Appendix 8

Name

VERITAS PRESS PHONICS MUSEUM PRIMERS *in sequence with the* VERITAS PRESS HISTORY CARDS

BOOK TITLE	VP HISTORY CARD SERIES	CARD #
Pan and the Mad Man	New Testament Greece and Rome	6
To the Rim of the Map	Explorers to 1815	8
Pepin the Not-Big	Middle Ages, Renaissance and Reformation	8
The Rig Ran On	1815 to the Present	8
A Pen for Ben	Explorers to 1815	26
The Dog, the Hog, the Rat, the Ram, the Hen and the Big Big Din	New Testament Greece and Rome	19
Dan of the Den	Chronicles to Malachi	85
In A Camel's Eye	New Testament Greece and Rome	17,18
Runs from Guns	1815 to the Present	13

Lower Case

a | begin at the center; curve around down, touch the ground, climb the column to close, down the column, and a curl.

b | begin at the top; down the column on a slant, touch the ground, curve around and up to close at the center.

c | begin under the center; curve up and around, touch the center and the ground, curve up, do not close.

d | begin at the center; curve around down, touch the ground, climb the column to the top, down the column, and a curl.

e | begin between the center and the ground, curve around and up, touch the center and the ground, curve up, do not close.

f | begin under the top, curve up and around, touch the top, down the column on a slant to the ground, cross at the center

g | begin at the center; curve around down, touch the ground, climb the column to close, down the column, underground, and a bend to the left in the tunnel.

h | begin at the top; down the column on a slant, touch the ground, climb the column, touch the center, curve around, down the column, and a curl.

i | begin at the center; down the column on a slant, touch the ground, and a curl; dot on top.

j | begin at the center; down the column on a slant, underground, and a bend to the left in the tunnel; dot on top.

k | begin at the top; down the column on a slant, touch the ground, climb the column, touch the center, curve around to close, to the ground with a curl.

l | begin at the top; down the column on a slant, touch the ground, and a curl.

m | begin at the center; down the column on a slant, touch the ground, climb the column, curve around, touch the center, down the column, climb the column, curve around, touch the center, down the column, and a curl.

n | begin at the center; down the column on a slant, touch the ground, climb the column, curve around, touch the center, down the column, and a curl.

o | begin at the center; curve around down, touch the ground, curve around and up to close.

p | begin at the center; down the column on a slant, underground, climb the column, touch the center, curve around to close on the ground.

q | begin at the center; curve around down, touch the ground, climb the column to close, down the column, underground, and a curl.

r | begin at the center; down the column on a slant, climb the column, touch the center, curve around with an arch.

s | begin under the center; curve up and around, touch the center and the ground, curve up, make a snake tail.

t | begin at the top; down the column on a slant, touch the ground, and a curl; cross at the center.

u | begin at the center; down the column on a slant, touch the ground, and a curl, climb a new column, down the column, and a curl.

v | begin at the center; down the column on a right slant, touch the ground, climb a new column on a slant.

w | begin at the center; down the column on a slant, touch the ground, and a curl, climb a new column, down the column, and a curl, climb a new column.

x | begin at the center; down the column on a right slant, and a curl; jump to the center, down the column on a left slant, to the ground.

y | begin at the center; down the column on a slant, touch the ground, and a curl, climb a new column, down the column, underground, and a bend to the left in the tunnel.

z | begin at the center; climb right on the center line, down the column on a slant, touch the ground, walk right along the ground.

Upper Case

A I begin at the top; down the column on a slant, touch the ground, jump to the top, straight to the ground, connect the columns on the center line.

B I begin at the top; down the column on a slant, touch the ground, climb the column to the top, curve around, close at the center, curve around, close on the ground.

C I begin under the top; curve up and around, touch the top and the ground, curve up, stop before the center.

D I begin at the top; down the column on a slant, touch the ground, climb the column to the top, curve around, close on the ground.

E I begin at the top; climb left on the top line, down the column on a slant, touch the ground, walk right along the ground, jump to the center and climb right on the line.

F I begin at the top; climb left on the top line, down the column on a slant, touch the ground, jump to the center and climb right on the line.

G I begin under the top; curve up and around, touch the top and the ground, curve up to the center, climb left on the line.

H I begin at the top; down the column on a slant, touch the ground, jump to the top, down a new column on a slant, touch the ground, connect the columns on the center line.

I I begin at the top; down the column on a slant, touch the ground, put a cap on the top, put a base on the ground.

J I begin at the top; down the column on a slant, touch the ground, and a bend to the left.

K I begin at the top; down the column on a slant, touch the ground, jump to the top, down to the center of the column, to the ground with a curl.

L I begin at the top; down the column on a slant, touch the ground, walk right along the ground.

M I begin at the top; down the column on a slant, touch the ground, jump to the top, down a new column on a right slant, touch the center, climb a new column on a right slant, down the column on a slant to the ground.

N I begin at the top; down the column on a slant, touch the ground, jump to the top, down a new column on a right slant, touch the ground, climb a new column on a slant.

O I begin at the top; curve around down, touch the ground, curve around and up to close.

P I begin at the top; down the column on a slant, climb the column, touch the top, curve around to close at the center.

Q I begin at the top; curve around down, touch the ground, curve around and up to close; give a tail on the right.

R I begin at the top; down the column on a slant, climb the column, touch the top, curve around to close at the center, to the ground with a curl.

S I begin under the top; curve up and around, touch the top and the ground, curve up, make a snake tail.

T I begin at the top; down the column on a slant, touch the ground, put a big cap on top.

U I begin at the top; down the column on a slant, touch the ground, and a curl, climb a new column, down the column, and a curl.

V I begin at the top; down the column on a right slant, touch the ground, climb a new column on a slant.

W I begin at the top; down the column on a right slant, touch the ground, climb a new column on a slant, down the column on a right slant, touch the ground, climb a new column on a slant.

X I begin at the top; down the column on a right slant, and a curl; jump to the top, down the column on a left slant, to the ground.

Y I begin at the top; down the column on a right slant to the center, jump to the top, down the column on a left slant, tag the first column, to the ground.

Z I begin at the top; climb right on the top line, down the column on a slant, touch the ground, walk right along the ground.

In a purely phonetic language there are as many letters in the alphabet as there are sounds. We might expect to have twenty-six sounds in our language, as we have twenty-six letters, but actually we have about forty-four sounds in our language. The vowels A,E,I,O and U represent many sounds, because the consonants with a few exceptions, do not vary the sounds they represent.

The list provided below is intended to help you know the various sounds that each letter makes. This is not here for you to spend hours laboring over, rather as a resource should you have questions.

Vowels are unobstructed sounds. Some would explain this by saying it is like water that flows from a garden hose. In making consonant sounds the breath is obstructed. To go back to the garden hose it would be like placing your finger at the end, partially obstructing the water. Consonants are referred to as voiced or unvoiced consonants. The pronunciation guide is intended to help you to make sure that you are saying each letter sound correctly.

Now that you have read over this list have fun as you begin your journey in teaching your child or students to read.

Aa *vowel*
Main sounds in order of frequency:
ă: apple, sad, pack
ā: late, nation, paste
ah: father, spa
(often sounds like a *schwa* in initial position)
PRONUNCIATION: *Open oral cavity, back of tongue raised, steady airflow*

Bb *Voiced consonant*
Main sound:
b: baby, about, cab
PRONUNCIATION: *Lips together, stopped airflow*

Cc *Unvoiced consonant*
Main sounds in order of frequency:
c(k): come, tactic
c(s): cent, acid, pace
Voiced equivalents: g, z
PRONUNCIATION: *Back of tongue raised to palate, stopped airflow (k); tip of tongue behind top teeth, steady restricted airflow (s)*
Common error substitutions: t

Dd *Voiced consonant*
Main sound:
d: doll, Adam, red
Unvoiced equivalent: t
PRONUNCIATION: *Tip of tongue behind top teeth, stopped airflow*
Common error substitutions: g

Ee *vowel*
Main sounds in order of frequency:
ĕ: end, fed
ē: me, emu, Peter
PRONUNCIATION: *Middle of tongue raised, steady airflow*

Ff *Unvoiced consonant*
Main sound:
f: fun, afar, puff
Voiced equivalent: v
PRONUNCIATION: *Bottom lip to top teeth, steady restricted airflow*
Common error substitutions: s

Gg *Voiced consonant*
Main sounds in order of frequency:
g: get, sugar, rug
g (j): general, diligent, rage
Unvoiced equivalents:
k, ch)
PRONUNCIATION: *Back of tongue raised to palate, stopped airflow (g); tip and sides of tongue behind top teeth, stopped and restricted airflow (j)*
Common error substitutions: d

Hh *Unvoiced consonant*
Main sound:
h: heart, ahead
PRONUNCIATION: *Open oral cavity, steady airflow*

Ii *Vowel*
Main sounds in order of frequency:
ĭ: ill, pin
ī: island, line
PRONUNCIATION: *Open oral cavity, middle of tongue lifted*

Jj *Voiced consonant*
Main sound:
j (g): jump, pajamas
Unvoiced equivalent: ch
PRONUNCIATION: *Tip and sides of tongue behind top teeth, stopped and restricted airflow*
Common error substitutions: d

Kk *Unvoiced consonant*
Main sound:
k: kitten, locker, sack
Voiced equivalent: g
PRONUNCIATION: *Back of tongue raised to palate, stopped airflow*
Common error substitutions: t

Ll *Voiced consonant*

Main sound:
    l: lips, salad, until
Tongue tip behind top teeth,
steady airflow
Common error substitutions: w, y

Mm *Voiced consonant*

Main sound:
    m: mother, animal, sum
Lips together, steady nasal
airflow

Nn *Voiced consonant*

Main sound:
    n: nose, panel, clean
PRONUNCIATION: *Tip of tongue*
behind top teeth, steady nasal
airflow

Oo *vowel*

Main sounds in order of frequency:
    ŏ: operate, not
    ō: open, total, no
    o move, into
PRONUNCIATION: *Open oral cavity,*
steady airflow, lips rounded or
pursed for second and third
sounds above

Pp *Unvoiced consonant*

Main sound:
    p: pink, taper, sip
    Voiced equivalent: b
PRONUNCIATION: *Lips together,*
stopped airflow

Qq *Unvoiced consonant*

Main sound:
    q (kw): quick, aqua
PRONUNCIATION: *Back of tongue*
raised to palate, stopped airflow,
lips rounded
Common error substitutions: k, t

Rr *Voiced consonant*

Main sound:
    r: run, arise, stir
PRONUNCIATION: *Back of tongue*
raised to palate, steady airflow
Common error substitutions: w, l,
y, and various distortions

Ss *Unvoiced consonant*

Main sounds in order of frequency:
    s: sin, listen, pass
    s (z): laser, was
    Voiced equivalent: z
PRONUNCIATION: *Tip of tongue*
behind top teeth, steady restricted
airflow
Common error substitutions: t,
various distortions

Tt *Unvoiced consonant*

Main sound:
    t: touch, later, sit
    Voiced equivalent: d
PRONUNCIATION: *Tip of tongue*
behind top teeth, stopped airflow
Common error substitutions: k

Uu *Vowel*

Main sounds in order of frequency:
    ŭ: up, such
    ū: tube, avenue
PRONUNCIATION: *Open oral cavity,*
middle of tongue raised, lips
rounded for second sound

Vv *Voiced consonant*

Main sound:
    v: vine, lever, save
    Unvoiced equivalent: f
PRONUNCIATION: *Bottom lip to top*
teeth, steady restricted airflow
Common error substitutions: b

Ww *Unvoiced consonant*

Main sound:
    w: wave, away
PRONUNCIATION: *Lips rounded,*
steady airflow

Xx *Unvoiced consonant*

Main sounds in order of frequency:
    x (ks): axle, box
    x (z): xylophone, xylem
    Voiced in initial position
PRONUNCIATION: *Back of tongue*
raised to palate, stopped airflow,
tip behind top teeth, steady
restricted airflow (ks); tip of
tongue raised behind top teeth,
steady restricted airflow (z)
Common error substitutions: k, t

Yy *Voiced consonant or vowel*

Main sounds in order of frequency:
    y *(as a consonant)*: yard, layer
    y *(as a vowel)*:
        î: pyre, my
        ē: duty
PRONUNCIATION: *Middle of tongue*
raised to palate, steady airflow
Common error substitutions: w, l

Zz *Voiced consonant*

Main sound
    z: zone, blazer, graze
    Unvoiced equivalent: s
PRONUNCIATION: *Tip of tongue*
raised behind top teeth, steady
restricted airflow
Common error substitutions: d

Dear Parents,

This week we will be studying the letter _____, as in _____. Please have your child fill their Museum Bag with at least one item that begins with this letter sound. We will be using these items to build our own class museum. Each child will have a turn during "Show and Tell" to tell the rest of the class about their special item.

When you are looking for these objects help your child to look through the house by asking questions such as, Look there is a cup, what sound does that begin with? /c/, that's right—cup begins with the letter C. Remember the reason for doing this is to help your child learn the sounds of the letters in the alphabet.

Please come and visit our classroom and see the items in our museum. The children always love to show their parents their work.

Thank you,

Dear Parents,

This week we will be studying the letter _____, as in _____. Please have your child fill their Museum Bag with at least one item that begins with this letter sound. We will be using these items to build our own class museum. Each child will have a turn during "Show and Tell" to tell the rest of the class about their special item.

When you are looking for these objects help your child to look through the house by asking questions such as, Look there is a cup, what sound does that begin with? /c/, that's right—cup begins with the letter C. Remember the reason for doing this is to help your child learn the sounds of the letters in the alphabet.

Please come and visit our classroom and see the items in our museum. The children always love to show their parents their work.

Thank you,

a

b

c

d

e

f

g

h

i

j

k

l

m

n

o

p

q

r

s

t

u

v

w

x

y

z

A

B

C

D

E

F

G

H

I

J

K

L

M

N

O
P

Q
R

S
T

U
V

W X

Y Z

a *b*

c *d*

e

f

g

h

i

j

k

l

m

n

o

p

q

r

s

t

u

v

w

x

y

z

A

B

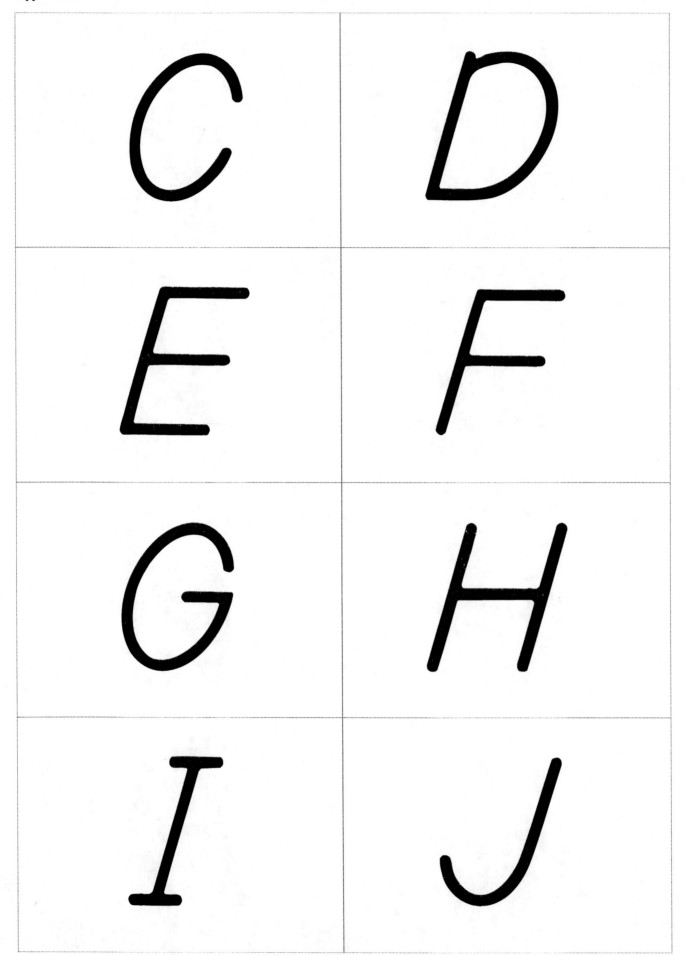

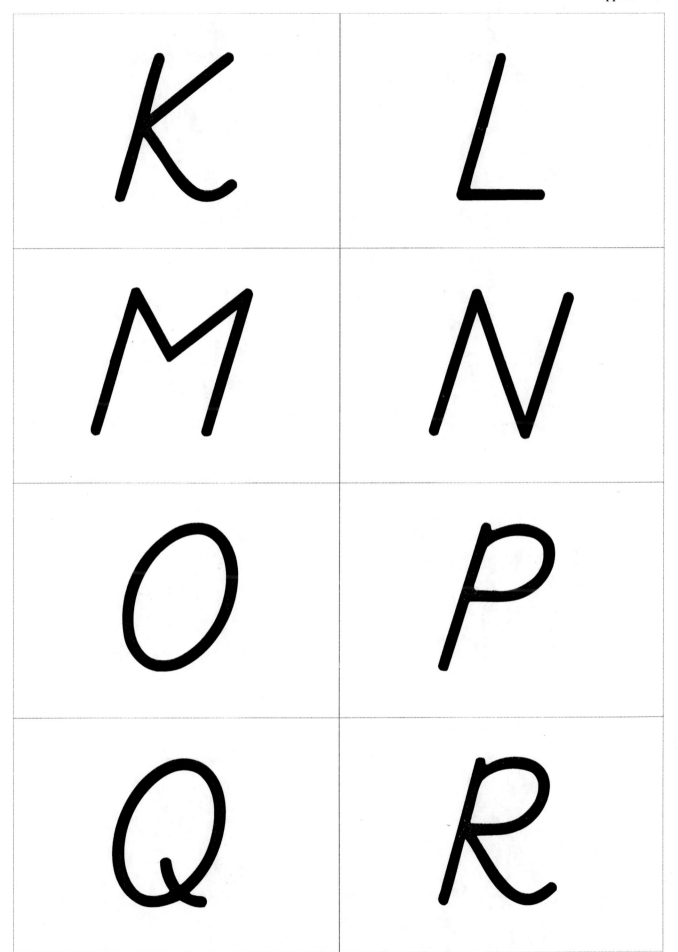

S T

U V

W X

Y Z

dim

gab

rap

pep

dip

fit

bin

tid bit

talk, discuss	**dark**
energy, vigor	**talk**
in good shape	**to sink or drop down**
small amount	**manger, feed trough**

tad bit

fib

sag

fit

bid

bit

nag

dim

lie	small amount
competent, able	bend or break at the center
piece in a horse's mouth used to direct it	desired, ordered
not bright	old horse

sob	rig
fig	ham
lob	lad
hem	din

a horse-drawn wagon	**cry**
meaty part of a hog's leg	**sweet fruit**
small boy	**to throw**
loud noise, commotion	**bottom edge of garment**

cuff	bill
ransack	combat
mull	lack
benefit	kin

document of law	part of shirt around the wrist
fight	attack, loot
be without	think about
relatives, countrymen	good result

jot	set
rat	caravan
vex	duck
timid	dim

determined, ready	**little bit, any**
travelers journeying together	**tattle, tell on**
stoop quickly to hide	**upset, bother**
hard to see	**shy**

shell	in shock
shucks	chap
gash	mush
havoc	hitch

unbelieving, incredulous	**bullet or casing**
fellow, man	**corn stalks**
hot cornmeal cereal	**wound, deep cut**
hook up	**confusion**

mutt

perish

sadness

die

dog

sad,
sorrowful

PHONICS MUSEUM ANSWER KEY

4A
alligator
apples
anchor
ax

5B
Row 1:
apple
Row 2:
alligator
Row 3:
anchor
Row 4:
ax

5C
Row 1:
apple
Row 2:
anchor
alligator
Row 3:
ax

7A
Row 1:
monkey
moon
Row 2:
mittens
Row 3:
mask
magni-
fying
glass

8A
Row 1:
moustache
moose
Row 2:
man
Row 3:
mermaid

9A
Row 1:
mermaid
mask
Row 2:
mittens
moon

10A
Row 1:
mule
Row 2:
mouth
Row 3:
mittens
mask

10B:
Row 1:
mittens
man
Row 2:
ax
alligator
Row 3:
moon
mermaid
Row 4:
anchor

12A
Row 1:
basket bat
Row 2:
bed
Row 3:
bucket
bench bell

13A
Bb:
baby
basket ball

Sounds
other than
Bb:
fish socks
zebra

13C
bed bat
bug big
bad

14A
Row 1:
bench
Row 2:
butterfly
boat

14 B
stamp
map ham
bat hat

15A
Row 1:
bat
Row 2:
ram
Row 3:
cat man

15B
Row 1:
barrel
bench
Row 2:
bear bed
Row 3:
bat
bicycle
Row 4:
bell ball

15C
barrel
bicycle
bird

17A
Row 1:
peacock
piano
Row 2:
pear

18A
Row 1:
potatoes
paint
Row 2:
pipes pot
Row 3:
penguin

19A
Row 1:
pizza pan
Row 2:
pin
Row 3:
porcupine
Row 4:
pirates

20A
Row 1:
m b p
Row 2:
b m. p

22A
Row 1:
tiger tie
Row 2:
tent

Row 3:
table
turkey
Row 4:
top

23A
Row 1:
b t t
Row 2:
a m. p
Row 3:
p b b
Row 4:
m b a

24A
tiger tacks
turtle

24B
Row 1:
rat cat
Row 2:
bat
Row 3:
hat fan

25A
Row 1:
dog
Row 2:
duck

26A
Row 1:
nose
Row 2:
necklace
nut
Row 3:
nail

27A
Row 1:
n b b t
Row 2:
d a p d
Row 3:
p a n t

28A
gun goose
globe

29A
Row 1:
nose nut
Row 2:
goat gun
Row 3:
necklace
nest
Row 4:
guitar girl

29B
Row 1:
m p b
Row 2:
p m n

30A
green:
goat golf
gun guitar
goose
red:
necklace
nest nose
nut

31A
Row 1:
sun
Row 2:
sunglasses
saddle

Row 3:
seal socks

32A
Row 1:
soccer
seeds
Row 2:
soldier
saddle
Row 3:
soccer
soap
Row 4:
saw sink

33A
Row 1:
faucet fan
Row 2:
feet
Row 3:
fist fork

34A
Row 1:
b m n p
Row 2:
d s g a
Row 3:
t b m n

34C
Row 1:
hat cat
Row 2:
rat
Row 3:
bat

PHONICS MUSEUM ANSWER KEY

35A
Row 1:
f s f s
Row 2:
s f s f
Row 3:
f s f s

35C
sad

36A
Row 1:
rat
rooster
Row 2:
razor
ring

37A
Row 1:
ring
Row 2:
rooster
rabbit
Row 3:
ram

38A
Row 1:
ring
rats
Row 2:
rabbit
Row 3:
rose
Row 4:
razor
rooster

42A
Row 1:
elf
Row 2:
elephant

Row 3:
eggs

43A
E:
eggs
elf
elephant
A:
alligator
apples
ax

44A
Row 1:
m g
Row 2:
b m
Row 3:
t r
Row 4:
f s

45A
Row 1:
web
leg
Row 2:
bed
Row 3:
pen
vest

46B
Row 1:
n d t
Row 2:
n n t

48A
Row 1:
man
pan
Row 2:
ten
rat

Row 3:
map
fan
Row 4:
bat
pen

50A
Row 1:
ram
picture
Row 2:
gap
picture
Row 3:
dam
picture
Row 4:
fan
picture

51A
A:
man cat
rat hat
E:
bell tent
pet bed

52B
Row 1:
men
bat
fan
Row 2:
bed
Ben
pet
Row 3:
pan
pen
cat

55A
Row 1:
ax
alligator
Row 2:
ball
basket
Row 3:
goat
guitar
Row 4:
mask
mouth

55B
Row 1:
nut
nest
Row 2:
rabbit
rooster
Row 3:
sun
socks
Row 4:
tie
tent

57A
Row 1:
Indian
Row 2:
igloo

58A
Row 1:
fish
lips
Row 2:
hills
Row 3:
pin
pig

59A
Row 1:
i a e
Row 2:
a e a
Row 3:
e i a
Row 4:
e a a

63A
Row 1:
man
sit
Row 2:
ten
bed
Row 3;
pig
fan
Row 4:
bat
pen

67A
Row 1:
otter
Row 2:
octopus
ox
Row 3:
ostrich

68A
Row 1:
pot
Row 2:
top
Row 3:
lock

70B
Row 1:
pig
Row 2:
monks

Row 3:
pen
Row 4:
father
and son

71A
Row 1:
ax
Row 2:
alligator
anchor
Row 3:
apple

72A
Row 1:
p o m
Row 2:
s m f
Row 3:
e i t
Row 4:
r o g

74A
Row 1:
p b d
Row 2:
f p d

77A
Row 1:
umpire
Row 2:
umbrella
Row 3:
up

78A
Row 1:
sun
Row 2:
cup

Row 3:
gun
Row 4:
nut

80A
Row 1:
u e i
Row 2:
e i o
Row 3:
a o a

81A
Row 1:
light bulb
Row 2:
lace
Row 3:
lemon

82A
Row 1:
lobster
lock
Row 2:
lemon
light
Row 3:
lion
lace
Row 4:
lamb
Light-
house

PHONICS MUSEUM ANSWER KEY

84A
Row 1:
lion
lemon
Row 2:
leg
lips
Row 3:
lobster
lamb

85A
Row 1:
p b. p
Row 2:
g l f

86A
Row 1:
hanger
Row 2:
hook
Row 3:
house
horse

87B
Row 1:
u r t
Row 2:
m i o

89B
Row 1:
l h e p
Row 2:
t b f d
Row 3:
m b a n

91A
Row 1:
cat
Row 2:
cup
Row 3:
cards
cow

92A
kangaroo
king
keys

93A
Row 1:
camel
cat
Row 2:
king
kite
Row 3:
cup
cow
Row 4:
kangaroo
keys

94A
Row 1:
duck
neck
Row 2:
sock
Row 3:
lock tacks

96A
Row 1:
e a o
Row 2:
u a i

97B
Row 1:
m b p
Row 2:
t d n

98A
Row 1:
g s f
Row 2:
r c c

100A
1. pen

100B
3. guns

102A
Row 1:
jump
Row 2:
jug
Row 3:
jewelry
Row 4:
jacks

107A
Row 1:
zebra
Row 2:
zipper

107B
Row 1:
u I o
Row 2:
a o e

109A
Row 1:
zebra
Row 2:
yo-yo
Row 3:
zipper
Row 4:
yarn

109B
Row 1:
z a e h
Row 2:
g j f d
Row 3;
c k m b

110B
Row 1:
a i o
Row 2:
e u a

110C
Row 1:
tacks sun
Row 2:
bed fan
Row 3:
gun lock
Row 4:
pig bell

111A
Row 1:
wink
Row 2:
walrus
wolf
Row 3:
wagon

114A
Row 1:
queen
Row 2:
quilt
Row 3:
quarter
Row 4:
quill

116A
Row 1:
vest vise
Row 2:
vase
Row 3:
violin

119A:
Row 1:
ax fox
Row 2:
box
Row 3:
six

120A
Row 1:
l t z
Row 2:
r w q
Row 3:
c m a
Row 4:
h p v

123B
Row 1:
u i o
Row 2:
a u a

123C
Row 1:
e e e
Row 2:
a i o

124A
pans eggs
cats bats

124B
Row 1:
d p
Row 2:
g f
Row 3:
z u
Row 4:
g. w

124C
Row 1:
m l
Row 2:
s h
Row 3:
m v
Row 4:
e r

125B
Row 1:
Boy
Row 2:
Camel
Row 3:
Eye
Row 4:
hills

126A
Row 1:
shoe
Row 2:
shell

Row 3:
shirt ship

127A
Row 1:
shell
Row 2:
shirt
Row 3:
ship sheep
Row 4:
shoe

130B
Row 1:
r d c
Row 2:
z b sh
Row 3:
l f g

131A
Row 1:
chair
Row 2:
church
Row 3:
chest
chicks

132A
Row 1:
church
Row 2:
chair
Row 3:
chest
chess
Row 4:
chicks

PHONICS MUSEUM ANSWER KEY

133A
red:
patch
hitch pitch
catch
ditch
botch
hatch
batch

green:
punch
lunch
bunch
hunch
pinch
bench
quench

136A
Row 1:
thirteen
Row 2:
thimble
Row 3:
thumb

138B
Row 1:
ch sh th
Row 2:
th sh ch
Row 3:
sh ch sh

139A
Row 1:
sheep
Row 2:
church
chair

Row 3:
shirt
ship
Row 4:
thimble

141A
Row 1:
whale
Row 2:
wheel
Row 3:
wheat

143A
Row 1:
wh ch sh
Row 2:
sh th ch
Row 3:
wh ch th

143B
Row 1:
sh ch ch
Row 2:
sh ch ch

151A
1. combat
2. Feds
3. radish
patch
4. Rebs
5. wagon

151B
Row 1:
3, 5
Row 2:
1, 4
Row 3:
6, 2

152A
c e h i l m
n q s v w
z

153A
Row 1:
duck
sock
Row 2:
pig
watch
Row 3:
fish
hat
Row 4:
dish
shell

154A
Row 1:
h f b
Row 2:
p f s
Row 3:
p c t

155B
Row 1:
sh ch wh
Row 2:
sh wh ch